Fit

Fitness today is not simply about health clubs and exercise classes, or meas-ures of body mass index and cardiovascular endurance. *Fit for Consumption* conceptualizes fitness as a field within which individuals and institutions may negotiate – if not altogether reconcile – the competing and often conflicting social demands made on the individual body that characterize our current era.

This is the first book to offer a comprehensive socio-cultural and historical analysis of the current fitness culture. Intended for researchers and senior undergraduate and postgraduate students of sport, leisure, cultural studies, and the body, the book utilizes the US fitness field as a case study through which to explore the place of the body in contemporary consumer culture. Combining observations in health clubs, interviews with fitness producers and consumers, and a textual analysis of a wide variety of fitness media, *Fit for Consumption* provides an empirically grounded examination of one of the pressing theoretical questions of our time: how individuals learn to fit into consumer culture and the service economy; how our bodies and selves become "fit for consumption."

Jennifer Smith Maguire is Lecturer in Mass Communications in the Department of Media and Communication, University of Leicester, UK.

D1421675

Fit for Consumption

Sociology and the business of fitness

Jennifer Smith Maguire

 Routledge
Taylor & Francis Group

LONDON AND NEW YORK

First published 2008
by Routledge
2 Park Square, Milton Park, Abingdon, Oxon OX14 4RN

Simultaneously published in the USA and Canada
by Routledge
270 Madison Ave, New York, NY 10016

Routledge is an imprint of the Taylor & Francis Group, an informa business

© 2008 Jennifer Smith Maguire

Typeset in Goudy by
RefineCatch Limited, Bungay, Suffolk
Printed and bound in Great Britain by
TJ International Ltd, Padstow, Cornwall

British Library Cataloguing in Publication Data
A catalogue record for this book is available from the British Library

Library of Congress Cataloging in Publication Data
Maguire, Jennifer Smith.
Fit for consumption : sociology and the business for fitness / Jennifer Smith
Maguire.
p. cm.
Includes bibliographical references and index.
ISBN 978–0–415–42180–5 (hardcover)—ISBN 978–0–415–42181–2
(softcover) 1. Physical fitness—Social aspects. 2. Physical fitness—Economic
aspects. 3. Physical fitness—Health aspects. I. Title.
GV342.27.M34 2007
613.7′1—dc22
2007006493

ISBN 978–0–415–42181–2 (pbk)
ISBN 978–0–415–42180–5 (hbk)
ISBN 978–0–203–94065–5 (ebk)

For Joe and Ruaidhri

Contents

Illustrations

Acknowledgments

In January 1998, faced with the need to come up with a research paper topic for a graduate seminar on the urban symbolic economy, and – in a flourish of new year's good intentions – having just joined a health club, I conducted a small-scale study of personal trainers. It proved to be a felicitous decision. That paper was the starting point of what would become both my doctoral dissertation at the Graduate Center of the City University of New York, and an ongoing body of research that has sustained my interest for nearly a decade and provided me with personal rewards as well as intellectual challenges. Given its lengthy germination phase, the book bears traces of a long line of people who have taken the time and energy to read or listen, and offer comments and support.

Those to thank include Sharon Zukin (who has unfailingly sent fitness-related clippings, and pushed me to make the most of this research), Stuart Ewen (a role model for engaged and engaging writing and teaching), and Patricia Clough (who never fails to remind me of the joys of a passionate engagement with theory), for their support and guidance as my doctoral dissertation committee members; the much-missed Bob Alford, for providing in his Logics of Inquiry seminars an exceptional environment for thinking and writing (with, among others, Randal Doane and Micki McGee); Jo Eberhard, Nadia Minian, Jack Levinson and especially Janet Mowat, for their peerless banter – intellectual and otherwise – in all manner of settings and, in the case of Janet, also for scouting around New York with a digital camera, looking for the perfect fitness scenes; Graham Knight at McMaster University, for his encouragement at every stage of my career; Marg McNeill at the University of Toronto, for the generous loan of her collection of personal trainer newsletters, magazines and manuals; and my friends and colleagues in the UK (especially Liz Pike, Louise Mansfield, Gavin Jack,

Gillian Youngs, Eric Dunning, Tom Maguire, and the recently departed Anne Witz), for making my transatlantic transition a delightful one, and helping me to examine the research from new perspectives. Thanks are also due to those conference participants, reviewers, and students who have shared insightful remarks and constructive suggestions on earlier versions of the arguments contained here, which appeared in the *Sociology of Sport Journal*, the *International Review for the Sociology of Sport* and elsewhere, and at conferences and invited lectures in Australia, Japan, Malaysia, Hong Kong, Sweden, Denmark, Switzerland, Germany, Ireland, and around the UK, Canada and the US; and to the interview respondents, who were so generous with their time, experience and enthusiasm.

My thanks to the Graduate Center of the City University of New York and the Social Sciences and Humanities Research Council of Canada (SSHRC) for their generous support through doctoral fellowships; to SSHRC and McMaster University for postdoctoral research and teaching fellowships; and most recently to the Department of Media and Communication at the University of Leicester for the grant of a study leave to facilitate the completion of the manuscript.

Nothing so undermines one's commitment to fitness and well-being as the final stages of completing a manuscript. I thus feel myself to be especially fortunate to have had the love and support of friends and family not only over the years, but most recently – thanks to the time zone differences and the pressures of writing – 24 hours a day. My mom especially deserves thanks for her patience with my far-flung life and inscrutable career choice, and her sense of humor during the awkward stages of writing. I am very sorry that my dad did not get to witness the end of my seemingly interminable student days, and advise me on all that's come since.

This book is dedicated to Joseph and Ruaidhri Maguire. Joe has put aside his own work and sleep on countless occasions to serve as research assistant, life support system, and confidence booster, as well as a tireless editor and sounding board. Rors, who has proven himself up to the unenviable task of living with two academics, has contributed much-needed levity in the fashion befitting a 2-year-old. This is for my boys.

1   Making sense of fitness

What is fitness? From the point of view of sports medicine, fitness is a combination of strength, flexibility, and cardiovascular endurance; it can be quantified and evaluated relative to established benchmarks. However, asking people what they mean when they say, "I think I'm fit," or "She doesn't look fit," often leads to a less straightforward definition. Certainly, fitness is experienced in part as physical ability, whether in the context of exercise or not – the strength to lift weights or groceries; the flexibility to perform a yoga posture or tie shoelaces; the endurance to power-walk or walk to work. But fitness is also associated with less tangible qualities: living up to expectations, or looking a certain way.

For Donna, a 30-year-old journalist who is trying to exercise more in order to lose weight, fitness is a visual category:

> I have this perception of fit, that when someone's fit it's almost like they're *clean*. And I don't mean "dirty versus clean." I mean clean, like put *together*. It's almost like it's an aesthetic. It's an Eames chair versus some overstuffed piece of crap from the '70s in your aunt's closet. It's sort of that *sleekness*.

Unlike Donna, Luke is a regular exerciser. A college teacher and entrepreneur in his mid-30s, Luke locates fitness somewhere between the medical definition and Donna's aesthetic quality:

> There are multiple aspects of fitness, I think. One is how I feel. For instance, walking up several flights of stairs – there's a bottom line, quantifiable understanding of fitness. After walking up several flights of stairs, I feel good, or out of breath, or so on. That is to say, do

I feel healthy, how do I feel after performing certain activities. And then there's one that's not so quantifiable, that at the end of the day can't be understood so clearly. And that has to do with you measuring up against . . . measuring up against images, measuring up against spoken or unspoken standards, measuring up against the covers of magazines.

The lived definition of fitness is not clear-cut. It involves feelings of capacity, notions of control (over ourselves; over how others see us), and understandings of societal norms and expectations, be they articulated in advertising and the media in terms of beauty and youth, or in medical and government documents in terms of risk and health. Fitness is a complex concept, its criteria and objectives varying within and between individuals.

Definitions of fitness also vary across time. Different aspects of bodies and selves have been problematized and valorized over time – character, attractiveness, happiness, strength, morality, intelligence, courage, honesty – and these changing bodily priorities reflect changing societal conditions. The contemporary value conferred on the fit body cannot be separated from the rise in the West of a largely sedentary way of life. Physical activity was once an integral part of everyday life; rather than an intentional leisure activity, strenuous exercise for many people was an unavoidable, unintentional aspect of daily life before the widespread use of vacuum cleaners, washing machines, computers and automobiles. Definitions of fitness have changed over the history of physical culture. In the nineteenth century in the United States, exercise was an important element of the military, childhood physical education, religious organizations such as the YMCA, the dieting industry, and the medical establishment. Moral reform movements of the late nineteenth century such as Muscular Christianity linked physical exercise to the development of a moral character feared to be lacking – or at least threatened – because of the changes to everyday life wrought by urbanization, industrialization, and immigration.

Over the twentieth century, however, individual fitness was promoted as a route not to social improvement but to self-improvement and self-actualization, concerns befitting the needs of burgeoning appearance and service industries for both consumers and producers. While the connection between individual fitness and national strength continues to resurface at times of war, the social construction of fitness has largely shifted from fears about protecting the country and its way of life, to fears about warding off disease and keeping up in an appearance-driven culture. Thus, fitness is a moving target, its definitions, criteria and associated goals inextricably linked to the particular social agendas, anxieties, and demands of the day.

This is a book about fitness in contemporary society. It concerns the ways in which individuals are encouraged to evaluate and work on their bodies in the context of consumer fitness culture – in commercial health clubs and the fitness media, and through personal fitness services. The focus is primarily on the US, and specifically New York City; however, consumer fitness culture is a global phenomenon. The US leads the way in the commercial provision of fitness services, as it has over the twentieth century in the development of consumer industries and mentalities more generally (Cross 2000; Ewen 1976, 1999; Zukin 2004). Furthermore, the juxtaposition between the mass marketization of fitness and an inactive and overweight population is nowhere more apparent than in the US. The US is thus a critical case study through which to assess the past, current and projected commercialization and privatization of physical fitness in other societies, where different sporting and leisure traditions – among other factors – mediate the tension between diversity and standardization in physical cultures.

Fitness in the US today is not simply about health clubs and exercise classes, or measures of strength and cardiovascular endurance. Fitness is best understood as a field of negotiations, within which individuals contend with the competing, and often conflicting, demands made of them by consumer culture and the service economy. In particular, the field of fitness provides opportunities to navigate, resist and comply with demands that the body be a focus of both work and leisure, that the body's function and form – its health and appearance – be maintained and improved, and that the body be disciplined as well as enjoyed. It is through such navigation and negotiation that individuals – both fitness consumers and producers – produce the body's status: as a status object *per se*, a site of investment, and an instrument of self-production. The book explores the opportunities, guidance, and rewards – as well as obstacles and penalties – that the fitness field offers to individuals in their negotiation of these demands. In an era in which health is a personal responsibility, appearances, and performances are occupational necessities, and leisure time is increasingly spent on the work of self-improvement, the fitness field is an example *par excellence* of the ways in which individuals learn to shape bodies and selves that are "fit for consumption."

FITNESS AS A CULTURAL FIELD

In the US, commercial exercise facilities and equipment have a history that reaches back into the nineteenth century; however, we can locate the take-off of this most recent boom in the commercialization of fitness in the late 1970s, which accompanied a surge in popular participation in physical activities. At work in driving the fitness boom in the 1970s was the convergence of a popular cultural interest in self-improvement and a political economic emphasis on individual responsibility. The body and its relative fitness were – and are – targeted by the consumer market promoting self-enhancing products and services, an expanding service market rewarding those "enhanced" selves with occupational and social status, and health policies and promotion strategies targeting "lifestyle" causes of disease.

A 1977 Gallup poll found that 47 per cent of all Americans were physically active on a daily basis – nearly double the percentage found in a 1961 poll (Leepson 1978). In the case of jogging, one of the most visible fitness trends of the 1970s, membership in the New York City Runners Club tripled between 1976 and 1978, as did the paid circulation (between 1977 and 1978) of *Runner's World* (Frum 2000: 173). The concept of fitness became one of the common-sense categories by which everyday information was organized. "Physical fitness" became an index heading in the *Reader's Guide to Periodical Literature* in 1973; previously, physical fitness-related articles were only listed under "exercise" or "health." In the 1975 *Yellow Pages*, "health clubs" replaced "gymnasiums" as a business category. These changes in cataloguing suggest the growing awareness of physical fitness in the *preceding* years, since indexing categories follow patterns of common usage. Thus, in the early 1970s, the growing cultural interest in physical fitness became institutionalized – "fitness" was a genre of news story, a category in the cataloguing of everyday life, and a commodity.

Over the past thirty years, three commodities in particular have shaped the fitness industry. First, in the 1970s, a new kind of exercise site emerged: the commercial health club. The health club combined old forms of exercise (such as calisthenics classes and weightlifting) with new exercise equipment in a coed and service-oriented leisure and lifestyle business. Second, in the 1980s and 1990s, as the health club industry expanded and consolidated, fitness was represented through the growing genre of lifestyle media. In addition to exercise manuals, consumers could turn to fitness magazines to advise them on the latest tips and techniques of the fitness lifestyle. Third, in the 1990s, commercial health clubs made a new kind of fitness service – personal training – available to a mass, middle-class market. Personal trainers are a new group of service professionals, providing exercise expertise in one-on-one sessions with clients. Underlying the transient parade of ever-new forms of exercise equipment and classes, health clubs, fitness media, and fitness service have become the institutional elements and stable points of entry for fitness producers and consumers.

Fitness in contemporary culture is primarily a commercial enterprise. However, rather than limit the analysis to the fitness industry, this research examines fitness through Pierre Bourdieu's concept of a *cultural field* – a network of sites, texts, producers and consumers that generates practices for and meanings of the body (Bourdieu 1984, 1990, 1993; Ferguson 1998; Jarvie and Maguire 1994; Jenkins 1992; Laberge and Kay 2002; cf. Becker 1982).

The analogy of a game provides an overall sense of a cultural field:

> We can indeed, with caution, compare a field to a game (*jeu*) although, unlike the latter, a field is not the product of a deliberate act of creation, and it follows rules, or better, regularities, that are not explicit and codified. Thus we have *stakes* (*enjeux*) which are, for the most part, the product of the competition between players. We have *investment in the game* . . . : players are taken in by the game, they oppose one another, sometimes with ferocity, only to the extent that they concur in their belief (*doxa*) in the game and its stakes; they grant these a recognition that escapes questioning. Players agree, by the mere fact of playing, and not by way of a "contract," that the game is worth playing . . . and this collusion is the very basis of their competition.
>
> (Bourdieu and Wacquant 1992: 98)

Fitness field participants – both producers and consumers – are thus not only involved in pursuing specific types of practices (such as working out with a personal trainer and reading fitness magazines), but also implicated in the production and reproduction of the social legitimacy of fitness as a mode of self-investment, and the social value conferred on the fit body and lifestyle. Before turning to the specific institutional elements of the fitness field, it is helpful to begin with a general overview of the dimensions of cultural fields.

First, the emergence of a cultural field is made possible through new social and cultural conditions that stimulate and sustain the production of new cultural goods, and popular interest and participation in new activities (Ferguson 1998: 601). External stimuli are necessary for fields to break with earlier traditions and institutions that are their foundation. A field is made possible by new political pressures, economic models, technological possibilities and social movements, and the same cultural and social conditions that stimulate the emergence of a field also continue to produce interest in it (Jenkins 1992: 85).

Second, in addition to the broader socio-cultural context, a field also requires popular passions: it requires a market of predisposed producers and consumers who regard the field's rules and rewards as both legitimate and desirable. Participation in a field, therefore, is not universal. The taste for certain fields (such as art, gastronomy or fitness) is patterned by an individual's habitus, his or her embodied, class-bound disposition (Bourdieu 1984: 190). Cultural fields make more sense to some people than others, depending on the skills required and the profits expected (Bourdieu 1984: 211). Actors within a field are thus stratified by preferences and tastes, through which a field will make sense (or not) to a prospective participant.

Third, the relative autonomy of a field from its antecedents in earlier traditions, and in its external relations to contemporaneous fields, is signaled by the production of "institutionally constituted points of entry" (Jenkins 1992: 85). These points of entry establish the boundaries around, and legitimate ways into, the arena of action. In particular, fields tend to develop a distinct social space, dedicated to production and consumption of new products and practices (Ferguson 1998: 601), such as the restaurant, art gallery or health club. By taking the field's activities out of the private space of the home and bringing participants together in a quasi-public space, these sites allow the mutual display and affirmation of membership, status and resources. The boundaries of a site – the physical parameters of the space, as well as the membership fees or costs required to enter – provide a literal division between participants and non-participants, while the competition between sites results in a hierarchy of elite and non-elite producers and consumers (Ferguson 1998: 605–6).

Fourth, actors in a field attempt to improve their relative position and control of resources through networks of authority and prestige. Such networks standardize and institutionalize a field's stakes, definitions, knowledge and hierarchy of positions. However, constructing such networks requires that field participants share stable channels through which they exchange views, debate practices, and confirm common assumptions. Fields thus require a "second-order" product of field-specific texts (Ferguson 1998: 600). Through the mass dissemination of popular and professional writings, forms of expertise, qualification and distinction are standardized and regulated

(Ferguson 1998: 611). Participation in the field can thus take the form of either immediate performance or textual appreciation – and, ideally, it takes both forms, as the latter provides a critical consciousness of the criteria for the former.

Fifth, the competition between sites and actors is illustrative of the more general principle that fields are inherently competitive social arenas. Some participants will be better at the field's activities and practices than others. Actors will attempt to gain access to and control over specific types of resources to better their chances of success in the field. Positions within a field are thus ordered by the relative concentrations of particular forms of social, cultural, and embodied capital – fields are "defined by the stakes which are at stake" (Jenkins 1992: 84). It is in the interests of the field's actors to try to legitimate and improve their own forms of capital: cultural goods, social connections, educational qualifications, aesthetic distinction, prestige, financial resources and so forth. Through strategies of legitimation and investment, participants set and institutionalize the value of particular forms of capital in the field as a whole.

In general, cultural fields are arenas of production, distribution, and consumption of particular forms of goods, service, knowledge and status (Laberge and Kay 2002: 253). Embedded in particular socio-cultural conditions, fields involve the interconnections between a core group of consumers, a defined set of nodes for participation and commentary upon participation (particular sites, products, and texts), and field-specific forms of capital that enable the struggles between actors – both producers and consumers – over relative positions of status.

A field approach offers distinct advantages to studies of cultural production and consumption. Such an approach helps to focus and empirically ground research on tangible and material products and practices, while encouraging an ecumenical, inquiry-based and multi-method approach to research framed by the dimensions of a field – producers, consumers, sites, texts, products, practices – rather than a strict (and illusory) separation of consumption from production, and culture from economy (du Gay and Pryke 2002; Ferguson 1998; Zelizer 2005; Zukin and Smith Maguire 2004). Fields are typically organized around a particular pursuit, the practices of which are delimited in social space and time; thus a field approach facilitates a close, detailed analysis attentive to both producers and consumers, individuals and institutions, subjectivities, and structures. For example, the creation and legitimation of a Scottish museum in the early nineteenth century (Prior 2000), the emergence of restaurants and cuisine in nineteenth-century

France (Ferguson 1998), the celebrity of British avant-garde artists in the late 1990s (Cook 2000), and the construction of French sport and physical education between 1960 and 1990 (Defrance and Pociello 1993), all provide substantive points of entry into broader socio-cultural conditions.

To take a field approach to fitness is thus to draw from and bring together the disparate roots of, and modes of engagement in, the practice of physical fitness. As such, the book brings together (predominantly sociological) studies of consumption, bodies, sport, media, and culture, including social histories of nineteenth- and early twentieth-century physical culture (Green 1986; Grover 1989); discourse analyses of fitness texts and videos (Duncan 1994; MacNeill 1994, 1998; Markula 2001); qualitative (largely ethnographic) studies of fitness spaces and their participants, such as health clubs (Crossley 2006; Fishwick 2001; Frew and McGillivray 2005; Glassner 1988; Sassatelli 1999a, 1999b), bodybuilding gyms (Klein 1993) and aerobics participants (Gimlin 2002; Maguire and Mansfield 1998); comparative studies of fitness in other countries (Ginsberg 2000; Spielvogel 2003; Volkwein 1998); theoretically driven and speculative analyses of contemporary political economy and culture, for which physical fitness serves as an illustrative example (Gillick 1984; Greco 1993; Howell and Ingham 2001; Ingham 1985; Pronger 2002; Sage 1998); and journalistic accounts of the fitness boom (Kolata 2003). What this existing body of empirical research on fitness lacks is a comprehensive analysis that takes account of the intersections between various elements of the field of fitness (health clubs, fitness texts, fitness producers and consumers), as well as the larger social processes to which definitions and practices of physical culture always refer. This is the contribution that a field approach can make.

Fitness may thus be understood as a cultural field: a set of relatively structured positions within which individuals and institutions, producers, and consumers struggle over the status and definitions of fitness and fit bodies. These struggles occur through the mobilization of particular forms of resources or stakes, some specific to the field – such as physique and sport science expertise – and some generic to consumer societies and services economies – such as impression management and the cultivation of status. The development of the contemporary commercial fitness field has involved the institutionalization of specific social settings (particularly, the health club), a variety of media forms targeting both the consumer (such as exercise manuals and magazines) and the producer (occupational texts and manuals), a cadre of professional producers (such as personal trainers and aerobics instructors), and a range of field-specific goods to signal participation. These institutional nodes are represented in Figure 1.1, with the fitness consumer at the center: the field's status rests on its market of affluent and informed consumers who generate and regulate the production and consumption of fitness. These field elements do not work in isolation, however, but in cooperation and competition; hence, the arrows interconnecting the various field nodes create an overall web of fitness consumption and production, so that, for example, health clubs reinforce the importance of fitness services (such as personal trainers) and exercise magazines promote fitness equipment.

Below, each node is briefly introduced with an overview of the types of data collection methods used in the research, which combined observations in health clubs, interviews with fitness producers (including health club and personal training managers, personal trainers, and advertising associates at fitness magazines) and consumers, and purposive sampling of fitness media (including popular exercise manuals and personal trainer occupational journals). Pseudonyms have been used for the names of respondents, and for the health clubs and fitness magazines mentioned in the interviews. A thematic analysis of the textual data (interview transcripts and producer and consumer fitness media) was approached both deductively and inductively: a

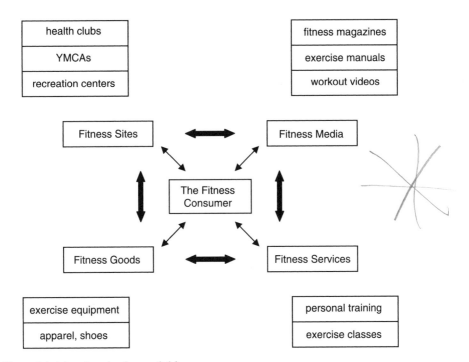

Figure 1.1 Mapping the fitness field.

priori templates of codes (Crabtree and Miller 1999; King 2004) for analyzing the data were derived from the cultural field framework and existing research on fitness and consumer body culture, and then refined over the course of the research through an iterative process that responded to data-driven inductive findings (Fereday and Muir-Cochrane 2006). For example, the problem of motivation (discussed in chapters 4 and 5) emerged as a theme both from the deductive templates and from the inductive findings, as the continuities between the content of fitness media and the work of personal trainers became clear.

Fitness sites

In the 1970s, a new kind of exercise site emerged: the commercial health club. The new health club drew from aspects of its forebears, such as men-only executive clubs, exercise salons, working-class gyms, and the YMCA, to offer a combination of old forms of exercise with new kinds of equipment, old notions of class prestige with new notions of gender inclusion. The health club offered to middle-class men and women a service-oriented space dedicated to the fit body. The health club market expanded and consolidated over the 1980s and 1990s, spurred in part by interest in group exercise such as aerobics, and in leisure goods and services more broadly that targeted the body and its appearance, and offered associations of status.

Various sources, including consumer reviews, exercise manuals, and fitness market research reports, as well as the health club industry organization and its journals, provided data about the growth of the health club market. *Yellow Pages* were used to conduct a census of the market in Manhattan, which increased from 67 health clubs in 1973 to over 200 in 2000. According to the International Health Racquet and Sportsclub Association (IHRSA), there were over 29,000 commercial health clubs in the US in 2005, outnumbering non-profit fitness centers (such as the YMCA) by 11 to one, as will be discussed in Chapter 3. Thus, although commercial health clubs are not the only site for the fitness field, their predominance makes them the logical focus for this research. Commercial health club industries are found around the globe in consumer societies, and the scale of those industries reflects local traditions such as the private provision of leisure services, and local demographics, such as the size of the middle class. For example, whereas the US had approximately 20,000 commercial clubs in 2002, the United Kingdom (with strong traditions of the collective provision of recreation centers) had less than 2,000, and China (with a small – but rapidly emerging – professional/managerial class; Flew 2006) had only 350.[1]

Market research reports and occupational journals (many from IHRSA) on fitness and the health club industry were consulted in order to grasp how the market viewed itself. Such producer-oriented texts helped to unify health club businesses into a coherent club industry, and reveal the challenges, issues, opportunities and strategies that fitness business owners regarded as central to their market success (cf. Roseberry 1996: 763; Vinikas 1992). This helped to prepare the ground for the interviews with health club owners and managers, and an IHRSA representative – a group that largely overlapped with the sample of personal trainers due to their career trajectories. Other second-order field products included consumer reviews of health clubs from the 1970s to 1990s, which were collected from *The New York Times*, lifestyle magazines (such as *Time Out New York*), and consumer guidebooks to fitness (such as *The New York Urban Athlete*; Goldman and Kennedy 1983). These reviews were analyzed for the recurrent criteria and descriptions used to rate or judge clubs, signaling the "stakes" for competition between health clubs.

Observations were also made of different health clubs, often in conjunction with interviews with fitness producers and consumers, and at other times as a participant. In total, 20 clubs were observed between 1997 and 2001, representing a range of options: high cost and low cost; single sex and unisex; family-oriented and young adult-oriented; chain branches and independent clubs; personal training only studios, a YMCA, and massive, multi-storied and multi-use clubs. Through these visits, I not only observed the clubs, but also recruited (directly and through snowball sampling) many of the interview respondents. I visited most of the health clubs only once; two branches of Apple Fitness were observed once a week over a period of months through the auspices of attending a yoga class as a guest of a member; and The Depot (at which I was a member) was visited at different times of the day and week over several years (with the frequency of visits reflecting the patterns of my life more so than an attempt at methodological rigor). Without delving into a discussion of the merits of, and obstacles to, assuming positions of involved detachment and detached involvement (cf. Elias 1987) in conducting social research, suffice it to say that my personal familiarity with sport and fitness – as a participant in both leisure and competitive forms of physical activity – proved a useful form of capital in the research, particularly in terms of establishing credibility in the eyes of the fitness producers interviewed.

Fitness media

Since the 1980s, fitness has been documented in an expanding range of media. For example, a Google search of the term fitness yields 4.85 million results,[2] ranging from links to online vendors of exercise equipment and nutritional supplements, to the websites of health clubs and fitness magazines, physical fitness-related government bodies and personal blogs charting different individuals' pursuit of fitness. Other fitness media include exercise videos, which have been one of the most profitable sectors of the home-entertainment industry since the mid-1980s. In 1992, eight of the ten top-selling videos in North America were workout videos (MacNeill 1998: 63–4). The book's focus, however, is on print media: fitness magazines and exercise manuals, both of which target consumers – predominantly middle-class women readers – with advice on the latest tips and techniques of the fitness lifestyle, including fitness goods and services. Consumer fitness texts are instrumental in drawing together various elements of the field into coherent consumption chains, highlighting for the reader the associated purchases that suit his or her interest in fitness. For example, an exercise manual by the American College of Sports Medicine (1992) features an endorsement from the editor of *Shape* magazine; and the exercise manual published by *Self* magazine (Billings 1998: 112) lists in its acknowledgments a variety of fitness products and services, including the health club and fitness equipment companies that had provided space and props for the book's illustrations.

To gauge the place of fitness in the general media in the years preceding the take-off of the fitness field, the *Readers Guide to Periodical Literature* was sampled at five-year intervals from 1950 to 1975 (representing material unavailable through online periodical databases), with attention paid to how fitness-related issues were indexed, as well as the topic and scale of coverage. The scale of media interest in physical fitness was also assessed (in November 2001) using a subject search for "physical fitness" in ProQuest, a database of magazine and newspapers content from the early 1970s. Although imperfect as a measure of press content – particularly given the addition of titles in 1986 – it shows a consistent increase in the number of physical fitness features. The number of features rose from 25 in 1980 to 63 (1985), 114 (1986), 331 (1990), 403 (1995), and 717 (2000); a sixfold increase between 1986 and 2000.

An analysis of a sample (four issues per year at roughly five-year intervals, from their inception – 1979 and 1981 respectively – to the late 1990s) of *Self* and *Shape* (the two leading women's fitness magazines) was carried out with regard to the construction of lifestyle. This data was complemented by descriptive circulation statistics from fitness magazine media kits, and formed the background for telephone interviews with advertising associates at fitness magazines. Advertising associates, in a markedly different fitness production role from the health club managers, sell their magazines to advertisers by presenting an ideal image of their readers. The construction of the ideal-type consumer is part of the production and legitimation of fitness as a consumer lifestyle. The interviews focused on their characterization of the ideal fitness consumer, including age, income and education, as well as other descriptors offered by the respondents.

In addition, a sample of 13 exercise manuals was purposively selected to reflect a range of dimensions shaping the fitness field, including: gender (manuals targeted directly at women, at men, and at both); class (by and large manuals are a middle-class product, but some are more explicitly directed at the professional/managerial class); links to other lifestyle media (manuals published by fitness magazines); changes over time (between manuals from different decades, and different editions of the same manual); and orientation (manuals with a health-education focus, and those more explicitly linked to commercial fitness). The sample consisted of the American College of Sports Medicine's *ACSM Fitness Book* (1992 and 1998 editions); the American Heart Association's *Fitting in Fitness* (1997); the first and second editions of *Fitness Facts* (Franks and Howley 1989; Franks, Howley and Iyriboz 1999); *The Gold's Gym Weight-Training Book*, first published in 1978 (Dobbins and Sprague 1981); *Jane Fonda's Workout Book* (Fonda 1981); *Nautilus Fitness for Women* (Wolf 1983); *Gym Psych* (Levy and Shafran 1986); the first two editions of *Fitness for Dummies* (Schlosberg and Neporent 1996, 2000); *Stronger Faster*, from the publishers of *Men's Health* magazine (Kaufman and Kirchheimer 1997); and *Self* magazine's *Self's Better Body Book* (Billings 1998).

Fitness services

In the 1990s, health clubs and fitness magazines promoted a new kind of fitness service: personal training. Personal trainers joined the established occupation of exercise instruction, which had experienced large-scale growth in the 1980s thanks to the popularity of aerobics and the provision of exercise classes as standard features of commercial health clubs. Once a luxury of the wealthy, personalized fitness training became more widely available to a growing middle-class market over the 1990s. A ProQuest survey of press coverage of personal training from 1970 to 1995 provided background context for this shift towards a mass market service. Personal trainers are involved in translating the ideal criteria and practices of the fitness field into one-on-one service interactions. While the occupation has no mandatory level of qualification, there has been a standardization of the expectation of certification as part of a broader process of professionalization.

Interviews were conducted with 19 individuals involved in personal training, either as personal trainers (currently or formerly), managers of personal training programs, or representatives of occupational organizations (the American Council on Exercise – ACE). All were based in New York, with the exception of six working in Ontario, Canada. The sample consisted of nine men and ten women, and the ages ranged from early 20s to mid-40s. The interviews focused on the components of the individual's work, the determinants of occupational and market success, and the career biography.

In 1990, the International Dance-Exercise Association (IDEA) began publishing a newsletter, *IDEA Personal Trainer* (*IPT*), which became a magazine in 1994. A thematic analysis was conducted of all *IPT* issues from 1990 to 2000, as well as the first personal trainer manual published by ACE (Sudy 1991); an inductive analysis of a small, preliminary sample of *IPT* issues was used – in conjunction with the findings from the interviews – to establish a coding template. From this analysis there emerged four standard types of articles, dealing with: what counts (skills, certifications) as personal training; how to sell personal training services; how to motivate clients; and technical knowledge on program design and special populations.

Fitness goods

The contemporary fitness industry comprises a range of commodities, with the athletic shoe as one of the most iconic. Over the 1960s and 1970s, the number of pairs of athletic shoes sold annually in the US rose from 130 to 180 million; over the 1980s that number more than doubled to 380 million (Vanderbilt 1998: 13, 26; see also Bernzweig 1983; Brubaker 1991). Nike was started in 1972 as part of the growing interest in physical fitness and especially running. By 1980, Nike had an annual revenue of $270 million; this grew to $2 billion by 1990 (Brubaker 1991; see also Vanderbilt 1998). Nike is the largest shoe manufacturer in the world today, with over 20 per cent of the US athletic footwear market share (Euromonitor 2005). Despite a challenge in the 1990s from so-called "brown" shoes – hiking boots and loafers – the athletic shoe industry continues to grow. In 2004, athletic footwear had the greatest rate of growth of the sporting goods sectors in the US, with a market worth $14.8 billion (Euromonitor 2005).

Athletic shoes were not the only – or the primary – sector of the $48.9 billion US sporting goods market in 2004, 30 per cent of which was made up of footwear, 23 per cent of sports apparel, and 47 per cent of sports equipment (Euromonitor 2005). Although the sports equipment market is dominated by the health club industry and other institutional markets (such as hospitals and corporate fitness facilities), retail sales of fitness equipment to individual consumers were nearly $2.8 billion in 1999 (Sporting Goods Manufacturers Association 2000: 10).

Athletic shoes and exercise gear – and the more generic "sporty" clothing popularized in the 1970s – are not only suitable to the social space of the health club; they also carry the connotations of physical self-improvement from the health club out to the street. Such diffusion is necessary if a phenomenon is to enter social consciousness; a field must be recognizable to participants and non-participants alike if it is to have broad cultural significance. Nevertheless, as is obvious from witnessing the fashions of everyday life and not just the sporting field, the scale of the sporting goods industry is a poor measure of a population's interest and participation in fitness and other physical activities. Because of their diffuse popularity, fitness goods such as athletic shoes and apparel are relatively weak symbols of membership in the fitness field; stronger symbols include reading fitness media, using a membership (especially if regularly) at a health club, the use of specialized services such as personal training, and – strongest of all – the possession and display of fit body parts. As such, the research examines fitness equipment only incidentally, and instead focuses on the other field elements given their requirement of higher levels of involvement from both fitness producers and consumers.

Fitness consumers

Ways of working on the body through adornment, maintenance and manipulation permeate our culture and, in particular, our leisure industries. However, not everyone has the same taste for each form of body work. Bourdieu's (1984) research on the consumption patterns of the French suggests that different social groups (largely defined by social class and occupation) have different ways of thinking about the body; class habitus is reflected in different predilections for ways to work on the body. The profile of fitness consumes reflects broader sociological discussions of the ways in which the health and appearance of the body are undertaken as projects by the middle class, and how such projects thus feature in the production of a middle-class identity (Bourdieu 1984; Crawford 1984; Ewen 1999; Featherstone 1982, 1991; Hepworth and Featherstone 1982; Howell 2005; Shilling 1993). IHRSA statistics, fitness magazine media kits, and IDEA surveys reveal that half of commercial health club members make more than $75,000 annually (thus placing them in the top 20 per cent of annual income; see Bureau of Labor Statistics 2006), and those in professional/managerial occupations make up approximately a third of fitness magazine readers and personal training clients.

However, social class is not the only contributing factor to the formation of habitus, which reflects both one's "objectively classifiable conditions of existence" and one's "position in the structure of conditions of existence" (Bourdieu 1984: 171). In both cases, the milieu in which an individual is socialized, and the societal hierarchies that serve to locate that individual relative to others, are structured by class, but also by identity markers more broadly. Of these, gender is clearly a relevant factor to the fitness field, as it structures the ways in which non-paid time is more or less available for leisure pursuits, and physical activity and physical empowerment are represented and valorized. In the case of the fitness field, gender mediates both access to and the experience of participation. Unlike the direct and indirect exclusion of women from much physical culture of the past (Green 1986; Hargreaves 1994), women's rates of participation in the fitness field are greater than those of men (IHRSA statistics show that women's rate of participation as health club members is growing faster than men's; 57 per cent of health club members in 2005 were women). IDEA research suggests that approximately three-quarters of personal trainer clients are women, and magazine industry circulation statistics show that women constitute two-thirds of the readership of the top-selling fitness magazines, suggesting that gender not only configures the desire for specific bodily rewards (slimming down versus bulking up; toning versus muscle gain), but also the relative utility of sources of therapeutic advice and guidance.

Aside from studies of consumption that explicitly foreground the production of ethnic identities (for example, Chin 2001; Lamont and Molnar 2001; Zukin 2004), the issue of ethnicity tends to "drop out" when the focus is on middle-class, mainstream consumption, rendering invisible the whiteness of the field (cf. Dyer 1996). This is the case of the present study: ethnicity was not an explicit focus of the research, and the ethnicities of interview respondents (who, with the exception of the personal trainers

Frank, June, and Rob, all fell into the amorphous category of "white") have not been noted in the book's narrative. Despite an absence of specific market research on the ethnicity of fitness consumers, it is telling that an IHRSA report identified African Americans, Asian Americans, and Hispanic Americans as underdeveloped segments of the health club industry (McCarthy *et al.* 1999: 65). While ethnicity – like gender – will shape the ways in which individuals access and experience the field (creating different obstacles and opportunities), the stratification of the commercial fitness field is first and foremost cast in the terms of class: the inclusion or exclusion of ethnic communities is largely a question of the relative size of their middle class, and thus capacity to constitute a viable target market.

From the point of view of the commercial fitness industry, fitness consumers are a problematic group. For example, up to half of new participants quit within six months of taking up an exercise program (Franks and Howley 1989: 128). As such, the problem of motivation is a key organizing theme within the commercial fitness field. Health club managers must work to entice new members and retain old members; fitness magazines and exercise manuals attempt to stimulate readers to buy future issues, and prompt them to buy other fitness goods and services; and personal trainers must inspire clients to work out during their sessions, and encourage them to purchase further sessions. In short, the field must educate its participants to be good consumers (Smith Maguire 2002a), and the focus of the book has largely been on modes of consumer education – consumer health club reviews, fitness magazines, personal trainers. Nevertheless, interviews with a small sample of 12 fitness consumers – drawn from contacts made in observing the health clubs and snowball sampling – were conducted in order to provide supporting and sensitizing data, intended not as the basis of generalizations about the experiences of fitness consumers, but to illuminate the other research findings. The sample consisted of ten women and two men; ages ranged from early 30s to mid-60s, and all were members of the middle class, with occupations in fields such as teaching and academic research, publishing, financial services, and the arts.

FITNESS AND INDIVIDUALIZATION

What is not captured in the field "map" of Figure 1.1 is the socio-cultural context of individualization, against which the development of the fitness field and the body's status as a site of investment, a vehicle for self-production, and a status object *per se* should – and indeed must – be placed. That is, in addition to using the work of Bourdieu and others to frame fitness as a cultural field, the book also draws on a complementary body of literature to understand how the fitness field is embedded within processes of individualization: those ways in which individuals have come to be held responsible for the production of their own identities. This is a critical issue; without attention to the broader issue of individualization, a case study of fitness risks being little more than a catalogue of contemporary fads and fashions. At stake in the fitness field is the production of bodies and selves that are fit to bear the burden of self-production.

Historical accounts of the individual have called attention to the ways in which identity has become a problem – the defining problem – for the modern individual (Bauman 1996, 2000; Beck and Beck-Gernsheim 2002; Beck, Giddens and Lash 1994; Foucault 1986; Giddens 1991). As Zygmunt Bauman (2000: 31–2) puts it:

> To put it in a nutshell, "individualization" consists in transforming human "identity" from a "given" into a "task" and charging the actors with the responsibility for performing that task and for the consequences (also the side-effects) of their performance.

The fragmentation and weakening of traditional and collective sources of identity have shifted the conceptualization of identity from a relatively fixed set of characteristics determined by birth and ascription, to the reflexive, ongoing project of choosing to *"become* what one *is"* (Bauman 2000: 32). Crucial to an understanding of the fitness field is an appreciation of how the decline of ascriptive identity and the process of individualization are bound up with the same cluster of processes that have, over modernity, given rise to an increasingly sedentary way of life, including urbanization, industrialization and post-industrialization, migration, and globalization.

Individualization presents opportunities, particularly as traditionally narrow categories such as gender have been opened to challenge, allowing a greater range of normative possibilities for the performance of identity. Individualization has also presented individuals with anxieties and risks: freed from the strictures of traditional authorities and categories dictating their life paths, individuals are now shackled to the obligation to produce themselves through an endless array of options, with each choice bringing with it the possibility of getting it wrong. Individualization thus implies not only an intensifying, reflexive relationship of individuals with themselves, and a breakdown in traditional modes and figures of authority; it is also associated with the rise of new therapeutic experts and supplemental objects to assist in the process of self-production (Giddens 1991; Ilmonen 2004; Lears 1983; Rose 1996, 1999). The more we are "free" to choose, the more we turn to guides and objects to provide a sense of security, and to anchor a sense of self against the churning tumult of choice. Hence the interest – both everyday and academic – in the body, "our first and most unconditional possession" (Simmel 1950: 344); to work on the body *is* to work on the self.

It is thus not coincidental that consumer culture has become predominant in the age of individualization; structured by the core values of individual sovereignty and freedom of choice (Slater 1997), consumption provides both the tools and the opportunities for self-production (Falk 1994). Compulsory self-production has been harnessed as the engine of consumer industries and the framework for everyday lives. The task of self-production is not reserved for any one class group; however, the middle classes have epitomized self-work as a form of consumer leisure, and framing leisure, more generally, as the sphere for the obligatory production of the self. The fitness field not only offers solutions to the problems of the self and the body (be they framed in terms of health, appearance, or otherwise), but also does so within the sphere of leisure – a realm of freedom *and* obligation to make the most of oneself (Baudrillard 1998: 151; see also Bourdieu 1984: 367; Rose 1996: 17).

Since the 1950s, self-improvement projects have become the hallmarks of middle-class identity (Turner 1994: xiii; see also McGee 2005). The mission to improve the self through physical culture, intellectual stimulation and self-reflection – while not new – was traditionally limited to an upper-class elite with sufficient resources of time, money and knowledge. However, following the Second World War, rising living standards and the mass production of consumer goods transformed self-improvement into a mass, middle-class project. As Tom Wolfe (1982a: 277, 291)[3] acerbically observes of the 1970s:

> The new alchemical dream is: changing one's personality – remaking, remodeling, elevating, and polishing one's very *self* . . . and observing, studying and doting on it. (Me!) This had always been an aristocratic luxury [. . .] since only the wealthiest classes had the free time and the surplus income to dwell upon this sweetest and vainest of pastimes. [. . .] Whatever the Third Great Awakening amounts to, for better or for worse, will have to do with this unprecedented post-World War II

American luxury: the luxury enjoyed by so many millions of middling folk, of dwelling upon the self.

Weaving individualization together with consumption, the problem of the self has, over the course of the twentieth century, become the problem of the consuming self, with the body as its project. Our bodies are reflected back to us through the lens of products and services, and consumption is promoted as the primary arena in which we are to make and remake our bodies. Through consumption we are "free" to choose, create, and control ourselves – modes of activity in the world of paid work that are increasingly both rare (for those occupying the lower end of the service occupations), and instrumentalized (for those in the professional/managerial "creative class"; Florida 2002).

It is only in the context of individualization and consumer culture, and against the backdrop of an increasingly sedentary way of life, that fitness is configured as an individual choice – and thus an ethical and moral choice, affiliated with connotations of status, virtuousness and self-responsibility. Only when being inactive is a distinct likelihood can the choice to be fit serve to fulfill one's obligations to self-production.

THEMES AND ISSUES

Cultural fields are formed through the interactions between consumers, producers and products. Understanding the fitness field requires us to pay attention to the social and cultural conditions that make the field and its participants possible. The development of health club services, fitness media content and personal training expertise involves articulating the rewards and benefits of fitness in a language that makes sense to the field's participants – to both producers and consumers. The remainder of the book is organized around these constituent parts of the fitness field.

Chapter 2 examines both the long-term historical roots and contemporary conditions that have given rise to the fitness field in the US. In the first of three sections, the chapter reviews the physical culture of the nineteenth and early twentieth centuries, highlighting how industrialization, urbanization, immigration, and political and military conflict were reflected in the changing goals and practices of physical culture. The second and third sections outline two clusters of social anxieties – around the questions of health and appearance – that characterize the late twentieth and early twenty-first centuries and the way in which the body is framed as physical capital. Drawing from interviews with fitness consumers, the chapter explains how concerns about health and appearance serve as the wellsprings of popular interest in, and institutional support for, physical fitness. The issue of health has been brought to the fore by changes in the nature of disease, the economic rationalization of health care, and calls for demedicalization as well as greater personal responsibility for one's health; while changes in patterns of employment and the types of personal qualities demanded for service work, as well as a broader shift towards a culture of self-promotion and improvement, have done the same for the issue of appearance. Health and appearance have become central both to the social order, and to an individual's occupational success and social status. Given these elements, it is little wonder that fitness has been so successfully commodified in the past three decades.

Chapter 3 focuses upon the commercial health club, the primary site for the production and consumption of the fit body. Through a comparison with such antecedents as executive clubs, bodybuilding gyms, and dance studios, the chapter highlights what is new about the commercial health clubs that began to appear in the 1970s and have since spread around the globe. Catering to middle-class young professionals of both genders, and representing a lifestyle that weds notions of fitness to status, success and quality of life, health clubs have become part of a network of positional leisure goods and services, with some clubs counting for more than others in the status stakes. Based on data from interviews with club members and managers, health club industry journals and health club consumer reviews, and observations in clubs in New York City, the chapter demonstrates how the status of health clubs is structured by: their production, first and foremost, as leisure businesses; their vertical stratification according to membership cost and the quality of service; and their horizontal stratification through the symbolic capital of design and décor, amenities, clientele, and staff, which coalesce as a club's "personality."

Chapter 4 examines the fitness media's role as arbiter and therapeutic expert in consumers' self-improvement projects, using data from fitness magazines and exercise manuals from the 1980s and 1990s, and interviews with advertising associates at fitness magazines. Returning to the dual anxieties of health and appearance, the chapter discusses the significant role of middle-class – and particularly women – consumers in the boom in fitness publishing and lifestyle media more generally. The chapter reveals the ways in which fitness is officially constructed as a commercial lifestyle, for which fitness participants must necessarily buy into a web of goods and services.

The problem of motivation, and themes of enticement, discipline and reward, dominate the content of fitness texts, making clear the difficult status of the body as a site of investment, and the challenges for individuals trying to reconcile the demands placed upon them and negotiate the tension between an ascetic ethic of hard work and an aesthetic ethic of indulgence.

Chapter 5 examines the ideal construction and subjective experience of the occupation of personal training, drawing on data from interviews with personal trainers and their clients, and personal trainer manuals and journals. The chapter reviews exercise instruction forebears and the factors contributing to the expansion of the occupation, before turning to the incongruous aspects of personal training work, which combines quasi-professional expertise in exercise science, with entrepreneurial personal service skills. While knowledge of exercise and nutrition may be necessary for professional certification, trainers' occupational success ultimately rests on their social and embodied capital – they must "fit" their occupation in terms of physique, personality, performance, and disposition. The bodies of trainers serve as resources for the production of status – for the trainers themselves, the clubs in which they work, and their clients, who are encouraged to regard trainers as role models for the fitness lifestyle. Personal trainers thus exemplify the work of cultural intermediaries, who are the ideal producers and consumers of fitness, for it is their own lifestyle that they are selling.

The final chapter reviews how the fitness field provides an education befitting a consumer culture and service economy. Returning to the argument that through fitness, participants negotiate social demands and thereby produce their own bodily status, the chapter addresses the seemingly paradoxical coexistence of fitness and fatness within consumer cultures around the world. The US is the global exemplar of this paradox, with the world's largest fitness industry and, at the same time, the highest rates of population obesity and inactivity. However, when viewed from the perspective of the fitness field – rather than simply expenditure on exercise equipment or health club membership trends – it becomes clear that the fitness industry is well placed to benefit from, but ill-equipped to solve, the moral panics and problems of population obesity and inactivity. Not only does the fitness field's status orientation tend to exclude those lower down the socio-economic ladder (who are disproportionately more likely to be obese and physically inactive), but it also configures the pursuit of fitness as an individual, leisure-time activity, rather than a public health issue that requires environmental change and collective behavioral prescriptions.

2 The roots of fitness

Physical culture and physical capital

Notions of individual physical fitness reflect the particular problems of social fitness. As society is transformed through such processes as urbanization, immigration, industrialization, and deindustrialization, the problems and practices of the individual body symbolically reproduce the crises and rituals of the social body (Douglas 1966, 1982). At times of war, for example, when the social body comes under attack and must defend itself, physical fitness has been defined as the capacity for battle, and the individual's strength and endurance become the concern of the population as a whole. Fitness is thus best understood as a relative state, a level of competence or capacity to succeed in particular conditions. As conditions change – from war to peace, rural to urban living, manufacturing to service economies – so too do the body's capacities that are socially valued. Over time, some notions of fitness emerge and become dominant while others become residual, and may become dominant once again (cf. Williams 1977: 112).

The first half of this chapter explores the changing meanings and conditions for physical fitness and exercise from the nineteenth to the mid-twentieth century. These historic attitudes and ideas about the body's physical capacities – the ends to which they are directed and the means by which they are developed – form the foundations for the contemporary fitness field. This history, while not exhaustive, highlights several salient features of the long-term physical culture of the US, including the instrumental ethos that underlies much physical culture, the long-term process of commercialization, and the different ways in which the forms of and access to physical culture have been stratified by class and gender.

Thus, the contemporary fitness field draws on a long history of physical culture. Health foods, workout programs, sports clubs, and weightlifting equipment had all existed for at least a century (Green 1986) when the New

York Health Club, one of the first of a new breed of commercial health clubs, opened its doors in 1973. As such, it is important to begin with the traditional physical culture roots of the fitness field, if only to debunk the popular media's representation of the 1970s fitness boom as entirely new. Despite its long-term roots, however, the 1970s marks the "take-off" of the contemporary commercialization of fitness.

The second half of the chapter examines how the convergence of concerns about the body as a form of physical capital created the conditions for the take-off of an individualized and commercialized version of physical fitness. The concept of "physical capital" (Bourdieu 1986; Shilling 1993) refers to the ways in which the body's shape, size, deportment, physical ability, and so forth serve as resources that may be used for economic or social gain. Of particular relevance to the fitness field are two broad rubrics of physical capital that roughly correspond with the body's function and form – broadly speaking, its health and appearance – that were problematized in new ways and emphasized to new degrees around the start of the 1970s.

These forms of physical capital, and their associated values, criteria and problems, are not mutually exclusive and may even overlap, as is often the case in talking to people about why they want to be, or get fit. For example, consider the response from Paulina (the manager of an independent film theatre, in her early 50s) to the question of why she works out:

> You know what, I think it's fear of dying, you know. I just don't want to croak of a heart attack at 55. I want to be healthy, I want to look good. You know, I feel that altogether, it makes me feel much better than I would without it. . . . Sometimes it's torture to get up at seven o'clock in the morning and drag yourself here when it's cloudy outside and you want to sleep. But altogether it pays off.

In response to the same question of "Why work out?", Luke, a teacher and entrepreneur in his mid-30s, explains:

> Because, I've been doing it for so long, and generally as a result feeling healthy for a long time. I mean, there's a difference, I *feel* differently when I don't [work out]. You become accustomed to feeling a particular way, or looking a particular way. And I . . . want to keep pursuing that. So it's partly a health issue, but there's . . . it's a vanity issue also. But we're not supposed to be motivated so much by vanity, right? . . . So people say health, or "I'm doing this because I want to live longer," or

"I want cardiovascular improvement." All of which is probably true, but
. . . I wouldn't *do it*, I wouldn't be at the gym three days a week if there
were not also a vanity issue.

Health and appearance, and the perceived worth attached to them, are often
inextricably linked in people's understandings of the meaning and rewards
of fitness, and their motivations for participating in fitness activities.

To understand the particular nature of the contemporary fitness field
and the timing of its emergence in the 1970s, it is important to examine how
the material consequences of exercise (such as weight loss, muscle toning
and reduced risk of disease) fit the demands for particular forms of physical
capital, and the social, political, and economic conditions of the era: individual desires and anxieties about looking good, keeping up and staying
youthful and healthy; political health agendas around reducing the prevalence and cost of chronic diseases; commercial interests of appearance
industries; and a service economy labor market that placed a premium on
appearances and images.

A SELECTIVE HISTORY OF PHYSICAL CULTURE

Physical culture constitutes a vast subject, spanning different time periods,
societies, and groups within those societies. It is not the purpose of this book
to provide a comprehensive overview of the historical and global forms of
physical culture; however, a grasp of some of the long-standing traditions
within physical culture is helpful for understanding the conditions that made
possible and gave shape to the mass commercialization of fitness from the
1970s onwards. What follows is thus a selective account of physical culture
in the US since the early nineteenth century, drawing heavily on Harvey
Green's (1986) comprehensive history of fitness in the US from 1830 to 1940
(see also Mrozek 1989; Riess 1989; Whorton 1982). The account, here, highlights those issues and developments most pertinent to the contemporary
commercial fitness field.

A central thread running from nineteenth-century physical culture to the
current day commercial fitness field is the belief in physical activity as a
route to individual and social improvement. While the particular forms of
physical activity deemed legitimate (especially with respect to the gender of
the participants), and the goals and criteria for improvement, have changed
over time, the contemporary construction of fitness as an instrumental

means to some other end (reduced weight, improved appearance, and so forth) can be traced back to the nineteenth-century institutionalization of a "positive ideology" of sport (Riess 1989), which regarded physical activity as a means of developing an individual's moral fiber.

That sport and exercise could be positive influences on the lives of individuals and communities was a profound departure from earlier Puritan suspicion of athletics as idle distractions from one's worldly and moral duties (Adelman 1986: 269; Green 1989: 7). However, Puritan disdain for physical pursuits was not total; in the seventeenth century, they endorsed, for example, running and forms of calisthenics (Guttmann 1995). What is crucial is that the Puritan attitude towards sports was instrumental: sports were a means to an end (rest and recreation in the service of a moral life) and not ends in themselves, sources of pleasure or routes to bodily excellence. At the start of the nineteenth century, Puritan beliefs in predestination were giving way to the belief that, through intentional improvement, individuals, and the human race generally, could bring about a state of perfection (Green 1986: 10). This shift in perspective – from a predetermined fate to a perfectible self – placed the responsibility for physical and mental improvement, health and, ultimately, salvation on the shoulders of individuals, thereby providing a powerful justification for intentional exercise and physical activity.

Between 1820 and 1860, participation in athletics thus came to be regarded as a way to build a healthy body, good moral values, and a strong character. This shift in the dominant view of exercise came from both the changing character of religion and also the transformation of urban life. Cities were growing more dense and heterogeneous. As well, the industrialization of cities had increased the proportion of bureaucratic, mental labor occupations.[1] These changing social conditions posed both new opportunities and new challenges for physical culture. The positive sports ideology was applied through a range of moral and urban health reform movements, in which the negative consequences of sedentary living, immigration, and crowded urban dwelling were battled through exercise and "rational recreation" (Bailey 1978).

As large numbers of people migrated to the cities (both from the rural US and from other countries), opportunities arose for cross-cultural exchange. For example, Germans, who immigrated to the US *en masse* in the mid-1800s, brought with them social and political traditions in which gymnastics occupied a prominent part in community life and social reform. Friederich Jahn had started the *turnverein* – "Turner" or, literally, "gymnastic" society – in Germany, and an American student of Jahn's had introduced these "Turner societies" to the US in the 1820s. With the growing German immigrant population, fully fledged Turner societies were established in the mid-1800s (Riess 1989: 23). Due at least in part to the example of the Turners, cities built public gymnasiums – New York had 4 gymnasiums by 1840 (Adelman 1986: 259) – and organized exercises were a common part of the American school system by 1850 (Green 1986: 89). Other influences came from the British, whose contributions included the vastly influential Rational Recreation (Bailey 1978) and Muscular Christianity movements (to which the discussion will return shortly; see Riess 1989), and from the Scottish who, like the Germans, brought with them their own set of (Caledonian or Highland) games, which were often run as commercial spectator sports (Jarvie 1991; Riess 1989).

While Turner societies aided the institutionalization of a positive link between athletic exercise and personal and social development, the rising pace of urbanization and industrialization added urgency to the promotion of exercise. The social transformations involved with large portions of the population moving from rural to urban settings, and large numbers of immigrants joining the urban population, added fuel to an earlier critique of the degeneration of American society (Adelman 1986: 270). Social critics of the time highlighted two problems of urban pathology: for the working class and the poor, city life brought with it new dangers in terms of disease and injury, corruption and anomie; for the middle classes, urban life increasingly meant a sedentary and stressful life, and the threats of corruption and effeminacy through luxury and the loss of the rustic life (Adelman 1986; Green 1986; Riess 1989). Social and health reformers, physicians, and the popular press promoted physical activity for the individual as the panacea for the social ills of the day. Exercise and sport promised to return the pastoral values, masculinity, and physical strength of Colonial times to the middle class, while forming the poor, immigrant, and working classes into respectful, moral, healthy, cooperative, American citizens.

The perception that social problems stemmed from the nature of urban life was underscored by the state of medicine and disease in the early and mid-nineteenth century. Outbreaks of epidemics such as cholera raised concerns over cities' water supplies and sanitation, and the need for fresh air and exercise. Meanwhile, the spread of tuberculosis in the 1830s, given its association with crowded and insanitary living conditions, served as a further confirmation of social degradation for those already convinced that moral and health reform were needed (Green 1986: 88–9). As one historian studying health in Victorian times has suggested, "with both the causes and patterns of disease very much matters of speculation, it was difficult ever to feel comfortable about the state of one's health" (Haley 1978: 11). Moreover, since medical treatment was often as severe as the diagnoses were uncertain, it was little wonder that methods of prevention and self-help therapy found a receptive audience (Green 1986: 24).

The clearest articulation of the positive sport ideology – though neither the only nor the first – was the Muscular Christianity movement. Originating in Britain in the early 1800s (in much the same conditions of rapid urbanization and industrialization), Muscular Christianity sought to bring together the mental, physical and spiritual development of men. Women were not as central to discussions of social problems and reform as were men, in part because women were not regarded as a major force in the labor market and reforms targeting the working class and poor were concerned with the formation of strong, healthy, moral *workers*. Nevertheless, Catherine Beecher and others were promoting calisthenics – gymnastics for women – by the early 1800s as a means of ensuring healthy, moral women (Green 1986: 87, 91).

Muscular Christianity endorsed athletics as a substitute for the rugged rural life, a means for instilling the same values – manliness, individualism, sexual restraint – while providing fresh air and an alternative to the vile, corrupting amusements of urban life (Riess 1989: 30). The institution most associated with Muscular Christianity was the Young Men's Christian Association (YMCA), brought to North America from Britain in 1851 (Zald 1970). Despite the integration of mental, physical and spiritual development in its stated mission, the YMCA in the US remained predominantly focused, until the 1880s, upon the spiritual needs of rural young men moving to the city for the first time. Prior to 1880, the YMCA's facilities did not usually include gymnasiums: only two YMCAs had gymnasiums in 1876. However, the number exploded to 101 by 1886, and 495 by 1896 (Zald 1970: 33). The growing numbers of gymnasiums were not merely expressions of the Muscular Christianity philosophy, but were also an attempt to stabilize the financial base of the YMCA (Zald 1970: 43–4). Like other Protestant organizations, the YMCA used memberships, contributions, and fund-raising to support itself. As membership conferred no special status or services, and those offering support were also funding the churches, the YMCA's financial base was unstable. Efforts to promote a stable financial base focused on the development of gymnasiums and residences, and the impact of the gymnasiums in stabilizing finances and membership was significant, foreshadowing the commercial health club industry by a century.

The YMCA was not alone in building sites for physical culture in the nineteenth century. Public spaces for recreation were established through national movements, such as those for municipal parks in the 1860s, and playgrounds[2] in the early 1900s (Riess 1989). Semi-public sites like those of the YMCA were joined by the public gymnasiums built by entrepreneurs and local governments (Green 1986: 182). Sporting activity was also joined by sport spectatorship, with the development of numerous venues for spectator sports, such as Madison Square Garden, opened by William K. Vanderbilt in 1879 (Riess 1989: 204). In addition, the number of private sport spaces greatly increased in the 1880s and 1890s. These spaces ranged from the elite athletic and country clubs to modest sport clubs for immigrant communities (Mayo 1998; Riess 1989).

Dr Luther H. Gulick, Jr, was responsible for reforming the YMCA's mission to provide equal attention to physical as well as spiritual development.[3] A principal advocate of Muscular Christianity, Gulick transformed the YMCA into a leader in physical exercise, adopting the emblem of an inverted triangle to signify the commitment to developing mind, body, and spirit. The YMCA's physical program tended to emphasize sport over gymnastics; students of Gulick invented such indoor pursuits as basketball (1892) and volleyball (1895). At the same time, the Young Women's Christian Association's (YWCA) program included an increasing emphasis on athletics along with its original mission of saving respectable, single women from corruption in the city (Riess 1989: 158). While the YMCA's program was ostensibly aimed at all Christians (and would, as time passed, lessen its emphasis on the religion of its members), it was not aimed at all classes. YMCAs were located in middle-class neighborhoods, declared their mission to serve "better classes," and worked on a paid membership basis. Only those company-financed YMCAs (such as those of the railroad and steel[4] companies) had an explicit emphasis on recruiting working-class members (Cohen 1990: 180; Riess 1989: 83, 157; Zald 1970: 39).

In the early 1900s, Gulick further narrowed the YMCA's focus to athletics and team sports (rather than calisthenics and gymnastics), following his theory that humankind's highest moral principles and qualities were instilled through "higher" stages of play (Riess 1989: 159). This was prefigured in Britain in the 1860s, in what was called the "Games Cult," which had its most explicit parallel in the US with the later adoption of British games and their Americanization (for example, the transformation of rugby into American football) in Ivy League schools such as Harvard and Yale (Bailey 1978; see also Green 1986: 233). Gulick linked the YMCA to other, non-religious reform and educational movements, such as the public school system, for which he directed the physical training program and athletic league in New York City in the early 1900s (Riess 1989: 160). Reformers in the settlement house movement (notably, Jane Addams of Hull-House) further promoted athletics as essential to a healthy, moral, American way of life. Addams and other settlement house workers used athletics not only as a means of drawing youth into their institutions, but also as a way to promote proper character and bodily development; by 1890, Chicago's Hull-House had organized gymnastics and calisthenics classes for boys and girls (Riess 1989: 164–5).

Linking Addams' and Gulick's efforts on a national level was Theodore Roosevelt's Strenuous Life philosophy (Green 1986: 236). At the end of the nineteenth century, Roosevelt combined athleticism with nationalism,[5] promoting a vigorous life as the solution to the flagging strength of the American male and (to a different end) female:

> A life of slothful ease, a life of that peace which springs merely from lack either of desire or of power to strive after great things, is as little worthy of a nation as of an individual. . . . In the last analysis a healthy state can exist only when the men and women who make it up lead clean, vigorous, healthy lives; when the children are so trained that they shall endeavor, not to shirk difficulties, but to overcome them; not to seek ease, but to know how to wrest triumph from toil and risk. The man must be glad to do a man's work, to dare and endure and to labor, to keep himself, and to keep those dependent upon him. The woman must be the housewife, the helpmeet of the homemaker, the wise and fearless mother of many healthy children.
>
> (Roosevelt in 1899, cited in Briedland *et al.* 1996: 377–8)

Roosevelt was not alone in declaring the American middle class in need of regeneration. Urban labor unrest in the 1870s and 1880s, and the declining birth rates of Anglo-Saxon families, raised the fear of "race suicide," in which the "Puritan stock" would be overrun by unruly, inferior immigrant races, who were no longer controlled (and socialized) through the challenge of frontier living (Green 1986: 219–24). The "answer" lay in fortifying the Puritan stock. Roosevelt championed athletic competitions such as football and boxing as the mechanism for producing manly and courageous leaders in the middle class, which – according to Roosevelt – suffered from a reputation of "timidity and unwarlikeness" (cited in Lasch 1979: 201). To improve the stock of the middle class was to improve the reputation of the country.

Anxieties regarding the uncertain position of the middle class were further manifested in the identification of a new health threat in the late nineteenth century: neurasthenia. At the same time that a germ theory of disease was locating blame for illness outside of the individual, this resolutely middle-class disease reaffirmed the ideology that health was a matter of individual responsibility and physical development. Unlike other diseases, neurasthenia – a nervousness, or weakness of the nerves – could not be blamed on germs; it was a product of the stressful, competitive, *middle-class* life of the late nineteenth century (Green 1986; Whorton 1982). Dr George Beard, the leading medical (and popular) authority on neurasthenia, stated that "physicians, lawyers, inventors, etc. furnish proportionately the largest contingent to this class of patients," and that the disease was "oftener met with in cities than in the country, [and] is more marked and more frequent at the desk, the pulpit and the counting-room than in the shop or on the farm" (cited in Green 1986: 138–9). This was a disease afflicting men who were involved in mental labor – as Beard called it, "brain work" – rather than manual labor. Although the cause of neurasthenia was an over-taxing of the brain – through the complexities of work or city life – the symptoms were predominantly physical, not mental. Thus, neurasthenia required physical treatments (Whorton 1982: 149), including exercise, fasting, baths and eating regimens (Green 1986: 140–66).

Although Beard regarded neurasthenia as a man's disease, the symptoms of nervous disorders were more typically diagnosed in the "weaker sex." Such a plague of nervousness, though it might have laid an easier path for women's access to sports and physical culture, was instead used to further constrain their general emancipation. Reflecting the larger fears about women entering the masculine world of work, Beard argued that women's nervous exhaustion was caused by the greater mental effort required to compete in the men's world (Whorton 1982: 150–2). Thus, the cure was not exercise but a prescribed retreat from public life. Nevertheless, women's participation in physical culture increased greatly in the late nineteenth and early twentieth centuries, especially with the popularity of skating in the 1860s (Adelman 1986: 259) and bicycling in the 1890s (Green 1986: 229–31). Women's participation in bicycling, skating and calisthenics was endorsed by medical authorities also seeking to promote dress reform and the end of the health-impairing corset (Green 1986: 185–6). Bicycling was particularly recommended to women as a cure for neurasthenia – if done in moderation, of course (Green 1986: 231).

As an updated, medicalized version of the traditional view of urban pathology, neurasthenia provided further justification (indeed, imperative) for the middle class to participate in physical culture. This entrenchment of sports and exercise as part of middle-class life paved the way for the commercialization of physical culture. At the forefront of the sporting boom of the late nineteenth century were middle-class participants, spectators, and consumers. For the middle class, physical culture was not only legitimated by the positive ideology of sport

> but was also a product of the growing wealth of cities, booming urban populations, sufficient discretionary income and leisure time among non-factory workers, the positive example of English, Scottish, and German sportsmen, the rise of middle-class voluntary associations [such as athletic clubs], the development of sports entrepreneurship, and various technological innovations that improved interurban transportation and communication networks [to access facilities outside of the city].
>
> (Riess 1989: 47)

Moreover, athletics provided middle-class individuals – particularly men – with an opportunity for satisfaction, creativity, and individuality that was felt to be lacking in the increasingly bureaucratized, sedentary work world (Elias and Dunning 1986). As middle-class interest and participation in sports grew, so too did the middle-class market for athletic products and services.

The late 1800s saw a large increase in the number of health and fitness entrepreneurs, who laid the organizational groundwork for the mass commercialization of the 1920s and 1930s. Best remembered thanks to their corporate legacies are breakfast cereal pioneers Sylvester Graham, John Harvey Kellogg, and Charles W. Post, who prefigured the health food industry with their prescribed eating regimes and special high-fiber and "natural" foods. No less influential, however, were S.D. Kehoe and Dioclesian Lewis, whose gymnastic programs, pamphlets, and equipment were successful businesses in the late nineteenth century (Green 1986: 188–93). Kehoe and, even more so, Lewis were responsible for popularizing a form of exercise using equipment – a "new gymnastics" – that today's fitness classes would instantly recognize.

In addition, large-scale sport retailers and a sporting goods industry emerged in the 1870s and 1880s (Hardy 1995). For example, A.G. Spalding & Brothers began in 1876, and by 1900 (in competition with several other sporting goods manufacturers) were selling equipment for every major sport, sponsoring sporting events and contests, publishing sport books and

advertising their brand nationwide (Hardy 1995: 139–45). The Spalding catalog (200 pages in 1909) was an index not only of the growing variety of
sporting goods designed and marketed to meet the sporting boom, but of
changing bodily ideals as well (Green 1986: 240). One catalog cover featured
Eugene Sandow, one of the first promoters of bodybuilding, endorsing
a type of dumb-bell. Sandow parlayed his reputation as an extraordinary
physical specimen and legendary bodybuilder into a sideline career as a
product endorser (Green 1986: 213) – an activity that now eclipses sports
performance *per se* as the source of income for today's top sports stars.

Bernarr Macfadden was the exemplar of the early twentieth-century
physical culture entrepreneurs (Green 1986: 242–54). Macfadden's career in
health and fitness promotion began in the 1890s, and would eventually
include books, health resorts, magazines (in particular, *Physical Culture*), and
touring physical culture shows (following the early lead of Florenz Ziegfeld,
Jr, who had exhibited Sandow in the 1893 Chicago World's Fair). In a manner prophetic of today's norms, Macfadden's shows and magazines combined displays of bodybuilding and sexuality (earning him obscenity charges
in 1905). By the 1920s, *Physical Culture* contained articles on how to improve
every aspect of a man's being, from his diction to his body odor – the white,
middle-class man's companion to countless similar publications aimed at
women in the 1910s and onward.

In 1933, *Physical Culture* acquired a new subtitle: *The Personal Problem
Magazine* (Green 1986: 282), signaling a shift from the social to the individual
in the ends to which physical exercise was directed. Physical exercise had
become a personal problem and project, tied not to moral character building,
as it had been in the nineteenth century, but to appearances and personality.
The purpose of individual self-improvement was no longer represented in
terms of a better, stronger society, as it had been for Roosevelt. Popular
culture in the early twentieth century was concerned not with the pursuit of
a better society, but with convincing individuals to adapt and fit in (Ewen
1976; Green 1989; Lears 1989; Mrozek 1989; Sivulka 2001; Susman 1979).
Reflecting these changing attitudes were depictions of physical culture in
magazines, books, and photographs, which began to accentuate the pleasures
and positive experiences involved in physical culture, without reference to
moral reforms or national strength (Mrozek 1989). The self-discipline and
restraint associated with exercise in the nineteenth-century moral reforms
gave way to representations and messages of self-expression and fulfillment:
exercise was to be pursued for the "intense experience" and self-realization it
produced (Mrozek 1989: 20).

This is not to suggest that societal objectives ceased to be relevant to the history of fitness. Threats to external social boundaries at times of war coincided with rises in popular interest in, and government policies about, physical fitness over the twentieth century. The First World War brought about the institutionalization of mandatory physical education in schools – not as a preparatory move, but in response to the rejection of so many men (almost 82 per cent in 1915–16) from military service due to poor physical condition (Griffin 1982: 267). But, in a pattern that would continue, the interest in physical fitness (conceived as fitness for duty) declined with the end of the war. By the Second World War, fully one-third of draftees were unfit for duty (Griffin 1982: 267), leading to renewed calls for physical education (see, for example, Fine 1943). Tests of physical fitness showed how poorly Americans – especially children – compared to other citizens of the world. In the 1950s, in a climate of anxiety regarding the Soviet Union's technological lead, the unfitness of American youth prompted such political initiatives as President Dwight Eisenhower's President's Council on Youth Fitness (established in 1956 and reaffirmed by every president since), and President John F. Kennedy's 1960 article for *Sports Illustrated* on the problem of "Soft Americans."

What is striking about the relationship between war and fitness over the twentieth century is how short-lived was the public's interest in fitness for duty. News coverage and policy initiatives about fitness as a measure of national strength and preparedness fell off steeply between moments of crisis. It was not that the public was uninterested in fitness during times of peace and security, but that the popular media representations of fitness focused more on personal appearance and social acceptance, and less on physical fitness for military defense. However, even during times of war, the nation's survival was wedded to individual improvement. In a 1942 *New Yorker* advertisement for the Elizabeth Arden spa, readers were told of Susan, overweight and unhappy, who discovered the Arden "Physical Fitness Treatments":

> Now Susan breezes through her defense work . . . interested, alert, and physically fit. Susan is very much aware now that to look and feel your best you must first build your health and strength.[6]

The 1940s woman was encouraged to embrace both notions of fitness; by being strong *and* looking her best, Susan reconciled the tensions between the new and traditional roles of women. Thus, it is difficult to draw a stark contrast between notions of fitness during times of war and times of peace, especially with the ascendancy of consumer culture over the twentieth century in mediating concerns about individual and social problems. Research by the US Bureau of Economic Analysis, for example, showed that spending at health clubs, beauty parlors, and barber shops outpaced consumer spending during World War Two and the Korean War (Buckley 2001).

Of particular relevance to the historical foundation of the contemporary fitness field is the long-term and ongoing dialogue between the Protestant virtues of hard work, self-sacrifice, and deferred gratification – promoted heavily in the nineteenth-century producer society – and the ethic of self-fulfillment and self-gratification that came to the fore over the twentieth century (Campbell 1987; Mrozek 1989). In the early twentieth century, the growth of service occupations (especially sales), appearance industries (such as cosmetics and advertising), and Hollywood films and celebrity images facilitated an increasing emphasis on qualities such as charm, magnetism, attractiveness, and self-presentation as the bases for judgments in the business and social worlds (Decker 1997; Ewen 1976; Featherstone 1982; Marchand 1985; Peiss 1998; Susman 1979). In his 1936 manual, *How to Win Friends and Influence People*, Dale Carnegie's instructions captured the emergence of a performing self, who knew the importance of putting on a smile while retaining a traditional expectation of authenticity:

> An insincere grin? No. That doesn't fool anybody. We know it is mechanical and we resent it. I am talking about a real smile, a heart-warming smile, a smile that comes from within, the kind of smile that will bring a good price in the market place.
>
> (Carnegie in 1936, cited in Briedland *et al.* 1996: 385)

This transition, which Warren Susman (1979) describes as a shift from a culture of character to a culture of personality, is borne out in the changing construction of the values and rewards of physical culture.

The move in physical culture, and public culture more generally, towards an emphasis on the individual and self-actualization did not go uncontested; critics decried the artificiality of this new, appearance-oriented individualistic culture. Nevertheless, others took a more pragmatic view; for example, *The New York Times* ran an editorial in 1927 defending the cosmetics and beauty parlor industry as a source of national strength, which had made the means of social mobility – beauty – available to all (Haiken 1997: 99). In the same year, the beauty editor of *Women's Home Companion* published a beauty guide, *Any Girl Can Be Good Looking*, in which she told her young women readers: "Everybody is thinking more these days about good looks. . . . Being good looking is no longer optional. People who pass us on the street can't know that we're clever and charming *unless we look it*" (cited in Haiken 1997: 91; emphasis added). In a growing service economy, in the context of an increasingly bureaucratic and impersonal world, having good looks and making a good first impression superceded character as the basis of upward social mobility (Featherstone 1991; Susman 1979). Advertisers added messages stressing the importance of those first impressions, and offered a universe of goods as the tools of upward mobility (Marchand 1985).

The promotion of physical self-improvement as a means to social mobility and individual fulfillment was not limited to women. Indeed, one of the best examples of the early twentieth-century transition in physical culture from the goal of societal health to individual improvement is that of Charles Atlas, whose bodybuilding manuals were directed explicitly at men. Atlas is an archetypal figure for the era. From a poor, immigrant childhood, Angelo Siciliano is "reborn" as Charles Atlas, through physical development and the legitimation of winning a bodybuilding contest (Gaines 1982): in Atlas, the twentieth-century formula of social mobility through self-improvement, appearance, and celebrity is privileged over the nineteenth-century vision of molding American citizens through physical culture.

Atlas began his career of popularizing muscularity and bodybuilding in the early 1920s. In 1921, based on a photograph of Atlas in leopard-skin briefs, Bernarr Macfadden declared Atlas the winner of his "World's Most Beautiful Man Contest" (Gaines 1982: 57–8). Based on the publicity, Atlas began a mail-order business for his exercise manual. Ironically, given his status as, literally, a self-made man, Atlas was a poor businessman, and his fledgling business nearly went bankrupt. In 1928, Atlas took on advertising writer Charles Roman as his business partner. Roman used Atlas' personal biography of a poor, scrawny immigrant kid who, through physical development, becomes a successful businessman and icon, to shape the advertising campaigns (Gaines 1982). The archetypal advertisement, which dates from the 1930s, featured "The Insult That Made a Man Out of Mac." In it, a skinny young man is bullied at the beach and loses his girlfriend to the better-built aggressor. Out of frustration, the weakling turns to Atlas' program, which – seemingly instantaneously – helps him to become a "new man." The newly muscular young man returns to the beach, takes revenge on the bully, reclaims his girlfriend, and is thus affirmed in his masculinity.[7]

Atlas advocated an overall regime for living, including instructions on posture, grooming, clothing, sleep patterns, breathing exercises, how to deal with constipation, diet and the proper "chewing" of milk and water, and the necessity of perseverance (Gaines 1982: 113). In short, he offered a manual for a total style of life, including an education in masculinity. The advertisement's parable of muscularity-as-masculinity was situated at a time of uncertainty for men. If male identity was bound to physique, the growing trend away from agricultural or manual labor meant that working hard no longer guaranteed a "masculine" body. As well, the Great Depression rendered uncertain what little was left in the workplace for defining a masculine identity as the sole and stable breadwinner (Kimmel 1996). It is no surprise that at a time of such uncertainty, Atlas' bodybuilding course found a large market, becoming, by 1942, the most successful mail-order business in US history (Kimmel 1996: 211). If *being* a man was wrought with uncertainty, then *looking* like a man became the solution.

Updating the nineteenth-century "rags to riches" novels of Horatio Alger, the "meek to muscles" myth of Charles Atlas highlights that women were not the only targets of the appearance industries. Playing on men's insecurities about being too scrawny and weak, Atlas' course promised a new, desired and admired identity through a new body. There was no need to justify bodybuilding with visions of national strength or moral virtue. Rather, Roman's advertising campaign tried to "reach into where people live, not into their abstract thoughts about good health and leverage over objects, but into their fears and longings, and dreams for themselves" (Gaines 1982: 69).

Throughout the 1940s and 1950s, Atlas popularized his "dynamic-tension" method of muscle development. During the same time – but targeting women as well as men – Jack La Lanne was also using fitness as the basis of a commercial venture.[8] La Lanne and his staff led people in an exercise program of calisthenics and weightlifting, both in his health spas and his nationally broadcast 1950s television program, *The Jack La Lanne Show*. La Lanne's links to exercise equipment and health spa memberships were far more developed than those of Atlas, whose exercise program required no special equipment. Indeed, Atlas' advertising boasted that the reader required no "weights, springs or pulleys. Only 15 minutes a day of pleasant practice – in the privacy of your room" (Gaines 1982: 71). By comparison, today's commercial fitness field deliberately cultivates dependence on memberships, machines, props, and apparel.

La Lanne was embedded within a leisure boom that arose at the intersection of postwar affluence, mass consumption, and popular interest in quality of life. One sign of such newfound personal affluence was the television set.

Watching television, an increasingly common part of leisure since the 1950s, not only involves no exercise, but also converts exercise and sport into spectacles rather than activities. Televised gridiron football rose in popularity in the 1950s, increasing the commercialization and competitiveness of both the college and professional games. As well, professional basketball was adapted to improve spectator appeal and increase television audience size (Sidwell and Kane 1990: 184–5), reinforcing the notion of a "degradation" of sport into commercial entertainment spectacles, and individuals into spectators (Huizinga 1955; Lasch 1979: 184–97). As in the nineteenth century, changing factors created the conditions for physical activity to become a "problem"; for the middle class, the issue was no longer the forms of labor ("mental" work), but the increasingly sedentary nature of forms of leisure.

With rising standards of living and increasing non-work time, the YMCA was well placed for the 1950s leisure boom. However, massive suburbanization brought several changes to the YMCA's clientele and challenges to its stated mission (Putney 1997). First, the intended audience for the YMCA (Christian, single, young men moving to the city for work) gave way to a new, suburban market of women and families from a variety of religious backgrounds.[9] While this market enlarged the prospective membership, it also created a lack of focus in organizing the various classes and programs. Athletics programs were often overshadowed by classes such as cooking and language instruction, intended to serve a diversifying clientele (Putney 1997). Second, the YMCA's moral mission and social relevance were challenged by the organization's growing secularization, and – as the 1960s progressed – the general cultural climate of distrust towards large institutions. Third, dovetailing with the general shift in physical culture from social reform to individual improvement, the YMCA's emphasis on physical training came to focus less and less on the effects of character-building and moral development. Rather, athletics was to be engaged in for its merits for the individual participant, further undermining the YMCA's original mission.

The YMCA's attention to athletics for social improvement returned briefly in the 1960s, following President Kennedy's lead, with a cautionary plea concerning the "softness" of American youth compared to their Soviet counterparts (Putney 1997: 240). The full reinvigoration of the YMCA's focus on fitness, however, did not occur until the end of the 1960s, when the public's growing interest in exercise was led not by the YMCA – as it had been in the 1880s – but by other "crusaders," such as Dr Kenneth Cooper and Dr George Sheehan, the "fathers" of aerobics and jogging. Responding to the rising popularity of exercise, and in keeping with the era's concerns with individual (rather than social) reform, the YMCA updated its social mission from character-building to "values clarification." These two programs – fitness and values clarification – were inherently linked:

> Both catered to the individual – values clarificationists ensuring that individuals felt good about where they stood on things and physical therapists seeing to it that they simply felt good. Moreover, the YMCA's growing interest in fitness and values clarification reflected the association's retreat from the idea that the individual's well-being is dependent on the well-being of society.
>
> (Putney 1997: 243–4)

In the 1980s, the YMCA also responded to the recession with corporate training programs aimed at improving the health of white-collar workers (Putney 1997: 245). Thus, the YMCA reproduced the link between employability and fitness, an issue of the nineteenth century now cast in the late twentieth-century consumer culture's terms of self-improvement. Since the 1980s, the YMCA has become increasingly commercialized; in many ways, YMCAs are now indistinguishable from their for-profit counterparts (cf. Miller and Fielding 1995).

Emerging from this selective history of physical culture in the US are several long-term features and patterns that helped prepare the ground for the contemporary commercial fitness field: the commercialization of the equipment, venues and guidance associated with particular forms of physical activity; the role of class and gender in shaping access to physical culture, the particular forms of activity deemed legitimate, and the ends (societal and individual) to which participation was directed; and the ways in which changes in the nature of work, leisure and everyday life have problematized physical activity in different ways, creating the conditions for exercise to be regarded as a choice, a status activity, and a panacea for a mutable collection of social and individual ills. Furthermore, this history is marked by a long-term shift, whereby physical fitness as a means to achieve individual improvement has been largely decoupled from notions of societal improvement. This has meant a transition in the objectives of fitness from building a better society (through healthy bodies and moral characters) to better adapting to society (through attractive bodies and charming personalities). Nevertheless, the shift from societal reform to individual experience and improvement has not displaced the central tenet of the nineteenth-century positive sports ideology: the rationale for physical fitness was, and remains, predominantly instrumental. Physical activity was prescribed not for its intrinsic enjoyment, but for the results (either from the exercise, the enjoyment, or both) of self-development, increased competitiveness in the marketplace, and improved social status: in short, fitness was an investment in the body's physical capital.

THE BODY AS PHYSICAL CAPITAL

To take the body as a form of capital, and thus a site of investment and work, is to take account of its function and form (Baudrillard 1998; Featherstone 1982; Shilling 1993). The *function* of the body is typically considered through the lens of health. In a society dominated by a "cultural imaginary of health" (Greco 1993: 257–8) in which health and disease are framed as matters of individual will or failure, investing in the body – through regular physical activity, for example – can help to minimize one's health risks. The *form* of the body is typically associated with outer appearances. In a consumer service economy, physical appearances are important for occupational success and social status; thus, investing in the body's form – through toning exercises, for example – is considered a way of maximizing one's competitive edge. These two facets of physical capital – of function and form, health and appearance – have become *idées fixes* in consumer culture, for the middle classes in particular (Baudrillard 1998; Bourdieu 1984; Crawford 1984; Featherstone 1982, 1991; Laberge and Sankoff 1988; Shilling 1993; Wynne 1998). Since the 1970s, the commercial fitness industry in the US has promoted exercise as an ideal route to both of these forms of physical capital: exercise helps you feel good and look good.

The ways in which physical capital, and specifically health and appearance, have been problematized and valorized in the late twentieth and early twenty-first centuries are connected to changing external conditions, including patterns of disease and health economics that highlighted the need for individuals to adopt healthier lifestyles, and the demands within the post-Fordist service economy and consumer culture that attention be given to aesthetic, imagistic, and appearance-oriented matters. Against this backdrop, an important element in the pursuit of physical capital – through the fitness field and any number of other body industries – comes to light, concerning status.

Status functions in contemporary culture not simply via the possession and display of exclusive positional goods, but through the cultivation and performance of a variety of capabilities and mentalities that are held in high esteem, and which cluster around notions of individualization and self-responsibility. The accomplishment of a youthful, attractive appearance brings status rewards; so too does the development of one's health. Both offer visible displays of investment in oneself, and thus can confer status, in the sense that the body is a positional good (Hirsch 1977). At the same time, both offer opportunities for the individual to exert control over himself or herself, his or her health risks, feelings of embodiment, and impression upon others, and thus can confer status – the status of being "properly" or "fully" an individual; in the context of individualization, the body is the individual's first and most important project. Thus, the role of status in the formation of the fitness field is not to be reduced to the competitive consumption habits of the professional/managerial class (what, in the 1980s, would have been called Yuppies; today the term – in the form of consumption patterns rather than occupational category – seems to characterize a vast swathe of the consumer market; cf. Howell 1990, 2005). The fitness field offers opportunities for the accomplishment of the all-consuming, lifelong task of the modern individual to develop oneself via working on the body's status *as* a vehicle for self-expression and identity production, and as a status marker *per se*. With this in mind, the chapter now examines how the status of health and appearance has been constructed relative to the context of the late twentieth century.

The value of health

The issue of health was a common one in discussions with fitness field participants – producers and consumers alike. Health is deemed a socially legitimate and individually responsible concern, unlike the (often accompanying) concerns about appearance and attractiveness, and interviewees often attached moral connotations to their attempts to keep fit: this was something that they *should* do. I asked Maggie, who is in her 60s, to explain what prompted her to first join a gym:

> What was I, 55 . . . I just needed to get myself together, you know. I think everybody as they approach 50, they think, "Ah! Got to do something!" . . . I think it's more . . . a sense of responsibility. That there's only me to look after me. And if I don't do it, no one else will. . . . I have osteoporosis a little bit more than I normally would do, for my age. And this [walking on a treadmill] is excellent for that. And I should do

more weights. That's one thing I should do for myself. But it is a responsibility.

When I interviewed Donna, a freelance journalist, she had quit smoking two days earlier and had resolved to rejoin her gym. I asked her what had prompted these changes:

> Probably because I turned thirty in September. And that was *good*, but it's *weird*, because it's definitely the first time I've been aware of my age. This is the first time I'm like, "Wow. I'm an adult. This is it." . . . I'm an adult and I feel like, sort of with the smoking, there's so much I want to do, and I haven't done yet. And I don't want something stupid to derail me, like emphysema, for example, or something that I could control. Granted, you know, you could be felled by any number of things in life, certainly. But I do think that you can certainly raise the bar on your chances [*laughs*] of lasting a little longer and having a good time, so I want to prolong my existence.

Despite their difference in age, Donna and Maggie express similar sentiments with regard to the role of aging in heightening awareness of the need to take control of one's body and health prospects. But the notion of health to which Donna and Maggie allude is a very particular one: health as something that can be controlled by the individual through behaviors such as exercise and smoking cessation, rather than a passive state dictated for the individual by the fates, genes, or age. This view is, in many ways, the product of the dominant approach to health over Donna's lifetime: health promotion and health education campaigns have stressed the importance of individual behavior for reducing the risk of disease, and have heightened public awareness of health-related issues.

The emergence of the fitness field out of the earlier physical culture was prompted, in part, by this new vision of health as the outcome of individual lifestyle choices, which itself can be traced to a changing context of disease. At the start of the twentieth century, the leading causes of death in the US were influenza, pneumonia, and tuberculosis; these three accounted for 23 per cent of all deaths in 1900 (Committee on Ways and Means 1971: 121). Thanks to the success of the nineteenth-century public health reforms targeting water and air quality, sewage, personal hygiene, and nutrition, as well as rising standards of living and new vaccines and antibiotics, many of these communicable diseases were brought under control (Rader 1997; Russell

1986). By 1967, only 3 per cent of deaths were attributable to influenza and pneumonia, but 56 per cent were caused by heart disease and cancer (Committee on Ways and Means 1971: 121), which remain the leading causes of death today and – significantly for the fitness field – are associated with factors such as obesity and inactivity (World Health Organization 2004).

The rise of these so-called "lifestyle" diseases is the mixed blessing of modernity's technological advances: people are now living long enough – and under the conducive conditions – to develop chronic, degenerative diseases. Agricultural productivity has largely removed the threat of starvation for US citizens, but has led to such an abundance of food – fast, cheap, fat-rich food – that obesity is a common occurrence. Technology, such as the car and telephone, and the shift away from manual labor have reduced the inadvertent exercise of everyday life, compounding obesity with inactivity. Leisure pursuits, too, have added to the rise of lifestyle diseases. Television, a factor in rising rates of inactivity, continues to contribute to the reduction of sport into passive spectacle. And smoking has been denounced for its ill-effects; first for the harm to the individual smoker in the 1950s and 1960s, and later, in the 1970s, for those inhaling "second-hand" smoke (Jackson 1995). When the US Surgeon General's first report on smoking was published in 1964, over half of the men in the US smoked; by 1975, that number had dropped to 39 per cent (Lehmann 1979).

Growing public awareness of health issues – and consumption of health products – was also connected to issues less directly related to disease. Like the breakfast cereal pioneers Graham, Kellogg and Post of a hundred years earlier, the health-oriented consumer in the 1960s and 1970s was responding to a crisis of the social and individual body. The burgeoning environmental movement, the counter-culture – which spurred new interest in vegetarianism and sustainable agriculture – and the 1973 and 1979 energy crises all called attention to the health of both the planet and the patterns of social life (Gottlieb 1993; Schulman 2001), and spurred interest in possible solutions. A 1973 article in *New York Magazine*, for example, suggested isometric exercises, tennis, biking and exercise classes as a way to survive the winter during the oil crisis (Schoen and Cohen 1973). Not surprisingly, health food experienced massive retail growth over the 1960s and 1970s (Whorton 1982). New York City, for example, had only one health food retailer in 1960; that number had jumped to 43 by 1965, and to 81 by 1973.[10] More broadly, consumer and media industries have used the language of health to sell an increasing range of products and information (not all of them necessarily healthy).

Rising rates of chronic disease are not simply a matter of carcinogens, longer life-spans, technology, and environmental degradation, but are also deeply connected to the social etiology of disease. Good health involves factors such as eating better, exercising more, and cutting down on alcohol, tobacco and fat; but it also involves issues of class, poverty and inequality. Although the precise nature of the relationship between class and health is a continuing debate, one suggested factor – and an echo of the neurasthenia experts of the nineteenth century – is "social stress," the combined result of perceived relative deprivation ("I'm not as well off as my neighbor"), lack of control over one's life ("I have to do what my boss tells me; I can't afford to do what I want"), and lack of social bonds ("I don't have a close connection to my community") (Epstein 1998; see also Blaxter 2003; Schwartz 2001). Given the material conditions of everyday life, it is little wonder that stress is an issue: income inequality has grown steadily since the 1970s, with poverty rising and the average middle-class income shrinking (Frank 1999; Sassen 1990; Strobel 1993); the labor market has increasingly moved away from manufacturing (which has undergone massive deskilling) towards service jobs, the bulk of which are low-end positions which offer little in the way of control and creativity (Braverman 1974; Sassen 1990; Strobel 1993); even higher-end service positions require the managing of attitude and emotion, reducing control over one's appearance and expression (Hochschild 1983); and commentators have suggested that there has been a significant atomization of society since the 1970s, with declining social cohesiveness marked by decreasing membership in church and community groups and rising crime and divorce rates (Fukuyama 1999; Putnam 2000).

Class position affects health as a determinant of access to good nutrition, recreation facilities and adequate health care, and of the experience of stress. Furthermore, health attitudes vary across classes, with the middle classes taking a more proactive approach based on a belief in their ability to effectively manage health (thereby incorporating health as a key element in identity construction), and the working classes taking a more passive view of the inescapability of health problems (Crawford 1979, 1984, 1994). In general, class has an almost linear relationship with health: no matter where on the social ladder, if all other variables are held constant, individuals are more likely to be healthier than the person on the rung below, and less healthy than the person above (Epstein 1998). Given these factors, it is little wonder that stress levels and lifestyle-related diseases are on the rise.

The transition from infectious to chronic, lifestyle-related diseases provided the impetus in the 1970s to rethink health care as disease prevention.

This change in policy reflected the higher overall costs associated with chronic diseases, and came at the same time that the US government was facing a general fiscal crisis *and* an increasing share of the costs of health care, particularly after the implementation of Medicare in 1966 (Committee on Ways and Means 1971; Lehmann 1979; see also Crawford 1979; Ingham 1985). Trying to *prevent* disease was thus an economically prudent policy. President Jimmy Carter, in his foreword to the Surgeon General's report, *Healthy People* (1979), endorsed prevention as a means to "substantially reduce both the suffering of our people and the burden on our expensive system of medical care" (cited in Russell 1986: 2). Health insurance industries and corporations also had a vested interest in promoting exercise, which was shown to decrease health care claims and employee absenteeism (see, for example, Drury 1983; Fisher 1985; Greene 1986). The US was not alone in the reorganization of health care; Canada and the United Kingdom were at the forefront of implementing health-promotion strategies (Lalonde 1974).

Underlying the new health promotion policies were growing numbers of cost-benefit analyses of prevention strategies, as well as medical studies supporting the epidemiological benefits of a healthy lifestyle, which included enough sleep, proper nutrition, abstention from smoking, and exercise (Hardman and Stensel 2003; Lalonde 1974; Russell 1986; Shephard 1986). Chronic diseases such as heart disease and cancer have proven themselves resistant to "passive" prevention, such as drug-based cures. However, medical research continues to support the role of "active" measures in lowering the risk of disease, meaning that the individual must participate through behavioral changes. For example, physical exercise was shown to protect against heart disease and, in a reversal of once-accepted opinion, to aid in the recovery of cardiac patients. Whereas health reformers in the nineteenth century stressed passive intervention (such as improving water and air quality), health promotion efforts since the 1970s have emphasized active measures – a shift from fluoridated water to better tooth-brushing, iodized salt to better nutrition patterns, inoculation to exercise. Exercise thus became a legitimate and heavily promoted way for the individual to minimize the risk of the ill-effects – obesity, inactivity, diabetes, cancer, heart disease – of modernity.

The move from passive to active management of disease involves a historic tension between individual empowerment and social control, which is bound up with long-term processes of modernization and individualization. Since the sixteenth century the balance of responsibility for, and enforcement of, social control has shifted from external, top-down measures (such as those of the priest and pastor, or the police) to internal, self-induced measures

(Elias 1978; Foucault 1977, 1978), with more directly invasive forms of social control reserved for those who fail to manage themselves appropriately (Foucault 1991). The contemporary manifestations of this dialogue between authority and individual freedom have been marked by the individual's increasing responsibility for addressing problems that have been identified for him or her by authorities. That is, authorities "act at a distance" (Rose 1999: 49) by laying out problems and solutions for the individual, rather than directly intervening in the individual body. Facilitating this mode of expert power – as advisory or therapeutic, rather than directly intrusive – was the loss of confidence in the traditional voices of power (such as politicians, business leaders, police, teachers, doctors, priests) and a range of critiques of the dominant structures of power and prestige.

Against this backdrop, exercise and a balanced diet represented means for individuals both to achieve good health *and* ease the financial burden on government, corporations and insurance industries (Crawford 1980; Sage 1998). As individual behaviors became the linchpin in health economics, there arose new political implications for consumers' lifestyle choices (Howell 1990; Howell and Ingham 2001; Ingham 1985; White, Young and Gillett 1995). Consider the following from a speech by President George W. Bush in 2003 regarding an initiative to promote daily exercise:

> And so our job as a country, at a federal level, the state level and the local level is to get people started and realize the great benefits of exercise. . . . One of the things I talk a lot about is the need to really work on cultural change in America to encourage a culture of personal responsibility, to encourage people to be responsible for the decisions they make in life. . . . By exercising every day, . . . no matter how busy you may seem or how boring exercise may seem initially, it's a part of a responsibility culture.
>
> (Bush 2003)

By managing their own bodily health, individuals reduce the costs of health economics: individual behavior becomes the means to minimize socially borne risk, thereby inserting political and economic priorities into individual lifestyles (O'Brien 1995).

Public health promotion since the 1970s can thus be understood as a combination of increasing both individual empowerment *and* social control over individual behavior (Foucault 1978, 1980b), both of which "work" through an ideology of individual responsibility. However, the delegation of responsibility for health to the individual is deeply problematic: health is perceived as a personal problem of choices and motivation, despite the fundamentally social and structural causes of illness and attitudes towards health. Nevertheless, illness is regarded as the outcome of a failure to make the right choices and the individual is held responsible – indeed, blamed – thereby continuing the long-held tradition in western culture to regard health as a natural state and an individual responsibility (Whorton 1982). This ongoing confusion between the individual and structural causes of health has meant that the root causes and solutions to public health problems are represented as personal troubles rather than public issues (Mills 1959: 14).

The economic rationalization of health care has necessarily involved the attempt to make disease rational and accountable. Through medical researchers' calculations of relative risk, for example, the infinite variations of individual health are reduced to seemingly objective projections of likely outcomes. Much of the focus on lifestyle factors such as smoking, exercise, or eating high- or low-fat foods is thus directed at calculating the relative risks of certain behaviors, or relative payoffs of others. Despite the difficulties in quantifying risk when it comes to the variability of individual bodies, health promotion utilizes this calculus of risk in the "selling" of a healthy lifestyle (Bunton and Burrows 1995). For example, the Department of Health and Human Service's 1996 Surgeon General's report on physical activity and health informed individuals that through regular exercise they could reduce the risk of diabetes, high blood pressure, and colon cancer, as well as control their weight, maintain healthy muscles and bones, and relieve depression and anxiety. Exercise also improves teenage girls' body image and self-esteem, and reduces the pain of arthritis for postmenopausal women (Laurence 1996). The marketing of risk allows consumers a sense (however tenuous) of control over their health outcomes, sometimes with the unintended consequence of creative health accountancy: if fitness and smoking are equally significant factors, then fitness may be rationalized as a way to "cancel out" the fact that one smokes (cf. Gilbert 1996).

The rationalization of disease through the logic of risk has entailed a broadening of the concept of health, from the absence of disease to a continuous process of risk-management. Even the healthy individual is still "at risk." This has important consequences for the field of fitness. As the sick person is replaced with the at-risk person, the sphere of health necessarily expands, absorbing more forms of behavior and more bodies into the realm of medical authority (Greco 1993; Petersen 1997). This expansion of the concept of illness, and the professional power of medical practitioners, gave rise in the 1960s and 1970s to a popular critique of the medicalization of society (Crawford 1979, 1980; Fox 1997). The advocates of demedicalization reflected the broader disillusionment with authorities and institutions, and the decreasing tolerance of state intervention in everyday life (Goldstein 1992). Calls for patient rights, the declassification of certain conditions as illnesses (such as homosexuality), and alternatives to the technologization of childbirth were bound up with distrust of, and dissatisfaction with, dependency on the medical professions (Fox 1997: 416). A declining reliance on experts such as doctors, however, does not remove the functions that they fill, including the providing of guidelines, rules, and reasons for conducting everyday life in certain ways. The turning away from traditional moral and expert authority brings with it an increasing need for individuals to assess and monitor their own lives, not simply for the "large" questions of faith and philosophy, but also for such mundane, intricate questions as the care of the body and the self.

Demedicalization – as a rejection of formal medical authority – has the intertwined effects of reconfiguring medical authority within the sphere of services (such that the patient takes on the qualities of the client/consumer); and, ironically, promoting a far-ranging process of medicalization, such that ever more aspects of everyday lives are thought about through the lens of health (Bunton 1997; Crawford 1980; Fox 1997; Goldstein 1992). Calls for demedicalization *enhanced* more than undermined the medicalization of everyday life, by encouraging people to become their own health experts. To regard health as yet another sphere of consumer choice (between products, therapies, doctors and hospitals) is not to decrease the authority or reach of the traditional medical experts. Rather, expert authority is reformulated as assistance. Individuals, increasingly responsible for their own moral direction and health choices, are not left to their own devices to discover themselves, but are inundated with assistance and advice from a whole range of traditional health experts and their new, commercial counterparts: commercials and talk shows, news programs, and self-help books. These therapeutic and educative experts mobilize individuals to examine, know and act upon themselves in certain ways (Miller and Rose 1997; Rose 1996), thereby recasting an ever-widening range of choices and behaviors in the language of health and risk (Crawford 1980: 370).

The push towards increasing "medical self-competence" (Crawford 1980: 374) relies on popular medical education – lessons in do-it-yourself health care, such as those found in *Our Bodies, Our Selves*, the best-selling book from 1974 to 1976 (Justice 1998), daily and weekly newspaper sections on health and well-being, and self-help style books (and more recently websites) covering such topics as diabetes, nutrition, allergies and asthma, thyroid conditions, healthy hearts, pregnancy, and so on. These media, and the exercise and lifestyle habits they endorsed, were (and are) presented as routes to empowerment. This was an appealing message, not only to those looking for ways to cope with stress and take control of their health. In the 1960s and 1970s, quests for bodily empowerment took on explicitly political forms, with feminist calls for women's rights explicitly tied to the right to control one's own body and health. Similarly in the case of civil rights, physical culture was a contested site for negotiating issues of race and ethnicity. For example, Muhammad Ali and Tommy Smith and John Carlos used their prominence in sports to speak out about US race relations at the 1968 Mexico City Olympics (Coakley 2001), while boxing (cf. Wacquant 1992, 1995) and martial arts were promoted to black youth as ways to learn self-respect and self-defense. Exercise, sport and popular health education combined messages of self-control and self-esteem, appealing to political and non-political platforms alike.

During the 1970s, the private sector began to support exercise as a way to decrease the risk of ill-health, further entrenching the individual's responsibility for adopting a healthy lifestyle. Following the earlier lead of Xerox, Mobil and Exxon, which had executive wellness programs, corporations began to offer exercise facilities and health seminars as a standard fringe benefit for the middle class (Gillick 1984: 378; see also Cavanaugh 1979). In addition, health professionals from the American College of Sports Medicine endorsed exercise guidelines (in 1978), and the government established an Office of Health Information and Health Promotion in 1976 (Lehmann 1979). Unlike the concerns over national strength and external boundaries that had motivated President Eisenhower to establish the Council on Youth Fitness, the crisis of the 1970s was internal – to the nation's fiscal health and the individual's physical state.

The emergence of the commercial fitness field in the 1970s can thus be traced in many ways to the question of health. Changing patterns of disease, the limited effectiveness of passive cures for chronic, lifestyle diseases, and the government- and medical research-led emphasis on active measures of disease prevention have placed individuals' lifestyle choices and an ideology of individual responsibility at the center of health economics and health promotion. Exercise and physical activity are key features on the list of endorsed active measures, perpetuating (and scientifically substantiating) the nineteenth-century construction of exercise as a panacea for individual and social problems. The health field has contributed medical legitimacy and political currency to participation in physical activity and exercise. (If the commercial field benefits in this way, it behoves us to ask how effective it is in addressing health concerns – an issue taken up in the final chapter.) In addition, the reformulation of health authorities as therapeutic helpers prefigured the emergence of fitness instructors and personal trainers; and calls for popular empowerment through health education created a ready market for fitness advice in magazines and manuals. Prompted by medical research and health policy initiatives, the media publicized the health implications of everyday behavior and the benefits of exercise, helping to create a population of consumers who looked to health as an area of self-improvement and control.

Health, however, was not the only factor at work in the emergence of the fitness field in the 1970s. Market surveys, for example, suggest that the motives for "getting fit" are as much about the appearance of the outer body as they are a matter of the inner body and reducing the risk of disease. For many, increasing the chances of success in the social and occupational markets required an investment in one's looks.

The value of appearances

Concerns over health and appearance are not mutually exclusive and, indeed, interact in complex ways: to look healthy is one aspect of a pleasing appearance; to feel confident in one's looks improves an overall sense of well-being; to pursue an attractive appearance may result in unhealthy behaviors. When asked in a 1998 survey why they join health clubs, 74 per cent of men and women said that they wanted to improve their health (McCarthy *et al.* 1999: 53). However, it is often unclear where the rubric of health leaves off, and that of appearance picks up. For example, the same survey found that 68 per cent of respondents wanted to improve their muscle tone, and 63 per cent wanted to lose weight (McCarthy *et al.* 1999: 53); another survey found that 60 per cent of women and 40 per cent of men devote at least half of their workout time to losing weight (Garner 1997: 44). Losing weight and improving muscle tone can have health benefits, but in an appearance-oriented culture in which unrealistic representations of perfect bodies dominate the media, such pursuits are difficult if not impossible to disentangle from concerns about appearance. Furthermore, such activities may actually undermine health, as when associated with body dysmorphia – an exaggerated or distorted emphasis on appearance, and destructive patterns and practices of body work (see, for example, Bordo 1993; Klein 1993). Therefore, the emergence of the fitness field can be understood only if in relation to both the changing definitions of health, and the intensification of the value of appearances in an image-driven economy.

Whereas individual efforts to improve health are typically applauded as responsible, improvement to appearance is often regarded as narcissistic and self-involved. Social critics such as Christopher Lasch (1979) and Tom Wolfe (1982a), for example, have observed of the 1970s a cultural obsession with self-discovery and self-improvement, the logical extension of what David Riesman (1950) diagnosed in the 1950s as the change in American personality from inner-directed to outer-directed, in which self-worth was to be found through the eyes of others. However, this other-directed personality was not, as Riesman feared, overly conformist; rather, for Lasch, the individual became more adept at manipulating interpersonal relations for his or her personal benefit (Lasch 1979: 127–8). A less derogatory but essentially similar analysis is offered by Andrew Wernick (1991: 193) of the contemporary promotional subject:

> a self which continually produces itself for competitive circulation: an enacted projection, which includes not only dress, speech, gestures, and actions, but also, through health and beauty practices, the cultivated body of the actor; a projection which is itself, moreover, an inextricable mixture of what its author/object actually has to offer, the signs by which this might be recognized, and the symbolic appeal this is given in order to enhance the advantages which can be obtained from its trade.

For such a mode of subjectivity, identity and social status are ongoing constructions that require concerted effort and investment: status won not through birthright or self-denial, but through the realization of one's capacity to be "fascinating, stunning, attractive, magnetic, glowing, masterful, creative, dominant, forceful" (Susman 1979: 217).

Appearance and performance are the tools by which the promotional subject exerts influence over others and accomplishes belonging. In this context, health (a vital appearance) and beauty (an attractive appearance) are valuable bodily resources to be managed and developed. As such, exercise was an ideal pursuit – the benefits of exercise are written on both the internal organs (strengthened heart, improved lung capacity) and the body's surface (toned muscles, slim waist). The shift from a culture of character to a culture of personality (Susman 1979), which had helped to reconfigure the physical culture of the US in the early twentieth century, also impacted upon the social and market value of the body's appearance, in turn facilitating the mass commercialization of exercise through the fitness field. The two motivations of health- and appearance-improvement are mutually reinforcing engines for the field of fitness. Improving one's health and appearance has become an obligation, linked to an ideology of individual responsibility as well as a logic of status display in promotional culture.

The rise of a promotional subjectivity is bound up with the move towards a service economy. Unlike the early twentieth century, when manufacturing was to the fore, services now eclipse it in the generation of businesses and jobs, a symptom of the shift from a Fordist to post-Fordist economy (Lash and Urry 1987; Slater 1997). This change in the organization of the economy and work, from creating things to creating interactions and images, involves a shift in productive capacities. For service jobs, appearance and attitude are necessary skills, which – like any capacity – must be produced through training and discipline (Foucault 1977). Like the factory worker who must learn the habits of routinized movements and time schedules, the service worker must be disciplined to acquire the capacities of appearance management and self-presentation. The education of the service worker is very much the education of the modern individual. In consumer culture and the service economy – in the roles of consumer and producer – individuals are exhorted to create and express identity through lifestyle (the assemblage of one's consumer patterns and choices), and to maximize market competitiveness through self-improvement. This social transformation has been described as the rise of an "entrepreneurial" (Keat and Abercrombie 1991) or "promotional" (Wernick 1991) culture. It is one in which each individual is at the helm of the enterprise that is his or her life: "individuals are incited to live as if making a *project* of themselves" (Rose 1996: 157). It is in the context of a labor market and consumer culture so attuned to images, that the fitness field emerged and in which it continues to develop today.

Many of the occupations that define the middle class grew out of the field of scientific management in the early part of the twentieth century. By 1930, almost half of the US labor force was employed in the tertiary sector of services (Lash and Urry 1987: 172).

Not only did the rearrangement of the labor process remove decision-making from labor; it also gave rise to a complex hierarchy of managerial positions, and a network of universities and occupational associations responsible for the reproduction of white-collar employment and the institutionalization of its education-based system of occupational stratification (Lash and

Urry 1987: 163). The middle class continued to grow and change over the twentieth century, as the shift towards a post-Fordist service economy brought with it changes to service occupations. Bourdieu's discussion (1984: 359) of the French service class – the new petite bourgeoisie – summarizes their occupations as those

> involving presentation and representation (sales, marketing, advertising, public relations, fashion, decoration and so forth) and in all the institutions providing symbolic goods and services. These include the various jobs in medical and social assistance (marriage guidance, sex therapy, dietetics, vocational guidance, paediatric advice etc.) and in cultural production and organization (youth leaders, play leaders, tutors and monitors, radio and TV producers and presenters, magazine journalists) . . .; but also some established occupations, such as art craftsmen or nurses.

The post-industrial middle class is thus bound up with the growth of consumer service industries, which has created new and expanded existing occupations at both ends of the service class, from the professional/managerial positions to the clerical and sales positions in industries such as advertising, fashion, media, and health.

Importantly for understanding the development of the fitness field, Bourdieu (1984) suggests how class mediates the ways in which individuals take up the project of the self. For Bourdieu, cultural intermediaries – the exemplars of the post-industrial middle class – are characterized by a sense of unease or embarrassment about their social position, which manifests as an uneasiness towards the body. As they possess little of the economic and cultural capital of the established, dominant class, the cultural intermediary class adopts a learning or investment attitude towards life, educating themselves in tastes, styles, and lifestyles (Featherstone 1987: 65). They are pretenders, but keen social mimics and quick studies, who are intensely aware of their bodies as they watch others and correct themselves accordingly – this is particularly pronounced for those working in occupations of display and performance, for which social mimesis is a necessity (Featherstone 1987: 64–5). As such, the middle class is assumed to be disposed towards investing in the body-as-symbol, or what Bourdieu (1984: 213) calls the "body-for-others," making them natural consumers for dieting, cosmetic and exercise fads, health foods, and self-help manuals. It is not simply that they are concerned with the body and its improvement through consumer goods and services, but that the middle-class body is treated as a sign rather than an instrument (Bourdieu 1984: 368), through which status and social position may be communicated and reinforced. In this regard, the middle-class body is best understood as an enterprise, and fitness as a mode of investment in the corporation.

The growth of the service class over the twentieth century is inseparable from the growth of consumer industries. The proportion of the US labor market made up of services climbed to 62 per cent by 1970, 72 per cent by 1990, and 75 per cent by 2000 (Godbout 1993: 8; Bureau of Labor Statistics 2001), while consumer spending constituted two-thirds of the gross domestic product by 2001. Service occupations, despite their somewhat monolithic depiction in Bourdieu (1984) and elsewhere (cf. Featherstone 1991; Lash and Urry 1987; Lury 1996; Wynne 1998), however, are not an undifferentiated mass. Over time, there has been a deepening bifurcation between low-wage service jobs (representing the largest source of employment), and high-end professional and producer services (Sassen 1990: 475). Of the three largest service sub-sectors of the US economy, the rate of growth between 1970 and 1990 of the high-end sub-sector – financial, insurance, real estate, and business services – was at least twice that of the numerically larger wholesale, retail, restaurant and hotel services, and community, social and personal services, which, combined, constitute over half of all service employment (Godbout 1993: 12–13). As such, the emergence and development of the fitness field must be understood relative to the class position and disposition both of its consumers (especially the professional/managerial class) and its producers (the personal service occupations, such as personal trainers and aerobics instructors).

The size and division of the service sector have changed over the last three decades, as has its gendered composition. Men's labor participation has declined since the 1950s, in part due to the loss of traditionally male-dominated manufacturing occupations. At the same time, women's labor participation has increased. After women's record levels of involvement during the Second World War, their labor participation dropped off steeply in the postwar reassertion of traditional femininity in suburban America. It was not until the late 1960s that women's rate of participation reached its 1945 high (Blau 1978: 56). Following traditional patterns, women continue to be concentrated within pink-collar services, but have also made great gains in higher-ranking service occupations. In 1998, women occupied over 58 per cent of financial, insurance and real estate service positions, and 69 per cent of professional and related services (Bureau of Labor Statistics 1999b; see also 1999a).

It is easy to appreciate the central role that women have played in the development of consumer culture in the late twentieth century. Women – white, middle-class women in particular – acquired the opportunity and means to consume not as the family provisioners, but as self-directed consumers, investing in themselves because they had the means to do so, and often without competing family obligations given the postponement of marriage and childbirth. When they did have families, women were often still in the labor market; the percentage of dual-income families has risen steadily over the past thirty years (Jacobs and Gerson 1998). As such, many of the traditional domestic duties of the homemaker have been outsourced, from the baking of the birthday cake to the cleaning of the house (Oropesa 1993). Women's labor market participation has thus fueled both consumption of goods, and the demand for low-end service occupations, as the jobs that a middle-class working mother no longer had the time or inclination to perform were outsourced to (usually poorer, minority women) service workers.

Improvements in the social position of women, especially white middle-class women, were facilitated by their increased labor market participation, as well as by new reproductive technologies and the consciousness-raising of the women's movement. Media milestones for women's bodies included coverage of legal victories regarding abortion rights (most notably with Roe *v.* Wade in 1973), magazines such as *Ms.*, launched in 1972, and the pioneering health and self-awareness manual, *Our Bodies, Our Selves*. The political call for women to claim control over their bodies was also given governmental support in terms of gender equality in physical culture. In 1972, Title IX of the Educational Amendments Act outlawed sex discrimination in athletics, providing women (at least on paper) with equal access to sport participation, scholarships and facilities. In the 1960s, before Title IX, fewer than 300,000 women participated in high school athletics; by the mid-1980s, the number was nearly 2 million (Sidwell and Kane 1990: 187). The women's movement gave to appearance management a political agenda and defense: taking care of one's body was a reclamation of power and a way to progress up the occupational ladder. Exercise and fitness also provided a non-political avenue of participation in the women's movement, creating opportunities of (literal) empowerment, without the often complex identity of a politically active feminist.

Moreover, women's rising labor market participation reshaped gender roles and norms for men as well. As many authors have noted, the late twentieth century has witnessed an intensification of emphasis on *men's* appearances (see, for example, Bordo 2001; Kimmel 1996; Luciano 2001). Economic security was no longer a unique selling point in the social market; a financially independent woman could demand an attractive and attentive partner (as *Cosmopolitan* magazine, among others, proclaimed). And occupational competence and qualifications were no longer sufficient for successful competition in a labor market, in which men now had to compete not only with other men, but with women as well. The cultural production of fitness consumers – individuals with an elective affinity for the practices and meanings of a fit body – has been significantly shaped by the interconnections between the women's movement, women's labor market participation, and the growth of service occupations, such that the value of an attractive appearance has increased for both women and men, in both occupational and social contexts. Such trends are relevant to the growth and character of the fitness field, as well as to other appearance industries like cosmetic surgery, which have witnessed a marked increase in participation, both by women and men in recent years (Davis 2002; Luciano 2001).

Matt is a journalist in his mid-30s; his answer to the question, "Why work out?", touches upon the issues raised above. His somewhat rueful reflection on the reasons for working out in his younger days highlights not only the social pressures on men to work on their appearance, but also the attitudes towards the body that Bourdieu (1984) suggests are typical of cultural intermediaries like Matt:

> *Definitely* I would go to the gym when I was feeling less good. . . . When I did weights, I was feeling like I wanted to . . . you know . . . compete. Like in Manhattan, for men and women, it is a very competitive environment. Especially for people in their twenties, I think. And especially where I was living at that time, downtown. . . . I mean, there were *models* in my building. You know, real, working models. And . . . you kind of felt like you had to have a whole package. I had the job going on, and I was smart. But, is that enough? You look around, and you think, "No, not really." You need the cash, you need the clothes, you've got to have the buff body . . . At least that's what you're thinking.

Matt's account also suggests the exceptionalism of New York: in a city with local industries and a global reputation both focused upon image, an attractive appearance is, unsurprisingly, a highly tradable form of physical capital. However, New York is less an exception than it is a magnifying glass on phenomena that cut across contemporary society. As such, New York makes a useful setting – Oliver Stone's *Wall Street*; Tom Wolfe's *The Bonfire of the Vanities* – for critiques of the hallmarks of the late twentieth century: competition through appearances and status consumption. In *American Psycho*, Bret Easton Ellis' condemning portrayal of the 1980s Zeitgeist, anti-hero Patrick Bateman exemplifies the obsessive attention to looks and logos as markers of personal identity, and the "new" masculinity:

> Once out of the shower and toweled dry I put the Ralph Lauren boxers back on and before applying the Mousse A Raiser, a shaving cream by Pour Hommes, I press a hot towel against my face for two minutes to soften abrasive beard hair. Then I always slather on a moisturizer (to my taste, Clinique) and let it soak in for a minute. . . . Afterwards splash cool water on the face to remove any trace of lather. . . . Next apply Gel Appaisant, also made by Pour Hommes, which is an excellent, soothing skin lotion. If the face seems dry and flaky – which makes it look dull and older – use a clarifying lotion that removes flakes and uncovers fine skin (it can also make your tan look darker).
>
> (Ellis 1991: 27)

Bateman and his 20-something Wall Street peers debate the intricacies of designer clothes, business cards, apartments, cuisine, shampoos and shaving creams – all in the quest for the right image. If Ellis' portrayal veered towards the excessive (Bateman is, after all, a serial killer), his analysis was firmly grounded in the everyday practices of competitive status consumption, into which fitness was readily adopted.

Returning to Bourdieu (1984), both Matt and Bateman are exemplars of the bodily disposition of the service class. The transition to a post-industrial service economy has encouraged the growth of industries and occupations that do not simply require, but *produce*, appearances. This "symbolic economy" (Drucker 1969; Zukin 1995) has given rise to new cultural intermediary occupations for which self-presentation is a necessity, and to new consumer products that rely on the added value of symbols and design. The use-value of products has been overshadowed by their expressive qualities (Baudrillard 1981; Falk 1994; Slater 1997; Wernick 1991), so that product differentiation is increasingly accomplished through images, such as those conferred by branding strategies. In 1998, for example, cigarette company Philip Morris bought Kraft for $13 billion, a value largely based on Kraft's brand recognition (Keller 1998: 30–3). Just as the exchange-value of products (and companies) is more and more determined by symbolic assets, exchange-value on the labor market increasingly rests on symbolic and physical capital. The growth and character of the fitness field in the late twentieth century is inseparable from the intensification of consumption as the basis of the reproduction of both the economy and identity. This social and political-economic climate shaped the production of fitness as a field of consumer leisure rather than a health or educational field, focused upon the symbolic value, rather than the use-value, of the body.

Over the twentieth century, the necessity of creating new markets for consumer goods gave rise to a range of market research data and niche marketing strategies, which have subdivided the consuming public along ever-finer lines of distinction (Turow 2000; Zukin 2004). This fragmentation of the consumer market dovetailed with social movements in the 1960s and 1970s, in which groups – particularly women's and minority groups – challenged the mass to which marketing attempted to reduce them. Consumer industries, in turn, assimilated and repackaged the identity politics both of the women's and civil rights movements and of the 1960s hippie and counter-cultures, and subjected them to the logic of fashion and its cycle of innovation and obsolescence. This has, in turn, shaped the field of fitness, which presents not a single version of exercise, but a variety of services, classes, machines and gimmicks (updated regularly) to appeal to and address ever-more finely defined markets: older people, young families, straight and gay singletons, pregnant women, and so forth.

To summarize, the fitness field's development is linked to the growth of occupations for which images, appearances and performances are fundamental, and more broadly to the increased emphasis on style and appearance in everyday life. The physical capital of the fit body "counts" in contemporary society: a good physique and an attractive appearance can be converted into social capital (a more affluent circle of social peers), or economic capital (a better-paying job). Indeed, a recent study by two economists reported that better-looking individuals earn 10 to 15 per cent more than their less attractive co-workers, an effect in part of the way in which employers interpret attractiveness, and the greater self-confidence of attractive people as signs of competence and productivity (Mobius and Rosenblat 2006; see also Hamermesh and Biddle 1994).

Rather than regarding fitness and other forms of self-investment as symptomatic of a narcissistic personality, *à la* Lasch (1979), one might instead recognize them as arising out of economic pragmatism: in image-oriented occupations, investments in physical and cultural capital are more likely to bring profits, through conversion into other forms of capital. The institutionalized and embodied forms of cultural capital (Bourdieu 1986: 243) of a formal education, good diction and social graces thus become occupational necessities for both ends of the spectrum of service occupations – from waiters (Zukin 1995: 154) and receptionists to stockbrokers and marketers. The increasing emphasis on self-presentation as an element of service work and as the product of that work (such as in the image industries of advertising and fashion) gives rise to an increasing demand for physical capital – forms of prestige and social distinction to which the body and its appearance are central (Jenkins 1992: 85; Shilling 1993: 127). Investments in self-presentation – through fitness activities, as well as dieting, cosmetic surgery, fashion and so forth – can thus be understood as modes of developing one's physical capital in order to improve one's exchange-value. As Jean Baudrillard (1998: 132) suggests, "beauty is such an absolute imperative only because it is a form of capital."

In the 1930s, Dale Carnegie and Charles Atlas addressed their advice regarding personality and physical appearances to the service population, when its identity and hierarchy of stratification were still in formation; today, such lessons in the importance of a winning smile or the right physique are taken for granted. Since the 1960s, the American dream has increasingly moved from a meritocracy of hard work to one of "winning images" (Lasch 1979: 116), in which appearances and personality trump lineage and inherited wealth as the determinants of social and occupational success (Susman 1979). The development of consumer culture over the twentieth century, and of the field of fitness in the past thirty years, cannot be separated from the efforts of the middle class to legitimate and advance its social position through such investments.

CONCLUSION

By the close of the 1960s, several conditions were in place for not only the transformation of the YMCA into a "health club" (much to the chagrin of its commercial competitors and, to some extent, its own leaders and members; see Miller and Fielding 1995; Putney, 1997), but also the rise of an institutional field of commercial health clubs, fitness-and-lifestyle publications and products, and fitness services such as personal training. Other established lifestyle and appearance industries, such as health food (Whorton 1982), cosmetics (Peiss 1998), and dieting (Stearns 1997), presented the fitness field with an already identified and participating set of educated and devoted middle-class consumers. In addition, this middle-class market was distinguished by its demands for a good quality of life over a longer period of time, thanks to medical advances; by its growing interest in self-improvement as a path for upward social mobility; and by its high expectations in terms of experiences, pleasures, and the expressive quality of products, guided by increasingly sophisticated delineations of taste and lifestyle identities (Bourdieu 1984; Featherstone 1991; Wernick 1991).

In the specific case of the fitness field, the material consequences (reduced health risks; loss of weight; improved muscle tone) and practices (such as attending a health club, with its connotations of status) of participation align with the social conditions and individual anxieties and aspirations of the day. The producers of the fitness field do not invent an interest in the body as capital; they tap into longstanding themes in physical culture and contemporary demands for specific kinds of physical capital, and thereby mobilize potential fitness participants towards specific ends, from the purchase of fitness equipment to the enactment of an ethos of self-responsibility (cf. du Gay 2004; Miller and Rose 1997).

Comparing the vision of Theodore Roosevelt in 1899 with that of Charles Atlas in 1930 and the accounts of today's fitness participants, the rationale for working on the body in dialogue with social ideals and norms has continued to change: "what is really new in the pursuit of happiness of modern (consumer) society is that the utopian project is reduced in scale to the individual, into a modern mode of self-building" (Falk 1994: 130). In contemporary society, physical fitness is directed by entrepreneurs, not reformers; the primary goal self-improvement, not national strength. What has not changed is the underlying assumptions regarding the instrumental value of exercise, and the dynamic interplay of body and self – that is, to work on the body is to transform the self. Such a belief reaches back into the history of humankind. For the ancient Greek and Greco-Roman cultures, the regimes of physical development were essential to the "arts of existence" (Foucault 1985: 11); today, working on the body continues to be an important avenue of self-transformation. However, contemporary consumer culture has intensified the instrumentalization of the body (Falk 1994: 50), draining body-development and care of the self of their once deeper associations with ethical existence and moral communities (Foucault 1985, 1986).

To maximize success in the contemporary labor market – as well as the social market – one must build a better body, and surround it with better trappings. This is not to suggest that the consumption of body products is entirely instrumental; the jogging craze of the 1970s, for example, had a strong sense of the religious (such as in James Fixx's *Complete Book of Running*, or

George Sheehan's *Running and Being*). However, such spiritual connotations are not incompatible with an instrumental mentality regarding physical capital. As Wernick (1991: 185) suggests in his analysis of the promotional character of consumer culture, it is not that there is a particular ideology being promoted (crass materialism or spiritual asceticism), but that what is being promoted is the logic of advertising itself: appearance sells.

Contemporary consumers are encouraged to construct themselves – and judge each other – based on the messages communicated through bodies, lifestyles and performances. Social interactions are anchored in the belief in a malleable self, the recognition of the interactive character of service occupations, and the consumption and deployment of sign values. Fitness is thus no different from fashion:

> In the Sixties, fashion stopped being clothes and became a value, a tool, a way of life, a kind of symbolism. It became human packaging. You don't have to work in an advertising agency to know that packaging sells the product. Any product.
>
> (Bender 1967: 43)

Individuals are encouraged to approach themselves and others as products – products to be exchanged, and which will become obsolete without upgrades and improvements (McGee 2005; Watkins 1993). Such an attitude towards the self, rooted in the transformation of production, spreads outwards to areas of life traditionally considered beyond competitive exchange. As social interaction increasingly takes on the form of commodity exchange, individuals are faced with anxieties concerning their market value, and the rate of conversion for their physical capital. And as with the physical culture of the nineteenth century, the primary site of the resolution of such anxieties remains the physical body.

3 Health clubs
The stratification of fitness sites

The body – as physical capital to be honed, augmented and displayed – is central to leisure in contemporary consumer culture. And just as the body is a status object, the places in which the body is tended, maintained, and improved are also spaces of status. Health club membership is marketed as not only a leisure pursuit and a healthy use of discretionary income; membership is also an investment in your status profile: membership in the "right" club is an indispensable element of the lifestyles of the status-conscious.

Commercial health clubs have become the primary site for the production and consumption of the fitness field in the US and, increasingly, in consumer societies around the world. By locating exercise in a semi-public venue for which membership is required, health clubs construct fitness as an opportunity for the social display of status (cf. Ferguson 1998: 606), thus associating body work with other status-oriented activities. In linking exercise to the purchase of a membership (and other equipment, advice and accessories), health clubs produce fitness as yet another aspect of lifestyle and leisure consumption. Finally, by positioning themselves explicitly as leisure businesses, health clubs reconcile the mismatch between cultural connotations of leisure as a time of ease and relaxation, and the hard work of exercise, thus positioning body work as a means of negotiating the conflicting demands made of the individual body: to be a focus of work and leisure; to be disciplined and enjoyed.

The chapter proceeds with a review of the historical antecedents of the contemporary commercial "lifestyle" health club. Only by looking back does it become fully apparent what is – and is not – new about today's fitness field. What is certainly new is the range of options available to today's fitness consumer: choosing a health club in a major urban centre like New York can involve hundreds of possibilities. Thus, the chapter draws on the experiences of health club consumers as a means of sensitization to the range of factors that differentiate the health club industry. Against this background, the contemporary health club industry emerges as a field of choices structured by three key distinctions: first, health clubs are leisure business; second, those businesses differ in their quality of service and membership cost; and third, those businesses are further differentiated through symbolic added value – what might be thought of as a club's "personality." Health clubs can only serve as status markers if they are stratified – if the differences between them are "mappable" according to various criteria. Only then can the difference between Club A and Club B be socially translated into an evaluation of which is *better*.

LOOKING BACK

In 1973, advertisements appeared in *New York Magazine* and *The Village Voice* for a new health club: the New York Health Club, opening in uptown Manhattan and Greenwich Village. The ads encouraged customers to "Shape up your shape!" with Nautilus machines, exercise classes, and efficient and individualized workout programs both for men and women. They also promised prospective members the chance to relax in the Finnish sauna or at the Guru Garden Health Bar. Ads in the following years' *Yellow Pages* featured the slogan "Health and Beauty Through Pleasure," and the promise that "[t]his is the club where exercise is a pleasure and fitness is your reward. New York's truly complete, luxurious and reasonable health club for vital and discriminating people."[1] With its initialed crest, menu of options, and appeal to young, affluent men and women, this health club was marketed as unlike any other of the time: a symbol of, and point of entry into, an entire lifestyle, of which a fit physique was only one part.

The commercial health club is a relatively recent product – middle-class and service-oriented, without the social, educational or religious missions of municipal recreation programs, physical education classes, or the YMCA. The "lifestyle" health clubs that emerged in the 1970s focused on individual activities rather than group sports and games, and combined what were considered to be typically male (strength) and female (flexibility) exercises. Furthermore, unlike existing health spas that offered separate facilities for men and women, the new clubs were typically unisex, bringing an added social dimension to the fitness lifestyle. The high-tech machines, mirrored walls, aerobics studios, and whirlpools of health clubs were ostensibly open to all. However, by virtue of stratified membership fees, clubs retained an air of exclusivity, something which could not be said for exercising in the school gymnasium, in the living room, or at the local YMCA.

Two years after it opened, the New York Health Club had 74 competitors, some of which also boasted Nautilus machines, health bars, personalized exercise programs and "Physical Fitness in Style."[2] But these lifestyle clubs were not the first businesses to sell exercise space. By the late nineteenth century, consumers had a number of options for physical exercise, depending on their budget – choices ranged from the YMCA to exclusive, expensive athletic and country clubs. In the early twentieth century, the commodification of physical culture continued. The Health Roof Club for Men, targeting Manhattan's business executives, opened in 1931. In 1936, Jack La Lanne opened his first health studio in Oakland, California; La Lanne's chain of health spas were a forerunner of the unisex health club.[3] Between the 1930s and late 1960s, four particular types of exercise businesses were found in urban centers: executive clubs, gyms, exercise salons, and the YMCA. Each had a specific, limited clientele (typically defined explicitly by class and gender, and implicitly by ethnicity), and was associated with a particular form and goal of physical activity. These four types of exercise business laid the groundwork for the contemporary commercial clubs.

Executive clubs

Executive clubs, like the nineteenth-century elite athletic clubs that they echoed,[4] targeted predominantly middle-aged businessmen. Such clubs were equipped with courts, gyms, and instructors to keep the executive fit, and were often located near the clients' offices. For example, the Health Roof Club for Men sat atop the Grand Central Palace Building, and the Barclay, "The Business Man's Health Club," was located in the Woolworth Building, targeting the midtown and downtown businessmen, respectively. The exercise facilities on offer, however, were often overshadowed by the relaxation and grooming facilities, such as the Roof Club's "Turkish baths, snooze rooms, sunlamps, massage, snack bar, sunbathing on roof."[5] In these plush surroundings, the executive could relax, enjoy the perks of his position, and network with his similarly privileged peers. He could also hope to outrun death. According to the popular press, businessmen were a species under imminent threat of heart attack, tension and stress. Since at least the 1950s, articles in business and women's magazines declared the sorry state of health for the executive, and focused on how men could take better care of themselves (and on how women might keep their husbands alive). These articles multiplied over the years, so much so that "executives – health and hygiene" became an indexing category of its own in the *Reader's Guide to Periodical Literature* in the late 1960s.

By the 1970s, the President's Council on Fitness and Sports (formerly, the President's Council on Youth Fitness) estimated that US businesses were losing $25 billion a year from the premature deaths of employees (Leepson 1978: 271). Businesses were also tracking the increasing costs of employee medical benefits, and sometimes passing these production costs on to the consumer. General Motors, for example, claimed that it spent more in 1975 on employee health claims than on its primary supplier, US Steel. The result was a $175 increase in the cost of each truck and car (Crawford 1979: 251–2). Thus, the specter of executive stress was reinforced by research on its fiscal implications.

In the context of such findings, companies discovered that providing exercise programs (either at corporate facilities or through subsidized memberships at commercial clubs) was good business practice. Corporations such as Xerox and Kimberly-Clark endorsed executive exercise programs in the 1960s and 1970s and, broadening the concern with executive health to include all employees, the late 1970s saw a boom in company fitness clubs (Cavanaugh 1979). While this continued and expanded the notion of an executive club, it was certainly not the first time companies had provided exercise and recreation facilities to their workforces. National Cash Register, for example, had an employee health and hygiene program in 1898 (Green 1986: 295). However, such programs did not become standard fringe benefits for white-collar workers until the late twentieth century (Gillick 1984). From 1974 to 1988, the number of company fitness programs in the US rose from 30 to 12,000 (Barbato 1988: 24). Executive and employee fitness programs clearly articulated the purpose of exercise (and health) as an improvement in productivity. This form of exercise was linked not to recreation and leisure, but to the preparation for work and the management of production costs (Brodeur 1988: 228).

Gyms

The second precursor to the lifestyle clubs were the gyms frequented by boxers and weightlifters. While "gym" and "health club" are today used interchangeably, these terms carried much different connotations in the past. Almost exclusively the domain of men – and largely working-class men – until the 1970s, gyms had none of the amenities of health clubs. Bobby Gleason's boxing gym, Mr Universe Health Studios, and the more mainstream Vic Tanny gyms and Charles Atlas Institute all catered to the man who was serious about his strength and muscles.

The tradition of working-class muscle building was enhanced by developments taking place within the bodybuilding subculture (Klein 1993). In the 1970s, competitive bodybuilding gained a wider audience thanks to movies such as *Pumping Iron* (1977), charismatic spokesmen and entrepreneurs such as Arnold Schwarzenegger and Joe Weider (Goldberg 1975; Johnson 1976; Roach 1977), and the successful expansion of California-based Gold's Gym. In addition, new user-friendly weightlifting systems such as Nautilus entered the exercise equipment market in the early 1970s (Roach 1978). Unlike exercising with barbells or "free weights," Nautilus equipment removed the need for weightlifting technique. The user sat on an adjustable seat, placed his or her arms and legs on the designated pads, and moved the bars or pulleys in the set tracks. The only decision the user had to make was how high to put the seat and how heavy to set the weight.

While competitive bodybuilding remained an extreme and relatively marginal subculture, recreational strength training gained in popularity. Gym owners stressed the differences between the serious bodybuilder and the "less extreme gym-built body" (Brady 2000: 12). Weightlifting gained respectability through this corporeal difference between the toned muscles of the gym user and the hyperbolic bodies of Mr Universe and Mr America.

Gold's Gym, once the headquarters for serious bodybuilders, helped to bring weightlifting from the margins to the centre of fitness (Klein 1993: 14). In 1978, Gold's Gym published a weight-training manual that pitched bodybuilding to a broad market:

> Although Gold's is synonymous with strong, healthy, and beautiful bodies, if you go there expecting to see a room full of super bodybuilders only, you are in for a surprise. The professionals are much in evidence, of course, but these days you could just as well run into a next door neighbor, the family doctor, or the supermarket produce man. Add to the list numerous dancers, actors and actresses, athletes of all kinds, factory workers, housewives, and even the physically handicapped, and you have a better idea of what's really happening there.
>
> (Dobbins and Sprague 1981: 1)

At Gold's, and at gyms more generally, weight-training was becoming an acceptable activity for more than just working-class men or competitive bodybuilders. Not only was it increasingly popular with middle-class "pencil necks," but also – for the first time – with a growing number of women (Klein 1993: 14). It was not simply that women were interested in their bodies, but that muscular development was associated with women's interest in empowerment.

Ellie, an academic in her early 40s, highlights these issues in her recollection of her first experience with weight-training:

> I was kind of an adamantly feminist anti-diet person, and this was before women were widely lifting weights, in 1979. A friend and I decided that we were going to take the weight-training class that only men were in. It was very, very interesting, because we *were* the only women, of course. And it was *great*. . . . In ten weeks, I lost 2 clothing sizes, and no weight. I gained 5 pounds [2.2 kg]. And I looked *totally amazing*. In ten weeks! . . . It was a very minimal time investment, no counting any calories, no thinking about any diet, not even losing weight, but I looked like I'd lost 25 pounds [11.3 kg]. And I was *really strong*. No one ever thought a woman would ever want to lift weights. It was a feminist thing at the beginning – my friend and I were the only women. We were laughing, and the guys thought we were so weird, but you know, we got the goods! [*laughs*] So you got to conform and not conform, which is always the best.

For Ellie, lifting weights was a means to challenge traditional gender norms; but it produced an unexpected benefit: feelings of physical empowerment and individuality, accompanied by the satisfaction of a new appearance. Not only did she inch closer to societal norms for the feminine body (to which she ostensibly objects), but she did so without feeling that she had capitulated to those norms. Working out thus allowed Ellie to negotiate (however temporarily) the double bind of feminist and feminine ideals.

Ellie is not alone in making the connection between fitness and female empowerment. Lucille Roberts started her chain of women-only health clubs in 1970; in a CNN interview, she reflects on the start of her business and makes an explicit link to the politics of the era:

> I was an exercise nut and there was a need for women to have their own space and to become strong. And one of the ways you can become strong is to get physically strong – to take charge of your own destiny.
>
> (van de Mark 1999)

The media also participates in constructing the link between physical exercise and women's empowerment. For example, an exercise manual from the editors of *Self* magazine – aimed at professional women – suggests that "muscle lib" (cf. Bordo 1997: 28) is the proud inheritance of today's women:

> Weight-training. It once called to mind bodybuilders with swollen chests, protruding veins, overstuffed limbs. The image was crude. The word: musclebound. Now, the words conjure all manner of streamlined athletes. The image is beautiful, often sexy. The word: strong. Muscle is empowering. We know that now. We don't gawk at strength. We go after it.
>
> (Billings 1998: 16)

Popular manuals and magazines encouraged the symbolic link between women's emancipation and empowerment through muscles. This link, however, was ambivalent; the ideal of physical empowerment could be employed to reproduce, as much as to challenge, traditional notions of the feminine form.

Consider, for example, how exercise manuals promoted the benefits of weight-training to women:

> If you are worried about developing bulging muscles, don't be. Women – 99.9 per cent of us – do not have enough testosterone, the male hormone that governs muscle growth, to develop bulgy muscles. But something muscle-like does happen and I like it. Since you are reading this book, you are probably like me and appreciate a woman's body on which the muscle cuts and contours are evident. This is what you will get with regular workouts.
>
> (Fonda 1981: 69)

Observations of this kind, from Jane Fonda's highly popular aerobic workout book, also found expression in manuals geared explicitly towards weight-lifting. In a guide to Nautilus equipment, women are promised equal access to strength training, but gender-specific versions of strength:

> And because you're a woman, with unique body chemistry, you can get all the benefits that men get *without* growing big muscles. How's that for an offer you can't refuse? . . . If you're among the 95 per cent of all women with 30 times less male sex hormone flowing through their veins than the average man, you just won't be able to grow big muscles. You

will . . . be able to tone, or firm, or reshape any body part you wish and show the same "per cent strength gain" that men will.

(Wolf 1983: 2–3)

These two passages emphasize the gap between a woman's physical and political strength; being strong was acceptable, being hyper-muscled was not. Nevertheless, women's participation in weightlifting shifted from the fringe pursuit of the female bodybuilders in the 1985 film *Pumping Iron II: The Women* to a popular activity for women who exercised (Penney 1977).

The gay community also played an important role in bringing weightlifting to a larger market. There is a long history of the homosexual aesthetic cult of the body (Dutton 1995), which has exulted several different ideal body shapes. Of them, the muscular body is perhaps the most spectacular, represented in the artwork of Tom of Finland, gay pornography and "displayed on the beaches, cruised at the clubs, and . . . worshipped on the go-go platforms of South Beach and San Francisco" (Long 1997: 20). Brian Pronger (1990: 128–9) suggests that the homoerotic appeal of hard, muscular bodies lies in the eroticization of masculinity; whatever the psychodynamics, however, it is a "truism in gay publishing that a muscled body on the cover . . . sells more copies than any other image" (Pronger 1990: 154). The homosexual attention to the muscled body was given new meaning in the early 1980s as a sign of health in the face of AIDS, which had begun its wasting attack on the body of the gay population. Gay men's muscle-building – as a real or symbolic act of health – and women's muscle-building – as a real or symbolic act of empowerment – are significant departures from both working-class body-building, in which the function of muscles was, literally, bulk and strength (Bourdieu 1984: 200–12), and competitive bodybuilding, in which the function of muscles was cosmetic and spectacular (Klein 1993; Pronger 1990).

Exercise salons

While executive clubs and gyms were "male preserves" (Dunning 1986), exercise salons were predominantly feminine, middle- and upper-class sanctuaries. Exercise salons emerged in the 1960s and 1970s, born in an age of boutique commerce in which consumption was framed as an intensely personal experience (Zukin 2004: 134). Often run by former dancers, gymnasts, or their disciples, the most high-profile of Manhattan salons included those of Nicholas Kounovsky, Lotte Berk, Manya Kahn, and Marjorie Craig (at the Elizabeth Arden salon). There, women would stretch and tone in their leotards: Lee Radziwill favored the Berk Method; Kounovsky followers included nearly every socialite in town (Taylor 1972, 1974). Journalists and social commentators linked exercise salons to a particular lifestyle: these were places for the "Beautiful People" (Bender 1967), and a mark of distinction for "the woman who has everything" (Wolfe 1982b: 113).

Exercise salons, however, did not only attract the rich and famous. At the Kathy Grant salon at Bendel's, for example, the course of a day might bring in several types of women. As one reporter observed: "Ballerinas come for 8 A.M. workouts, while businesswomen sneak in for an hour during the day, using the self-propelled machines under Miss Grant's watchful eye" (Taylor 1974: 49). And despite Lotte Berk's popularity with fashion models (Taylor 1974), classes included a range of women: "A midday class recently was made up of a couple of college girls, a new mother, and a former record company executive who is the mother of a 19-year-old" (Taylor 1972: 36). This was a space of social networking and body improvement for white, middle- and upper-class women. The function of exercise was largely instrumental, an investment in one's "body capital" (Bourdieu 1984: 206), on which social position and occupational success depended.

Socialites as well as housewives, secretaries and businesswomen – and a small number of men (Taylor 1972) – were using exercise salons, and paying between $6 and $12 per class (Kaye 1977). Health clubs, when they began to open, had a competitive advantage in that they offered similar classes but at a lower cost. The NYHC, for example, had classes in calisthenics, yoga and belly dancing; for the monthly cost of membership (approximately $50), clients could attend as many classes as they liked (Taylor 1974).

The YMCA

The YMCA is one of the longest-standing providers of exercise space in the US, and the most enduring alternative to commercial health clubs. Despite its long history (reviewed in Chapter 2), however, the YMCA's role in physical fitness has not been constant. Postwar suburbanization challenged the organization's original religious and urban mission, and the disillusionment with large institutions in the wake of Watergate and Vietnam created difficulties for the YMCA's explicit social program. With the rising popular interest in fitness, the Y was provided with a new focus; or rather, its focus returned to what was an old objective: promoting physical fitness.[6] Between 1968 and 1978, the YMCA's national full-time membership grew 16 per cent. Not only were more people joining, but they were joining to enroll in fitness programs: attendance in YMCA exercise classes increased 26 per cent between 1971 and 1976 (Leepson 1978: 275).

As part of their renewed focus on fitness, some YMCAs began to invest in updating their facilities in the 1970s. For example, both the Vanderbilt and Westside YMCAs of New York City opened new facilities for women, and YMCAs in New York and California added facilities to accommodate women's new interest in weightlifting and strength-conditioning (Johnson 1976; Penney 1977). In addition, the YMCA was one of the first facilities to offer Jazzercise classes – the forerunner to the 1980s aerobics classes. Judi Missett, who designed the Jazzercise program for women in 1969, began offering classes at the YMCA in La Jolla, California in 1972.[7] Alongside the contemporaneous growth of the commercial fitness industry, the YMCA retained its definition of exercise as a means of moral self-development and family- and community-development. Advocates and leaders of the YMCA promoted fitness as the glue to keep society together; however, the organization's morally strict nineteenth-century view of (Christian) character-building had been updated and broadened to the more encompassing mission of "values clarification" (Putney 1997).

Despite such leading examples as New York's Vanderbilt and Westside branches (and the 92nd Street YMHA), most YMCAs in the 1970s did not invest in updating their facilities, leaving locations looking "dated . . . spartan . . . unattractive," according to a *New York Times* review of health clubs (Hinds 1980: 48). Moreover, what the YMCA offered in affordability could also be regarded as a lack of exclusivity – "bargain priced" (Hinds 1980: 48) can mean both easy access and lack of status.

The lifestyle health club

By the 1980s, the lifestyle-oriented commercial health club had become a standard feature in the urban landscape. Club membership was the perfect accoutrement in the lifestyles of both the health- and status-conscious, fitting in with the decade's Zeitgeist of competitive individualism and conspicuous consumption, as captured in Bret Easton Ellis' novel *American Psycho*. Ellis' psychotic anti-hero, Patrick Bateman, obsessively details his various status credentials, including his designer suits, luxury furnishings, high-flying Wall Street job, boutique grooming products, and membership in an aptly named health club:

The health club I belong to, Xclusive, is private and located four blocks from my apartment on the Upper West Side. In the two years since I signed up as a member, it has been remodeled three times and though they carry the latest weight machines (Nautilus, Universal, Keiser) they have a vast array of free weights which I like to use also. The club has ten courts for tennis and racquetball, aerobics classes, four aerobic dance studios, two swimming pools, Lifecycles, a Gravitron machine, rowing machines, treadmills, cross-country skiing machines, one-on-one training, cardiovascular evaluations, personalized programs, massage, sauna and steam rooms, a sun deck, tanning booths and a café with a juice bar, all of it designed by J.J. Vogel, who designed the new Norman Prager club, Petty's. Membership runs five thousand dollars annually.

(Ellis 1991: 67)

In today's New York City, the equivalent is the flagship location of the Equinox health club chain. Located in the new Time Warner Center, Equinox offers a club-within-a-club: the exclusive E Club, limited to 200 members at an annual cost of $24,000 (Cerulo 2006). In comparison to more affordable alternatives, Xclusive and its real-world counterparts such as E Club offer more equipment, more services, and, most importantly, more status.

This new breed of health club combined the elite privilege, luxury facilities and social networking of the executive club; the gym's traditionally male strength-training activities like boxing and bodybuilding and the exercise salon's female toning exercises of calisthenics, dance and yoga; and the YMCA's organizational structure of membership, classes and multiple-use facilities. At the same time that new commercial clubs were adopting and adapting these elements, the function of exercise was being reformulated. Clubs sold fitness as a leisure lifestyle activity, promoting pleasure and recreation ahead of the executive clubs' and corporate fitness programs' goal of productivity, or the YMCA's promotion of community- and character-building. The new lifestyle clubs continued the emphasis, found in gay and women's weightlifting and exercise salons, on exercise as the means to improve one's physical capital, and amplified the concern – found in the executive clubs and exercise salons – with status and leisure: health club memberships and physical appearance were interrelated status markers in an overall lifestyle package. As testimony to the link between the new health clubs and notions of a desirable lifestyle, health clubs have been used since the late 1970s in property development strategies, serving as residential amenities to attract residents to high-priced apartment and condominium developments (Horsley 1977; Moss 1986).

The most obvious break between the older alternatives and the new clubs was material – that is, it lay in the equipment. In terms of exercise products and practices, the new clubs were at the forefront of making exercise machines a standard part of fitness in the late 1970s. Machines such as Nautilus and Universal removed the need for much (but not all) of the expert knowledge regarding body position and exercise sequence, meaning that fewer staff were required to supervise exercise. In addition, as only one person could use a machine at a time, health clubs required considerable floor space – not only for the machines, but also for exercise class studios (especially with the 1980s aerobics craze). The need for space coincided in the late 1970s with the waning of the racquet sports boom. In terms of the use of space, health clubs are more profitably organized than tennis or squash clubs: a racquet court can accommodate a maximum of 4 people, while the same space in a health club can accommodate between 20 and 80 people, depending on the configuration of the equipment or studio.

In the early 1980s, large club chains began to emerge, particularly as older spas and racquet clubs were acquired and converted into multi-use health clubs. With the growing number of health club owners came the development of a trade association. First organized in 1981, the International Health Racquet and Sportsclub Association (IHRSA) is the leading trade organization of the commercial health club industry. IRHSA[8] represents over 6,500 clubs worldwide – including a variety of fitness facilities, spas, and sports clubs, as well as suppliers. The organization compiles industry statistics, organizes an annual trade convention, publishes a trade journal (*CBI – Club Business International*, launched in 1987), and lobbies for policy initiatives, including increased funding for physical education in schools, and the end of the tax-exempt status for YMCA fitness facilities (see Miller and Fielding 1995).

According to IHRSA industry figures,[9] the number of commercial health clubs in the US had grown from 6,000 in the early 1980s to over 29,000 at the end of 2005, with 2005 revenues for the total US health club industry of nearly $16 billion. While the book's focus is on the fitness field in the US, it is important to note the globalization of the consumption space of the health club. Selected statistics from the global spread of commercial health clubs are outlined in Table 3.1, and reflect 2005 data (for the US, Asia-Pacific and Latin America), and 2002 data for Europe and Canada.[10] Health clubs, like gourmet coffee shops and day spas, are an example of the urban leisure and lifestyle amenities that have multiplied to capitalize on the discretionary income and image-consciousness of the professional/managerial class. It is

Table 3.1 The global commercial health club industry

Country	# Commercial clubs	Country	# Commercial clubs
United States	26,830	Mexico	1,800
Brazil	7,000	Netherlands	1,700
Germany	6,500	Canada	1,658
Italy	6,072	Australia	1,335
Spain	3,500	New Zealand	450
Argentina	3,000	China	350
France	2,500	Malaysia	225
Japan	1,951	Taiwan	220
United Kingdom	1,943	Korea	200

Source: International Health, Racquet and Sportsclub Association and the Canadian Business Directory.

little wonder that health clubs have sprung up in major cities across the globe: they are part and parcel of a globalized service economy for which images are increasingly the primary product.

IHRSA's industry figures also show that US membership at all forms of health clubs has grown from 17.3 million in 1987 to 41.3 million in 2005, with more than 52 per cent belonging to commercial clubs – more than double the number of members at YMCAs/YWCAs. More to the point, the privatization of the provision of fitness facilities in the US is gathering pace. In 2000, commercial health clubs outnumbered YMCAs by a factor of seven; by 2005, that factor had increased to eleven.[11] Once a new alternative to traditional sites of exercise, commercial health clubs dominate the contemporary fitness field.

Who are health club members? According to the 2005 IHRSA / American Sports Data Health Club Trend Report, 57 per cent of US health club members are women – a rise in recent years due possibly to the emergence of more women-only health clubs. As with other leisure industries for which Baby Boomers are central, the age profile of health club consumers is becoming more diverse: in 1987, 53 per cent of members were 18 to 34; in 2005, they accounted for only 35 per cent, while 33 per cent were 35 to 54, and 20 per cent were 55 and older. Despite the increasing age diversity, commercial health club membership remains predominantly middle-class: 73 per cent of members have household incomes of more than $50,000, whereas only 40 per cent of the general US population makes more than $50,000.

Moreover, a full 50 per cent of health club members make more than $75,000 annually, whereas only about the top 20 per cent of the general population makes that amount (see Bureau of Labor Statistics 2006). The lifestyle health club of the contemporary fitness field is not only a specific kind of leisure business offering a particular vision of the means and goals of fitness; it is also characterized by its consumer market, which is becoming increasingly female and older, but which remains middle- and upper-middle-class. It is thus useful to consider the experiences of those consumers in choosing and using health clubs, as a means of sensitization to the ways in which the contemporary health club industry is constructed.

CHOOSING AND USING HEALTH CLUBS

Julie is in her early 30s and works at a non-profit organization while pursuing a PhD in philosophy. In addition to running in Central Park, Julie works out in a health club at least five times a week – usually a combination of yoga classes, free weights, and cardio machines. Through friends and guest passes, free trial memberships, and changing membership between clubs, Julie has sampled from a wide range of New York City's health club chains, including the low-cost, women's-only Strength & Beauty; the mid-level multi-use Apple Fitness, which targets a younger, co-ed crowd and offers a wide range of classes but few service amenities; and the more expensive but no more luxurious Champion's, once a bodybuilding gym and now multi-use. I asked her to recount her health club biography:

> I started out working out at Strength & Beauty, which I deliberately chose because I wanted to be in a women-only environment, because I really like being able to be in my own world, and be uninterrupted. So I noticed, very dramatically, the difference when I first joined Apple Fitness, how being checked out *bothered* me, and did affect me.

Combining Julie's comments with health club industry statistics, gender emerges as a factor that shapes the question of how, more so than if, one is involved in the fitness field. The health club environment – including sweaty exercisers, mirrors, and a focus on the physical form – amplifies the sexual dynamics of everyday life, mediating types of use and feelings of comfort/discomfort within the space of the club. For some, like Julie, this may be experienced as an unwanted intrusion of the logic of the dating market into the self-focused time of working out; for others, the sexual dynamics of the gym is central to its appeal. Spaces of physical culture have long been a "pick-up" spot for gay men, who used YMCAs, health spas, and bath houses as sites for sexual cruising from the early twentieth century. In the 1980s, the role of health clubs as "meat markets" was signaled by a 1983 *Rolling Stone* cover story that declared the health club the "new singles' bar" (Ryzik 2006), and epitomized in the John Travolta and Jamie Lee Curtis 1985 film *Perfect*. However, health club users do not passively accept gendered norms regarding their behavior within clubs or the ideal fit bodies[12] to which they are encouraged to aspire; rather, societal norms – in terms of gender, sexuality, age, class, and so forth – intersect within the space of the health club, making options more or less available to different users (cf. Fishwick 2001).

Julie continues with her health club biography and the discussion of Strength & Beauty:

> Strength & Beauty used to be run by less well-paid folks. The kids – and I mean *kids* – who would open the doors were frequently late and left people out on the street in the mornings. They were not qualified trainers, but they were supposed to take people around and show them how to use machines, even though they were just the door people. They would play their Madonna music as loud as they wanted. And we would often have to go and ask them to turn it down. It doesn't happen that way, as much, at Apple Fitness, which is far better staffed. There were two people on duty generally at Strength & Beauty, whereas there are probably more like fifteen or twenty at Apple. And I'm very lucky because I'm at Apple so regularly, at least a couple of people on staff not only know my name, and not only know me to see me all the time, but they know my *number*, and so when I walk in I don't even have to pull out my membership card. They just say good morning, and put my number in for me, and it makes all the difference.

Julie's assessment of the clubs employs the typical criteria used to judge consumer leisure businesses more generally: the added value components of interior design, staff professionalism, and the quality of service. She continues:

> I've also been taking yoga classes at Champion's, at the one in midtown, so it's full of a lot of actresses and folks who are in the midtown area who are highly competitive. So it's a very, very different energy [*laughs*]

than yoga at other places. I also thought Champion's was a far less expensive gym, but my friend Sarah who teaches there says it's not. In fact, it's more expensive, but it still has a less expensive feel: everything's *metal*, and everything's got a very fast food, sort of McDonald's – as opposed to nice restaurant – edge to it. They have a juice bar and stuff at the front though, and they sell some clothing. Strength & Beauty doesn't sell any, and Apple Fitness sells a handful. My friend Sarah actually teaches at several different gyms, and she says Champion's has the best classes of *any*, including the high-, high-, high-priced places in New York. You will have a selection of two or three *great* classes every day, instead of a couple great classes a week, which is what it is at Apple Fitness. And even less at Strength & Beauty! And the yoga classes are a big part of why I'm paying ten times as much to go to Apple Fitness as I was to go to Strength & Beauty.

Here, Julie's comments highlight how perceptions of quality mediate definitions of value: excellent, professional service may mean that a high price is experienced as good value.

Julie is typical of the people I spoke to in that she has used several different health clubs and brings a critical consumer eye to choosing and using health clubs. While Champion's remains out of Julie's reach because of the membership fees, the great classes, friendly staff and "right" atmosphere legitimize the cost of upgrading from Strength & Beauty to Apple Fitness.

Service quality and environment were not the only factors at work in Julie's move from Strength & Beauty to Apple Fitness. In the course of working out at Strength & Beauty, Julie became friendly with a group of women in their mid-50s to late 60s, whom she has come to call the "gym ladies": "I didn't join a gym for the social dimension; it was just this wonderful, added fringe benefit." One of the women, Teri, was the first to move to Apple Fitness, and the group followed her there. However, as Julie recounts, the new space and cost of Apple posed challenges to maintaining the same social network:

A couple people came over and then went back to Strength & Beauty because it just wasn't the same. They weren't finding us as available because Strength & Beauty was so small that if it's an intimate group of five or six people, you can really have a conversation. And there are so many more machines at Apple and more things to do that we ended up more diffused than we had been.

Intrigued, I asked Julie to introduce me to the group.

My first stop was Apple Fitness, to meet Teri, a retired teacher, Paulina, who manages an independent film theatre, and Barbara, a travel writer. During the interview, Teri, Paulina and Barbara were working out alongside each other on treadmills. I asked how they met, and their responses underline the importance of the social dynamic in their use and experience of the health club:

Teri: Barbara and I live in the same building, and met there. The others I met at Strength & Beauty.

Barbara: The girls from the gym! I always call us the girls from the gym. And Julie's about 30, and Isabelle's 78 or 79. There's like a 50-year difference.

Teri: Yeah, I love that. The social part is important because it gets me here and it gets me doing it, because when I wake up in the morning, I don't really feel like working out. If there's nobody waiting for me here, I would just roll over. So, it also makes the time go by so much quicker. So I really like that.

Barbara: I'm not nearly as dedicated as these two women. I come because Teri calls me every morning, at eight-twenty.

Paulina: Or if she doesn't, I do! [*Laughs*] Especially at Strength & Beauty, we were very tight as a team, you know, and it was just something very ritualistic. We're still very, very close. We celebrate each other's birthday, we go out in the gym group.

Barbara: And we look for each other when we're at the gym.

For many, health club-based friendships can be a powerful incentive to remain committed to working out, as has been demonstrated in other research on health club users (Crossley 2006; Unger and Johnson 1995). However, as much as health clubs open up possibilities for social interaction and networking, they also pose particular challenges:

Barbara: We all moved gyms together too. But not everybody stayed here; some went back to Strength & Beauty. What's not happening is we're not making new friends *here*.

Jennifer: You're a clique!

Barbara: Yeah, we are! [*Laughs*]

Teri: I think people tend to keep to themselves much more here.

Barbara: Everybody's plugged in here. That's the other difference between Strength & Beauty – there, not everybody is plugged in.

Barbara's observations on the earphone culture of the club – with everyone "plugged in" to their own music device – suggest how technology facilitates the individualization of physical culture. It is not only that a treadmill is a more individualized mode of exercise than a team sport. It is also a matter of the norms of use of the treadmill: health clubs typically offer "cardio theaters," in which treadmills, stair climbers, and the like are surrounded by banks of television screens and music consoles that allow – indeed encourage – exercisers to plug in and tune out of the social milieu.

In further reflections on the differences in the health clubs, the women also highlight how age mediates the experience of the health club space:

Paulina: You know, I still have a membership at Strength & Beauty, and I periodically go for social reasons and I'll do a quick workout. But they blast the music so loud you cannot hear yourself think.

Barbara: There is this culture, that gyms are supposed to be loud. But the problem is that not everybody is part of that culture. The people who are working in the clubs seem to think everybody's twenty-something. I once said to the manager, "You need to come out of your office at nine thirty and look around. There's nobody who's twenty-something here. There's nobody who's thirty-something here. This is a different group. And we don't like loud music."

Health clubs are not static spaces; they are shaped by their clientele and as the demographic profile of users shifts over the course of a day and a week, so too does the social milieu of the space.

I later met with Maggie, one of the group who returned to Strength & Beauty after trying out Apple Fitness with Teri and the others. Maggie, a retired singer and singing teacher, is in her mid-60s. Despite Maggie's being impressed by Apple Fitness during her free trial membership, budgetary issues have meant that she has remained at Strength & Beauty, along with four others from the group. Although the classes and equipment cannot compare with Apple Fitness, a recent change in staff has meant that things have improved at the low-cost women only club:

Maggie: The two girls who work at the desk right now are *phenomenal*. They're *just delightful*. Because until they came, we had some really awful, *really awful*, sort of heart-trembling women there. They were extremely hostile. Maybe there have been so many complaints so maybe they sought out these *very, very* sweet, amiable,

polite, wise, young women. One of them is very *motherly* [*laughs*].
She's young enough to be my granddaughter, but she has this deep
voice and will say *"How are you, Maggie? Are you feeling all right?"*
You know, very embracing. So it's lovely to come in. That's very
welcoming, instead of this sort of anonymous, hostile stare.

When Julie and her friends describe their health club experiences, they highlight two different, but overlapping dynamics. The first concerns the ways in
which the choice and use of health clubs are mediated in different ways by
gender, age, and class. The second concerns the means by which the value of
a club is judged: service. Service, however, comes in many guises. A club's
atmosphere (friendly, intimate, loud, hostile), range, and quality of amenities,
equipment and classes, and the friendliness and professionalism of the staff
all contribute to a health club's service profile, and set the context within
which members can create social connections. Strength & Beauty, Apple
Fitness and Champion's are all selling the same notion of fitness, but they are
not selling the same services. Like other leisure businesses, the health club
market is stratified by service, which provides the basis for the cost of
membership (and a consumer's rationalization for paying more), and the
distinguishing feature between different clubs.

THE STRATIFICATION OF CLUBS

With the historical development of health clubs as the foundation, and
the subjective experiences of Julie and her friends as the sensitizing context,
the chapter now explores the commercial health club industry as a network
of choices structured along three lines. At the most general level, setting the
outer parameters of the grid, the health club choices available to consumers
are shaped by the social construction of fitness as a leisure activity and, thus,
fitness spaces as leisure businesses. Positions within the grid are structured
along both vertical and horizontal lines. Vertically, health clubs are stratified
according to the range of services they provide, which generally translates
into a question of cost. Horizontally, health clubs are stratified according to
the "personality" they offer – the added symbolic value that derives from a
club's décor, reputation, clientele, and so forth.

The stratification of commercial health clubs can thus be represented as a
relatively structured field of choices, as shown in Figure 3.1. The dashed
outer line marks the permeable boundary between commercial health clubs,

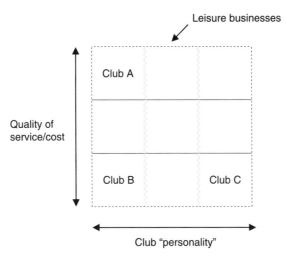

Figure 3.1 The field of choice for commercial health clubs.

which construct themselves as leisure lifestyle businesses, and other exercise venues that adopt a different frame of reference, such as health care (as in the case of the physiotherapy clinic) or economic productivity and occupational satisfaction (as in the case of the corporate gym). One of the most important consequences of selling exercise as a leisure activity is that fitness must necessarily contend with the constraints that characterize people's leisure. In other words, health clubs must orient themselves to competing for people's discretionary time and disposable income.

The matrix is also stratified vertically, with the different strata demarked by solid lines, indicating the relatively concrete difference between levels – Club A costs more than Club B; Club A offers a greater range of services than Club B. What is less clear-cut is the point at which the *quality* of service changes. In general in the health club industry, as the cost of membership increases, the role of services within the health club becomes more central for member retention and thus membership revenue.

Finally, the horizontal strata are separated by undulating lines, indicating the fluid boundaries between different types of club personality. Memberships in Clubs B and C cost approximately the same; what differentiates them is the "feel" of the club, with – for example – Club B aimed more at a young, urban social crowd, and Club C aimed solely at women. Although "personality" bands are rarely homogeneous up and down a cost band – the personality of Club A is not going to be articulated in quite the same way as that of Club B – there are continuities. Thus, Club A would also be aimed at the young, urban crowd but, given its higher cost and quality of service, would articulate its personality through markers of higher prestige, such as the use of a famous interior designer or exclusive social events for members.

Altogether, these elements form the fitness field's "stakes" (Bourdieu and Wacquant 1992: 98), or the qualities that matter. Since the 1970s, health clubs have not only expanded in number, but have become more sophisticated service and leisure businesses. Most health clubs now offer a similar range of exercise equipment and classes. Thus, differentiation increasingly depends on the quality of a club's services and its image. The advantages of membership are promoted in health club advertising, reinforced in consumer reviews, and actively constructed by health club staff: clubs provide motivation and instruction for exercise, and the status associated with *belonging*. But some clubs "count" for more than others, reproducing the social stratification of consumers in the range of health club options. The chapter now examines each of these facets in turn, in the stratification of the field of choice.

Leisure businesses and competition for time

Health clubs promote physical fitness as, first and foremost, a leisure activity. In contrast, the YMCA promotes physical fitness as an ethical mode of character-building, school physical education promotes fitness as a tool of vocational development, and corporate fitness programs endorse exercise as a means of ensuring productivity (cf. Defrance and Pociello 1993). Commercial health clubs are competing not only against these other exercise venues and programs, but with other leisure businesses as well and are, in turn, shaped by the logic of leisure industries that focuses upon status, identity, and the expressive value of goods. Within such a framework, the value of a health club may rest upon the affirmation of a member's social position and sense of self, irrespective of the accomplishment of health goals.

Many health club chains, like consumer businesses generally, have expanded their brands with parallel product lines and brand licensing. Crunch is a chain of clubs that began in New York's East Village in 1989; it has since expanded within the city and across the US. In a CNN interview, Doug Levine, the club's founder, explicitly locates his business within the leisure market, and understands his competition in terms of the options his members have for spending their leisure time:

> [W]e think that people are working longer hours under more stress in their life, both men and women in equal numbers. And we think that,

you know, you're no longer getting out of work at 5 or 5:30 but are now working till 6 or 8 o'clock at night. And some people are working on the weekends. And Crunch feels that it's competing with Blockbuster. It's competing with movie chains, with theme restaurants and bars and restaurants. And we think that when you're out of work at 7:30 or 8 o'clock at night, we think that we can eliminate stress in your life and entertain you through some of the things that we do. And it's – our competition is other forms of entertainment.

(Morris 1997)

This competition between health clubs and other retail and entertainment businesses is instrumental in setting the tone of the field as one of leisure, relatively autonomous from the related health and political fields that lend it support. In other words, membership sales at Crunch (for example) may benefit from the Surgeon General's endorsement of exercise, but the product that Crunch sells is ultimately cast not in the language of health, but in terms of leisure and entertainment value.

Thus, it is not surprising that health clubs are incorporating more entertainment value into their design and programming. The aforementioned cardio theaters have become standard in clubs, offering music, television, and web access hooked up to cardiovascular machines. Clubs also offer novel exercise programs, featuring the routines of ballerinas, firemen, and striptease artists. Overall, the health club industry adopts many of the same strategies as other consumer industries, focusing upon personality, status, brands, and experience in the delivery of their goods and services (Pine and Gilmore 1998; Sherry 1998).

This equation of fitness with leisure is reproduced in the market research reports commissioned for the health club and fitness industries. For example, the Great Waters of France company, makers of bottled water, commissioned a study in the late 1970s of the average American's knowledge and opinions on sport and exercise. The resulting report, *The Perrier Study* (Harris *et al.* 1984), explored popular attitudes towards, and participation in, fitness activities in the US. Half of the survey respondents felt that they were not getting enough exercise, and were asked for the main reasons why this was so. The most often-cited reason was "not enough time" (Harris *et al.* 1984: 51). However, active, moderately active, and inactive people were all found to have approximately 25 hours of leisure time per week (1984: 12); therefore, the report concluded that "the main obstacles to fitness lie with the people themselves" (1984: 51). The authors of the report represent fitness as a choice of how you spend your *leisure* time, without consideration of the different constraints placed on people's discretionary time, or of other possibilities such as building time for exercise into the workday. Instead, leisure is promoted as the unproblematic, unquestioned sphere in which self-improvement should take place.

Given the production of fitness as a leisure activity, it is important to understand the changing patterns of leisure and consumer spending. Spending on the body (at leisure, and as leisure) makes up a significant portion of a household's annual expenditures: food away from home, apparel and services, health care, entertainment, and personal care products and services account for over 22 per cent of annual consumer spending (Bureau of Labor Statistics 2006: 4). According to the Bureau of Labor Statistics' Consumer Expenditure Survey, the average high-income household (with an annual income of $70,000 or more, the group that represents half of all commercial health club members) spent $4,119 in 2004 on entertainment, a category that includes the costs of health club memberships, at-home exercise equipment, video rentals, admission to sporting events, recreation on trips, television and stereo equipment, pets and pet supplies, athletic shoes, boat rentals, and even fireworks. While such entertainment expenditures dwarf the amounts spent in households with incomes less than $70,000, the *proportion* of household spending on entertainment is quite close: entertainment spending was 5.4 per cent for households both over $70,000, and those between $50,000 and $69,999; 4.6 per cent for households both between $40,000 and $49,999, and those between $30,000 and $39,000; and 5.6 per cent for households between $20,000 and $29,999 (Bureau of Labor Statistics 2006: 10). The implication for the health club industry – and the fitness field – is that there is a lower-income leisure market. To reach this potential market, however, health clubs must provide lower-cost memberships, often at the expense of high-quality service (a point to which the discussion will return, with regard to vertical stratification). Nevertheless, the occupational group that spends the most on entertainment is, not surprisingly, the professional/managerial class (Bureau of Labor Statistics 2006: 20).

As the options for leisure activities have increased, several studies have suggested that leisure time is shrinking, especially for the professional and managerial workers (Cage 1989; Jacobs and Gerson 1998; Hochschild 1997; Schor 1991; Zuzanek, Beckers and Peters 1998). This "time crunch" is explained not by an increase in work hours (although unlike other occupations, the professional/managerial group has seen an increase in the average work week; see Jacobs and Gerson 1998), but by a decline in the amount of non-work time available for leisure. Since 1970, the rising participation of women in the labor market has meant that the percentage of dual-income households has risen from approximately 36 per cent to 60 per cent (Jacobs and Gerson, 1998). As a result, fewer families have a stay-at-home individual (traditionally, the woman) to look after the non-paid, time-consuming work of maintaining a household and family. Thus, chores like the laundry and vacuuming get done during one's "free" time, decreasing the amount of non-work time available for actual leisure activities (especially so for women, thus highlighting the role of gender in mediating the experience of and access to fitness and other forms of leisure). This is even more pronounced for families with one or more individuals in professional or managerial positions.

Bearing in mind that individuals in professional and managerial positions are the ideal target consumers for the health club industry, it is not difficult to appreciate the business problems for health clubs. On the one hand, health clubs must contend with other entertainment and leisure venues, as well as other investments of discretionary income, from apparel and personal care products to transportation and housing. On the other hand, health clubs are competing against the other demands on their consumers' time. Thus, the marketing of fitness must combine the trappings of leisure with efficient outcomes.

In 1987, John McCarthy, the director of the trade organization IHRSA, discussed the state of the health club industry. In an article published in the trade journal *Athletic Business*, McCarthy outlined both the industry's weaknesses and strengths, highlighting the concerns for health club owners. McCarthy (1987: 44–5) suggested that the industry was suffering from inconsistent quality, lack of professional standards, a high rate of member attrition (30–50 per cent), and a narrow age range of members (70 per cent were between 25 and 44). The strengths, however, lay in an emerging consistency in the production of fitness as a service-oriented, lifestyle and leisure industry. McCarthy highlighted the importance of the YMCA and other fitness facilities for "producing millions of people who are conditioned to an exercise-, recreation- and athletic-oriented lifestyle. These people are prime candidates to become members of private sector clubs" (1987: 40). More importantly, McCarthy declared, the industry was learning to position itself as part of that exercise- or recreation-oriented lifestyle:

[The] industry is, and is becoming even more so, a convenience industry. . . . Managed recreation is a repeat business, and any repeat business industry is a convenience industry. . . . In 1985, for the first time in decades, the average American employee began working more than 40 hours per week. . . . This time famine is both an opportunity and a limitation for the industry. It's an opportunity because clubs now have the real possibility of generating more money from amenity services than they do from their core membership services.

(McCarthy 1987: 42)

Such thinking reflected a wider business strategy, which had since the early 1970s targeted a "convenience-oriented customer" (Anderson 1971). The amenity services that McCarthy had in mind included dry-cleaning, banking and child-care – in short, converting the health club from a multi-use exercise facility into a multi-purpose leisure and lifestyle facility.

Several of the health club consumers I spoke to also highlighted the issue of convenience, particularly with regard to location. Ellie, for example, said that when it comes to choosing a club:

> It's almost always the location that matters the most, in terms of actually knowing that you'll be able to do a workout. If you have a crazy schedule like mine – where almost anytime that I'm not with my child, I'm *paying* someone to be with my child – it means that I don't waste any time traveling anywhere.

Luke, a teacher and entrepreneur in his mid-30s, emphasized a broader notion of convenience in his definition of a good club. He mentioned a very upscale health club that offered services such as pet-grooming, dry-cleaning, and travel bookings, which was, thanks to such amenities, out of his price range:

> It's very expensive. But I tell you what, if I *could* afford it, I would probably get my hair cut, and I would get massages and so forth at clubs. If I could, I would. Because it would save me a trip going to my barber. . . . It's one-stop shopping. There is something . . . it's an issue of convenience. It's an issue of time. And if money were not an object, then one-stop shopping for this kind of body- and self-improvement is . . . I mean it seems foolish not to.

The cultural production of the health club as the site of the fitness field does not rest solely on the shoulders of health club owners and managers. Consumers like Ellie and Luke must come to regard exercise as a leisure activity, and health clubs (and other fitness products) as the necessary tools for their leisure-time activity of "getting fit."

Media plays an important role in educating consumers to make this unquestioned association between exercise and the leisure market (an issue examined in more detail in Chapter 4). Over the past thirty years, sources of advice on health and fitness purchases (from athletic sneakers to personal training services) have multiplied. Consumer reviews, fitness magazine articles and exercise manuals produce a naturalized connection between fitness and leisure, and fitness leisure and consumption, by presenting choice as occurring between different health clubs and exercise products, rather than between commercial and non-commercial possibilities.

The naturalization of the connection between exercise and consumer leisure is not only found in unabashedly commercial magazines and manuals. The American College of Sports Medicine (ACSM), for example, has published an exercise manual with the goal of educating the public about fitness and debunking the association between exercise and consuming: "Becoming fit does not require hard physical activity, monotonous workouts, or a health club membership. To be physically fit, you simply need a regular program of exercise" (American College of Sports Medicine 1998: 9). However, the ACSM's interest in making physical activity accessible to a general population – through downplaying the necessity of consumer expense – is accompanied by the acknowledgment that fitness products and services are often regarded as an essential part of getting fit. As such, the ACSM ultimately reproduces the message that being a fitness participant involves being a fitness consumer: "Some people find home exercising lonely or boring and want the variety and socializing that a fitness center can offer" (American College of Sports Medicine 1992: 102).

In general, leisure time has become increasingly colonized by consumer products and services since the postwar leisure boom: hobbies and travel require equipment, clothing, admission passes, and guidebooks. While the fitness industry greatly benefits from the endorsement of such external fields as health promotion and physical education, and gains institutional support and scientific legitimacy from such non-profit organizations as the ACSM, health clubs and other fitness products ultimately profit by highlighting the differences between exercise-as-leisure and exercise-as-medicine. Unlike working out under the orders of a physician – or doing so in the setting of a physical therapy clinic – exercising in a health club is explicitly constructed as a leisure activity, with the associated perks of membership and entertainment. In market research reports and consumer reviews, the production and consumption of fitness are presented as part of the realm of leisure, rather than the by-product of work or housework, or as a prescribed or routine health-maintenance activity.

All commercial health clubs may be the sites of fitness-as-leisure, but they do not offer equal products. The ACSM manual (1992: 102), for example, is typical in that its discussion of health clubs combines objective measures of value (the equipment, cleanliness, fees) with a subjective description (the clientele, staff). Through the process of market consolidation and the education of fitness consumers in a set of common expectations, the expansion of the health club industry has been marked by increasing similarity in the types of equipment and classes offered. As with competition in other industries in which products – from automobiles to toothpaste – are highly similar on a material basis, differentiation thus comes to depend on the quality and cost of customer service, and the symbolic added value of a club's status and personality.

Services and membership cost

The vast majority – over 70 per cent – of health clubs' revenue comes from membership dues.[13] At the most basic level, health clubs generate profits along three avenues: acquiring new members, generating higher returns from existing members (through sales of ancillary goods and services such as equipment and personal training), and extending the duration of members' relationships with the club (cf. Grant and Schlesinger 1995). The quality and diversity of exercise programs, professionalism of staff, and variety of ancillary services (such as massage, dry-cleaning, restaurants and pro shops) determine a club's relative status, and rationalize a club's membership costs. The differentiation between health clubs based on service largely translates into a vertical stratification of cost. Good service, after all, is expensive.

In an interview with Jim, an IHRSA representative, I asked how the health club industry has changed during his ten years with the organization:

> We're a service industry, not something else. At one point, operators were focused on people coming through the front door, and not much after that. But [IHRSA] noticed that some clubs focused on service, on member retention, and they didn't suffer the same rates of turnover so they were more stable businesses. They were more profitable, because they could concentrate on selling to the members they already had,

selling services like personal training. So we would report that to other operators, share that information.

Jim's account of the development of the health club industry reflects a broader pattern in many consumer industries, such as banking, automobile manufacturers, and airlines, which have responded to intense competition by adopting the "quality model" for business management (Grant and Schlesinger 1995). This model was popularized most notably by the work of W. Edwards Deming, whose system of "Total Quality Management" was credited with changing the fortunes of Japanese businesses.

The quality model not only focuses upon service provision, but also involves workers and customers in product and service design so as to engender loyalty and productivity. Health clubs are thus interested in researching not only why people join clubs, but also why they do not join them, or why they quit. The identified problems can then be operationalized as the criteria for designing and delivering ancillary services in the health club, including programs geared to the handicapped, elderly, and chronically ill; child-care services; and the motivational and instructional services of personal trainers. IHRSA's endorsement of the member-retention type of health club is part of the business world's accepted wisdom about profitability – espoused in financial and information industries, grocery chains, automobile makers, and others – regarding client loyalty as a key to long-term profitability (Grant and Schlesinger 1995; Pine and Peppers 1995; Reichheld 1996). The commercial health club's attention to service is also a reflection of the operating model of another exercise site: the YMCA. Indeed, some health clubs have come to resemble multi-use YMCAs – particularly those large commercial clubs located in suburbs where memberships tend to include families. According to Jim, these commercial clubs "are 'out-Y-ing' the Y. Full service family clubs can do it better than the Y."

Despite Jim's suggestion that there has been a progression from one type of club to the other, the health club industry continues to be characterized by two business models: one focused on signing up new members, the other on keeping existing members (Howell and Minor 2000: 455–6). These two models – sales-driven and retention-driven – both emphasize service; however, the relative cost (and quality) of the service differs.

The sales-driven model emphasizes acquiring new members as the means of generating profit. These health clubs rarely limit the number of members, and memberships tend to take the form of long-term contracts, often sold at a heavily discounted rate to attract new members. This business model allows clubs to maintain low membership costs; however, the pressure on club staff to generate sales often degenerates into strong pressure on customers to sign up (and ensuing customer complaints). With the emphasis on drawing in new members rather than keeping existing ones, these clubs often have a high rate of turnover, which may see the same person join and quit and join again. Low prices also translate into lower wages for staff; consequently, the quality of service is also lower.

The retention-driven model focuses on keeping members for long-term profitability through a combination of higher-quality services (such as better-trained staff, or tie-in services such as social events) and superior surroundings (such as those designed by architecture firms). These high-quality services and added features are delivered at a higher price for the members, in part because better service requires better, more qualified service workers. Thus, retention-driven clubs have higher membership dues. This tends to translate, geographically, into locations in higher-income neighborhoods, either in the city or in the nearby wealthy commuting suburbs.

College physical education students – prospective fitness professionals and producers – are provided with an overview of the two business models in a recent kinesiology textbook (Howell and Minor 2000). According to the authors, sales-based facilities are characterized by their unrealistic advertising, which suggests "that exercise is only for individuals who are already fit and healthy," whereas retention-based facilities "make a sincere effort to meet the long-term needs of current members" (Howell and Minor 2000: 455–6). The prospective "physical activity specialist" is then asked:

> What do you think it would be like to be a professional physical activity specialist in a sales-based facility? Would you be likely to feel fulfilled and have a sense of helping people? Are professionals in a sales-based facility likely to adhere to a mechanical, market-driven professionalism or a social trustee, civic professionalism? . . . What do you think it would be like . . . in a retention-based facility? Would you be likely to feel fulfilled and have a sense of functioning as a social trustee, civic professional?
>
> (Howell and Minor, 2000: 456)

The sales- and retention-based health clubs are thus juxtaposed not only in terms of their operating strategies, but also in terms of their underlying ethos: mechanical and market-driven, or civic-minded and socially valuable.

In contrast to the retention-driven clubs, sales-driven clubs tend to be represented in producer and consumer fitness texts as bad businesses. For example, an article in the trade journal *Athletic Business* in 1987 reflected on the possibility of further state regulation of the health club industry. Rather than view regulation as a constraint upon business, however, the author suggested that health club owners take a positive view, as regulation would inspire greater public confidence in the industry. According to the author, the public image of health clubs had been tarnished by: "high pressure sales tactics and outright misrepresentation and fraud . . . abrupt club closings and bankruptcies that leave prepaid members holding the bag . . . [and] the industry's persistent reliance on long-term contracts, up-front fees and pre-opening membership sales to fuel clubs' start-up costs" ("More state regulation?" 1987: 20).

Consumer-oriented fitness texts also reinforce the low status of sales-driven health clubs. In a *New York Times* article, for example, readers in the early 1970s were warned of the "hard sell" tactics at Jack La Lanne health spas, at which a reporter was asked: "Wouldn't you like to be able to look yourself in the eye next time you put on a bikini? If you don't commit yourself, you're saying that you don't care about the way you look" (Lichtenstein 1972: 16).

As with earlier complaints against the dieting and health spa industries (Lichtenstein 1972), health clubs became the focus of consumer ire as unscrupulous business tactics were used to compete in an overcrowded market. Complaints of "deceptive advertising, high-pressure sales tactics, misrepresentations in sales presentations, contracts restricting membership cancellations and unexpected closings" led the Federal Trade Commission in 1975 to propose industry-wide regulation, and that members be able to cancel memberships at any time (Pagano 1985: 1). While such proposals never passed, 24 states had already adopted mandatory "cooling-off" periods by the mid-1980s, which allowed members to cancel without penalty within three days of signing a contract (see also Glassner 1988).

Despite such guidelines and regulations, fitness magazines and manuals continue to warn consumers of "slimy sales tactics" when they are looking for a health club. Meredith, in her early 30s and working in publishing, recalls her encounter with the low-cost health club chain, Hurley's. Attracted by an advertised sale on memberships that offered a significant discount on monthly fees for those who joined during a limited period, she went for a tour of the Hurley's club nearest her home:

They were *extremely*, extremely aggressive. And that is an immediate turn-off to me. While I was there, they were trying to make sure that I filled out a membership thing and they got my name and all that kind of stuff. They really didn't just accept that I wanted to look at it. They really wanted to have some kind of commitment. . . . Luckily I gave them a voicemail number that I never actually answer; it's just set up to take messages. And I would get a message a day, from the club's person, for two or three weeks after I went for a visit. I was there for 10, 15 minutes and they . . . I mean, on one hand, I credit them for follow-up, but it was overkill. It was the point of feeling [*laughing*] like I was being stalked!

Fitness producers who operate member-retention clubs have a vested interest in cultivating the status of their businesses by distancing themselves from the negative image of sales-driven clubs. In an interview with Dom, I asked about his view of the industry as a whole. Dom is the owner of Areté (a Greek word for virtue and reaching one's highest potential), a high-cost club that combines the services of fitness and health specialists. Reflecting his retention-driven approach to fitness, Dom observed:

> We're trying to create a totally new kind of business. There's nothing else out there like this. It just made sense. It was practically screaming to be done, it was so practical. It's ridiculous what this industry does. It's banal in every sense of the word. It markets to the weakest side of people's persona. It markets to them in the same way as an enabler. It tells you that you have to have perfect abs [abdominal muscles], or that you have to look a certain way. So of course, you'll never be satisfied. So, I didn't like what I was seeing.

The vertical stratification of clubs involves more than simply an equation of high fees with high status: clubs that charge less are not to be trusted, give the industry a bad name, and discourage people from getting fit.

Despite their low status, what sales-driven clubs *do* offer is a low-cost fitness option – an important aspect in opening access to commercial fitness for a wider portion of the population. Given that the average enrolment and monthly dues at commercial clubs in 2004 were $150 and $55, respectively, it is little wonder that membership at health clubs is largely middle-class. Nevertheless, 8 per cent of club members in 2005 made less than $25,000 a year, and 19 per cent made between $25,000 and $49,999.[14] The emergence of tiers of membership costs (so that, at a lower price, members can use clubs during off-peak hours) and an increasing number of "value-priced" clubs help to open up access to membership. In addition, some chains are targeting lower-income and ethnic minority neighborhoods. Indeed, health club owners have identified three groups as absent from their rosters: African Americans, Asian Americans, and Hispanic Americans (McCarthy *et al.* 1999: 65). As with other consumer industries, the move to include new communities of consumers is driven by the bottom line: a combination of a growing ethnic middle class attracting the interest of businesses, and the saturation of the existing middle-class market prompting expansion into lower-end markets.

The development of these two business models – of low- and high-cost fitness options – has been accompanied by the active construction of the relative status of sales- and retention-driven clubs. Various voices – including physical education textbooks, health club trade media, consumer reviews, and health club owners and staff – contribute to the construction of the relative position of each of these business models. The high status of expensive clubs is triply determined: retention-driven clubs employ the more respected business model; their higher fees ensure a more affluent, higher-status clientele; and they offer the sort of ancillary amenities and attention to personal detail that characterize other high-status leisure businesses.

Personality and symbolic capital

While the vertical stratification of status within the health club industry is structured by the range and cost of services, horizontal stratification occurs through a club's symbolic capital: distinctive assets in the form of images and ideas that can be converted into economic capital, as they provide the basis for membership costs. Factors such as décor, clientele, and the demeanor of staff are strategically cultivated by the health club developers, managers and staff to create an overall club "personality." Reinforced in the clubs' promotional material and other consumer reviews, the construction of club personalities helps to create a range of structured choices to meet consumers' various budgetary constraints, exercise requirements and lifestyle preferences.

Underlying the emphasis on symbolic capital is the assumption that today's consumers are versed in the importance of style and demanding of aesthetically pleasing goods and services to complement and contribute to the stylization of their everyday lives (cf. Featherstone 1991; Gronow 1997). The attention to the personality of a health club is thus but one aspect of a larger cultural interest in the expressive qualities of goods and their role in the production and representation of identity – an interest that is manifest in the consumer marketplace in countless ways: witness the growing markets in do-it-yourself home improvement, home style and lifestyle publishing, image and style consultancy, themed retail environments, and aesthetically augmented everyday household objects (such as toasters and juicers designed by famous architects). This is also in keeping with Gilles Lipovetsky's observations about capitalism and the contemporary "narcissistic cult of the body": "The market sectors that focus on the body tend to become fashion industries themselves, caught up in the process of marginal differentiation and product renewal" (1994: 244).

One element of a health club's symbolic capital is its physical setting or décor. Health club owners and developers invest in layout, decoration and design as part of the production of the club, and the cultivation of an intended market. The "look" of a retail or leisure space reproduces the stratification of the market: compare the polished wood counters of upscale boutiques with the plain glass cases of a mid-range department store and the piles of merchandise at discount stores. For health clubs, market competition is not simply about providing exercise equipment, but about reflecting the desired clientele in the health club's image – younger or older, trendy or traditional.

Thus, the design and style of the health club, and of retail and leisure venues more generally, are utilized as a way to compete for consumers. In a glossy coffee-table book about health club architecture, one of the owners of Equinox, the upscale Manhattan health club chain, commented on the importance of design:

> Design is one of the three most important factors [to a health club]: the others are customer service and programming. The machines are the machines. It's the architecture of how they are configured that makes the difference. Clients often spend two hours a day in the gym, and they want a pleasing environment. And they have trained eyes: their homes, offices, restaurants, and stores are professionally designed, and they are attuned to architecturally pleasing spaces. . . . Factors like service and price are essential, but good design is like a halo that sits over the customer while they're deciding whether or not to join the club.
>
> (Fogarty 1998: 2)

Commercial health clubs compete with, complement and are complemented by other entertainment and leisure venues – restaurants, retail stores, movie theaters, hotels – that are also produced as lifestyle environments, contributing to an inflation of aesthetic expectations.

The difference in status is immediately apparent through a comparison of the décor of clubs from different vertical strata. Earlier in the chapter, Julie and the "gym ladies" provided an introduction to Strength & Beauty, the low-cost, women-only club. The flagship location of Strength & Beauty was, until recently, painted in the club's signature colors – hot pink and bright yellow – which was made all the more intense by the bright, fluorescent lighting. Now it is painted a dull off-white, an attempt at a facelift for the club that has only made it seem, in Maggie's words, "rather anonymous, like a factory." The day I visited Maggie, there were only twenty cardio machines – a combination of stair climbers, treadmills and stationary bicycles. What is unique about these machines – the same machines you will find in almost all clubs – is that they are labeled with signs that show women (rather than a generic muscular man) performing the exercise, reinforcing the club's image as a women-friendly version of the masculine world of gyms. Unlike most larger clubs, there are no exercise studios; classes are carried out in the middle of the floor, surrounded by the mirrors and machines.

At the upper end of the market is Dom's club, Areté. Membership is limited and the interior bespeaks the status of the clientele, which includes several celebrities. Members can relax on leather sofas by the juice bar while enjoying the view over the workout studio: the converted ballroom of a former luxury hotel. The ornate columns and exposed brickwork combine with wood panels and a massive skylight to create a space of light and tranquility. Private changing and shower rooms, tiled with sand-colored slate and complete with plush towels and cotton swabs, are the ultimate sign of prestige. Not only does Areté trump Strength & Beauty's group locker rooms on counts of design and cleanliness, but also on the degree of privacy.

More telling, however, are the variations within the middle of the market, as they highlight how symbolic capital is used to differentiate between clubs of similar cost, range of services and physical facilities. In this range, the majority of clubs are unisex and multi-use, and many are chains offering anywhere from two to a couple of dozen locations within the city. They are characterized by economies of scale: large, often multi-floored clubs offering three to five times the number of machines available at Strength & Beauty, as well as several exercise studios and other services, such as steam rooms and massage. Such clubs also offer a range of classes, such as several varieties of yoga, dance and aerobics classes (including some clubs' innovative takes on the exercise regimes of firefighters and pole dancers). Members at chains are typically allowed to use all of the branches, increasing the convenience of facilities. Differences, however, lie in the packaging. Apple Fitness is a massive chain and its clubs evoke the young, urban market it tries to capture. Upon entrance, users are greeted by loud hip-hop music (to the dismay of Teri, Barbara, and Paulina, who left Strength & Beauty for Apple Fitness), which is often playing in tandem with MTV videos on the numerous video screens. Black rubber flooring and brushed metal accents are juxtaposed with the chain's colors: exposed pipes, walls and columns painted red, yellow, and blue. Row upon row of cardio and strength machines dominate the space. At the multiple locations of the Health and Athletic Club, by contrast, the impression is of having entered a university club: navy carpets and wood paneling, vases of flowers and brass plaques give the impression of a more upscale clientele, who work in financial analysis rather than acting and modeling. And at The Depot (an independent club in a condominium development, so named for the building's industrial past), members can enjoy views over the Hudson River from the rooftop pool and sundeck, and from the large windows on the club's two floors. There is no music piped in, and the soft blues and grays of the décor, along with the potted palms, create a calm and quiet space.

In addition to physical setting and décor, a club's symbolic capital is also constructed through its clientele, which furnishes the club with its social atmosphere. Consumer reviews and exercise manuals advise consumers to judge a prospective club by looking around and asking: "Would I be comfortable exercising alongside the other members here?" (American College of Sports Medicine 1992: 108). Determining what body of clientele provides the most motivation is a decision ultimately left to the consumer; the fitness magazines and manuals limit their intervention to describing the choices between member populations, and to asking the question, "Do they seem like your type?" (Schlosberg and Neporent 1996: 189). Such a mode of evaluating clubs leaves implicit the questions regarding identity, class, ethnicity, gender, sexuality, and age that shape the conditions under which individuals feel more or less comfortable and at home. Nevertheless, the rationale for assessing the membership lies partly in the perception that the social atmosphere of a club will assist in maintaining participation – a perception certainly supported by the experiences of Julie and the "gym ladies."

In her *Workout Book*, Jane Fonda tells her readers that the social atmosphere of the exercise class is as important as the exercise:

It is a lot easier for most people – and I am one of them – to work out in a class or a gym. You have made the effort to get there, and you are there for one reason only. There are no distractions, and the teacher and the rest of the class are there to motivate you. You huff and you puff and you all hurt together and feel great together afterwards.

(Fonda 1981: 67)

Similarly, another exercise manual tells readers that "[p]hysical exercise and socialization make a profitable combination. . . . Many people enjoy the social interaction with others, and a support group develops to help every-one continue the exercise" (Franks and Howley 1989: 128). Part of the chal-lenge facing fitness consumers – and fitness producers who are trying to reproduce consumption – is that fitness exercises (such as aerobics, weight-lifting, yoga) are inherently individualistic. Even if done in a class setting, the exercises tend to focus on individual improvement (rather than, say, team cooperation) and individual movement (rather than team coordination). The problem with such exercises is that they do not, in and of themselves, involve the mutual reinforcement and support of team sports and group physical activities; such support is supplied through the proximity of others in the club, or through the exercise instructor.

The caveat to the social aspect of fitness lies in the dilemma of popularity. The production of health clubs as a community of consumers has its limit in the physical space; clubs can only accommodate so many members at one time. Accordingly, the lessons of consumer education suggest that customers visit prospective clubs during the time of day they are most likely to work out, as clubs can be more or less busy at certain times of the day depending on the membership. As such, choosing a club based on clientele may take two very different directions. On the one hand, the implicit assumption behind choosing clubs based on member affinity is that there will be a signifi-cant amount of overlap in the kinds of occupations, income and educational levels of members. Members thus often follow much the same workday schedule, creating regular patterns of crowded hours – for a higher-income clientele, this means that, typically, a club is crowded before and after work, and during lunch. On the other hand, those who want to avoid crowds may choose a club with members who *don't* look like them, so as to take advan-tage of the lulls. For example, the freelancer, student and artist who make their own hours have the professional/managerial clubs to themselves during the off-peak (that is, regular business) hours.

While the individualistic nature of fitness exercises may stand in awkward relation to the notion of the health club as a social space, the clientele nonetheless creates a social backdrop for the pursuit of the fit body. The members are also mobilized in attempts to construct a club's "personality": conceptual shorthand for its entire package of symbolic capital. Judging health clubs based on their personality raises the ongoing dialogue in marketing between the personality of the consumer, which is difficult to categorize and control, and the personality of the brand, which can be controlled to a much greater degree through packaging and promotion (Plummer 1984). Health clubs, like other leisure sites, cannot separate the two, as they are fundamentally constituted through the people using them – an empty club, in other words, has no personality at all. However, a club's personality is not tied to *each* of its members; rather, health club promotional material and consumer reviews represent membership populations as if there was one, predominant (and ideal) member personality.

For example, print advertising for the luxurious Reebok Sports Club in New York in 2000 equated its status with its clients' wealth and fame by featuring in its advertisements famous club members (for example, the musician David Sanborn and the fashion designer Vera Wang), and the proclamation that "Our Members Know Why They Belong." Fiona, an academic in her early 30s, recounted why a friend had gone to considerable expense and inconvenience to join an elite club, The Studio, which was located miles from where she lived and worked:

> Part of why she joined was to meet men. She felt that it was a way to meet pre-screened people – people who could afford this gym. And the place is like, oh God, it's absolutely amazing. It's enormous, and just the luxury of it. And also the real sense that this was a *club* in more ways than just a gym membership, because the membership is so expensive. You know, [*laughing*] I never really identified with that mentality. I didn't want to care what I was wearing or what I looked like or any of those things. You're there, you're sweaty, and you're there to work out. And yet this woman at The Studio, a big part of her motivation was to meet someone. And they had these areas there that were socializing areas: they had two or three restaurants, and the lounge-y kinds of areas. So there was much more opportunity for non-gym socializing.

The social capital of the clientele is converted into symbolic capital for the club, and a prospective member can thus hope to benefit from both.

Besides links to the rich and famous, health club advertising invokes other markers of distinction, such as the connection – via the health club – to a way of life that brings together fitness consumption, social status and overall well-being (see Plate 3.1). Health club advertising may also mobilize the perceived attitudes of members, positioning the health club, for example, as edgy ("No Judgments"); dedicated ("Compromise is just a polite word for surrender" and "110%"); or image-conscious ("Look Better Naked"). Other gyms promote themselves as low-key ("All Fitness. No Attitude") and low-cost ("More gym, less money").[15] It is not that one health club has status and another does not, but that clubs attempt to cultivate a particular style or personality that differentiates them from other clubs.

Status is not a predetermined trait but a fluid quality, manufactured and engineered for the specific product/service/health club. Status engineering and personality construction, however, cannot be accomplished by clubs alone; status is a matter of socially conferred recognition and honor (Weber 1946: 191). Thus, health club advertising may make claims to status and distinction, but these must be affirmed – by other members and by other media. Consumer reviews are instrumental in this regard, in the development of consumers' self-consciousness about the criteria of their choices (Zukin 2004). The media literacy that comes with being bombarded with advertising

Plate 3.1 Health club banner, New York.
(Source: Janet Mowat).

in everyday life often results in a skeptical attitude towards marketing; why believe someone who is trying to sell you something? Consequently, consumers turn to trusted intermediaries, such as the Good Housekeeping Seal of Approval or Oprah's book recommendations. For the fitness field, consumer reviews of health clubs – in newspapers, websites, fitness and lifestyle magazines, and exercise manuals – consolidate the various symbolic elements of the club, such as the interior design, membership and promotional messages, and reflect it back through the language of lifestyle and personality.

For example, consider the example of the New York Health Club – with which the chapter began – later renamed the New York Health and Racquet Club (NYHRC). The following sketches of the membership and atmosphere of the NYHRC are taken from consumer reviews from the late 1970s onwards:

> The future is here: sparkling, very chic clubs with full Nautilus gyms. . . . The gym area, coed but divided by plants, is a bit crowded at times. All the branches are very popular, and they get quite busy. Good, social atmosphere. [Annual dues $275]
>
> (Roach 1978: C10)

> Excellent [rating]. Slick interior. Dating bar atmosphere, as in three other club branches. Spacious, well-equipped. [Annual dues $425]
>
> (Hinds 1980: 48)

> This [branch], the branch of the stars (Richard Dreyfuss, Cher, and Susan Sarandon are among the members), is the newest NYHRC – big, shiny, and filled with young, attractive people and the latest in exercise equipment. They've got the biggest pool in the NYHRC system, and four good racquetball courts. The place fills six levels . . . [Annual dues $795]
>
> (Goldman and Kennedy 1983: 411–12)

> New York Health & Racquet advertises itself as a "way of life," and though it doesn't specify *which* way of life that is, it's obviously one founded on money and privilege. The organization owns a 75-foot [22.8-metre] yacht, a summer beach-and-tennis club on the Long Island Sound . . . Secret reason for going: . . . If nothing else, this club will help you exercise your sense of entitlement. [Annual dues $1,175]
>
> (Damjanov *et al.* 1999: 12)

It's been almost a year since Wall Street went casual, but the folks at New York Health & Racquet are still holding out. The vibe at the downtown location is decidedly corporate, from the suits at the front desk to the ... TVs tuned to MSNBC [to] keep traders in the know ... Although plenty of women work out here, this is definitely an "old boys' network" type of club. [Annual dues $1,595]

(Kriegsman 2001: 18, 33)

Over the years as its dues have escalated, the personality of the NYHRC has crystallized, not only through its own advertising (which does, indeed, claim that the club is a "way of life"), but through consumer reviews such as these. In the market competition between health clubs, NYHRC is thus differentiated from similarly priced alternatives, providing added value for the member who identifies with the club's personality and who might otherwise have chosen a different (if not differently priced) type of club.

As much as clubs and consumer reviews portray personality as a stable category, consumers interpret the available choices through their own biographies, resulting in a variety of mixed readings. For example, Ellie explains why she quit using Apple Fitness:

The membership was very young. I don't think there was anyone there who was over 30. I never worked out there and saw anyone who was in their 40s at all. I mean, I *know* because I'm in my 40s and you look around and you go, "Well, is there anyone here who looks even remotely like me?" No! Everyone there looked like they walked out of a fashion magazine. And . . . that's weird. I don't want to go to a place where I feel like . . . like, I'm there with supermodels and stuff, which was really annoying.

Donna, a freelance journalist in her 30s, dislikes Pump for the same reason that Ellie dislikes Apple Fitness, but has a different read of the personality of Apple Fitness:

I went to Apple Fitness and I found it to be a little more dirty and grimy – not in a gross way, but in a not so *fabulous* – "we're all male model and actresses" – kind of way, which is what Pump tends to be.

Matt, another journalist in his mid-30s, has a similar perception of Pump as Donna, but finds this appealing rather than a turn-off:

After I got a new job, I was back in the market for a gym. And so I joined Pump because it was near my new fancy digs. And I had two friends who were going there. So the choice was pretty much straightforward. *And* there were clearly very attractive women going there. Pump has big glass windows, so I didn't have to go and visit to know what it was like. You can just walk by Pump and you can just see that it's *full* of attractive women. And they lay it out that way on purpose, I'm sure.

Consumer review personality profiles and consumers' perceptions of clubs' predominant clientele may thus serve to attract and repel prospective clients by narrowing the conception of who *belongs*. This can work in the favor of a club that hopes to consolidate its desired profile (which might be undermined if non-ideal members were to become the norm), but it is also a hindrance to attracting new members and diversifying one's member base.

Much of the typecasting of club membership is tongue-in-cheek: in a New York weekly lifestyle magazine's annual fitness issue, writers surely know that members of the David Barton health club aren't only "built Chelsea boys;" that there are more than just "cool, attitude-free downtowners" working out at World Gym; and that you don't have to be one of the "good-looking 20- to 37-year-olds who'd be perfect as extras on [TV show] *Jack & Jill*" in order to belong at Equinox.[16] However, gross generalizations, even if in the service of humor, aid in the production of clubs' reputations. Consumers are encouraged to see themselves through the same broad categories of personality and motivation, in order to choose the club that best suits them. Belonging as a member is not simply paying your monthly dues, but is also about fitting into the generic profile of the club.

Besides clientele, a club's symbolic capital and personality are also constructed via its staff (cf. Witz, Warhurst, and Nickson 2003). As such, the fitness service worker is doubly important to the health club industry (hence the focus in Chapter 5 on personal trainers). Front desk receptionists, sales staff, personal trainers and exercise instructors not only deliver the services that legitimize membership costs; they also help to produce the health club's personality through their demeanor, appearance, and interactions with members. The importance of service workers is not lost on the low-status end of the health club industry: even low-priced health clubs now offer personal training. However, membership prices – which translate into staff wages – are reflected in the professionalism and experience of personal trainers, just as higher-priced restaurants employ waiters with more cultural capital as part of the production of higher-status dining experiences (Zukin 1995: 154).

As Kimberley – the coordinator of personal training for the Apple Fitness chain – says, "member retention is just experience":

> If you walk in, and have a good experience . . . If the person at the front desk is nice to you, if you're greeted on the exercise floor, then that's a good experience. But if you come in, and you're getting attitude, you're not going to be happy. It's just like a restaurant. If you get some pissy waiter who gives you a hard time, you're not likely to go back to that restaurant; you'll go somewhere else, because there are so many in the city. So we focus on a positive experience across the board as a company.

This emphasis on customer service is disseminated throughout the company's ranks. Frank, for example, is the fitness program manager at an Apple Fitness branch. I asked him what he looked for when hiring staff members:

> You must be a people person, because our members come first, they're number one. They must have a customer service approach to the members. So, first thing: are you the kind of person who greets people? They must not be afraid to greet people, to approach people, even if they look like they've just come out of hell! [*Laughs*] You have to be able to say, "Hi. Good morning."

The personality of the club may draw customers in, but it is the affirmation of the members' individuality and personality that secures their long-term membership and elevates the club's status. As such, health clubs are an example of the "experience economy" in which the interaction with the product and the process of consumption supersedes the material product in determining value and price (Pine and Gilmore 1998).

Personality thus plays out on three levels in the production of the health club: as function, image and instrument. First, personality is a function of market differentiation. Through a variety of strategies, there is a cultivation of club personality – as corporate, alternative, women-only, young, family-centered, and so forth. Instrumental in this process of club identity formation is the second level of personality: the image of the stereotypical member, who serves to symbolically reduce the varied membership to one type of person. Prospective members are thus encouraged through consumer reviews and guides to recognize themselves in the descriptions of the different clubs. Finally, the personality or persona of the fitness workers – front desk, sales and instructional staff – is mobilized as an instrument of customization, creating value-added services that cater to the individuality (indeed, the personalities) of the members. Like other service industries such as restaurants and airlines, however, health clubs do not all offer the same quality of service. Good service comes at a price.

CONCLUSION

In attempts to differentiate commercial clubs from their antecedents, health club owners and managers have naturalized fitness as a field of leisure, and the health club as the site for the production and consumption of a fit lifestyle. The expansion of the industry has involved the standardization of two business models that create a vertical stratification of clubs according to price, and a horizontal stratification through symbolic capital and the language of personality.

Health clubs, if they are to compete within a leisure market, must compete according to the same stakes and on the same terms. Linked to the broader field of leisure, then, the health club industry reflects many of the developments in business philosophy and market strategy, focusing on the long-term retention of customers, the provision of high-quality services, and the production of fitness as an experiential product, which complements other leisure and lifestyle pursuits. Like restaurants, health clubs provide a social setting in which to display one's consumption and commune with similarly participating peers. Like *couture* fashion or elite airport business lounges, membership at a health club can act as symbolic capital for the consumer, marking the individual's position above the crowd. Like theme restaurants or the massive coffee-and-browse bookstores, health clubs offer entertainment as part of the consumption experience. And, like restaurants and airlines, commercial health clubs are also stratified by price. Thus, the stratification of the commercial health club industry reproduces fitness as a leisure activity, its options discussed and evaluated in the same way as other leisure options, from shopping and dining to tourism and movie-going.

The cultural production of health clubs as leisure businesses differentiated by different types of distinction reproduces the association between body work and status. To work on one's body is to work on one's status – both because the body itself is a potential status symbol, and because the site of that work is structured by status. Membership at a health club has become a symbol of the motivation to take care of oneself, and the possession of the means to do so. Membership at *particular* health clubs can be as potent a symbol of social position and distinction as monogrammed handbags and designer jeans (with similar possibilities for forgeries and poseurs). The competition between health clubs, from the sales-driven to the retention-driven, from the everyday to the elite, parallels the stratification – economic, social, physiological – of the consumer marketplace.

4 Fitness media

An education in the fitness lifestyle

A cultural field is characterized by struggles over the legitimate function and definition of an activity. The previous chapter examined how commercial clubs construct fitness as commercial leisure, affiliating working-out with status rewards as well as physical capital. Media such as fitness magazines and exercise manuals reinforce this definition by constructing a taken-for-granted vision of fitness as a lifestyle inextricably embedded in consumer culture. The development of the fitness field is tied to the emergence of these "second-order" products (Ferguson 1998: 600) of educative texts. Directed at the consumer, fitness media bring together the disparate elements of the field (health clubs, exercise programs, sporting products and fitness services), and order them through prescribed rules of engagement: how to choose a health club, how to lose the extra weight by swimsuit season, how to control your body's aging. The demarcation of the fitness field (from the health field, as well as from other leisure fields) involves the formation of critically minded, informed consumers who self-consciously participate in fitness and carry out socially visible activities of fitness consumption.

Thus, educative texts such as fitness magazines and manuals are not simply another fitness product; they are central to the cultural production of the fitness consumer (Smith Maguire 2002a, 2006; see also Pronger 2002). Such texts attempt to "mobilize" the consumer (Miller and Rose 1997: 2) by aligning individual anxieties and aspirations with the material consequences and practices of fitness and, ideally, with the larger agendas of consumer industries, health promotion strategies, and the service economy, for which the ideal figure is the individual working on his or her health and appearance, via goods and services provided by the market. Just as the material consequences of regular exercise fit contemporary social conditions – an emphasis on individual responsibility for health and physical capital in the form of a pleasing appearance – so too do the social and material practices of fitness suit today's consumer society. Working out at a health club or reading a fitness magazine provides opportunities for the cultivation of a particular attitude towards the self, means for addressing anxieties about appearance and health, and pertinent symbols for the construction and display of the body's status.

This chapter first explores the conditions that contributed to the growth since the 1970s of fitness publishing, and lifestyle media more broadly. Focusing on fitness magazines, the chapter then investigates the construction of fitness as a lifestyle, and its affiliations with consumption and an ethic of self-improvement. Of particular interest are the ways in which fitness magazines – in their content, and in the work of their advertising associates – employ different connotations of lifestyle, and position themselves as advisory experts for individuals' body projects. Despite the proliferation of advice, however, many fitness field participants do not successfully translate their reading into regular exercise. Turning the focus to exercise manuals, the remainder of the chapter concerns the ways in which fitness has been framed as a problem of motivation. An analysis of the content of a sample of exercise manuals reveals how the lessons for fitness readers are as much about the means of self-discipline as the actual practices of physical exercise. Manuals deploy a range of techniques for enticing readers to become participants and disciplining participants to persist in their exercise, providing an education in both the fitness lifestyle and the broader challenges of negotiating the tension between an ethic of hard work and an ethic of indulgence, both of which intersect in the task of self-management.

READING ABOUT FITNESS

Much as the designers of abdominal exercisers try to build a better sit-up, the type of physical exercise required to achieve health benefits is relatively straightforward. Current recommendations suggest that individuals should engage in moderate-level activity for 30 minutes on at least five days of the week, or vigorous activity for 20 minutes on at least three days of the week.[1] Efforts to make physical exercise appear less daunting to growing legions of the overweight and inactive, and changes in medical opinion, have resulted in a somewhat erratic history of officially endorsed exercise prescriptions; for example, in the 1990s, people were told that three ten-minute sessions of mild physical activity per day were sufficient (Critser 2003). This has arguably contributed to confusion about how much exercise is needed; nevertheless, what is required for achieving health benefits can consist of nothing more elaborate than brisk walking, gardening or housework,[2] in addition to a proper diet. However, fitness is not simply a question of exercise, and the benefits sought are not merely matters of health; hence, the fact that there is no magic formula to fitness-as-health does not prevent the production of a seemingly endless stream of advice on the fitness lifestyle, on websites and in instructional videos, fitness magazines and exercise manuals.

In 1979, *Self* magazine was launched, billing itself as the first women's fitness magazine. In the editor's inaugural statement, she located the magazine at the centre of several contemporary social currents:

> Why SELF? Very simply, there was no fitness magazine for women – until now. Fitness is America's No. 1 enthusiasm, and this exuberant concern for body and mind is what SELF will focus on. An extraordinary spirit and energy are emerging in women today. Fitness is the fuel. We have acquired a strong appetite for the full experience of life – the exhilaration of the outdoors, the challenge and success of professional work, the honest enjoyment of sex. SELF will be a guide to the vitality we need to do all the things we want to do.
>
> (Wilson 1979: 6)

The *Self* editor reflects a number of issues central to understanding the growth of fitness publishing and the fitness field since the 1970s. First, there is explicit reference to the key role of women consumers. As Table 4.1 indicates, women made up over 63 per cent of the readers of the top-selling fitness magazines in 2001, in keeping with earlier research that showed that

Table 4.1 Circulation of the four top-selling US fitness magazines, Fall 2001

Publication	Paid circulation (000)	% Women readers
Men's Health	1,639	15.8
Shape	1,609	85.3
Self	1,428	92.5
Fitness	1,172	64.6
Total percentage of women readers		63.4

Source: Mediamark Research Inc., MRI+ (http://www.mriplus.com [accessed November 2001])

women outnumbered men as consumers of diet, health and fitness advice by approximately two to one (Wood 1988; see also Dahlin 2001).

Women's taste for the fitness field stems in part from the ways in which physical empowerment and control over one's body and health have been associated with women's gains in social, political, and economic empower-ment. The taste for fitness advice can also be understood as a pragmatic response to changing material conditions: at the same time that increased labor market participation, especially in professional work, and shifting pat-terns of marriage and childbirth presented women with new opportunities to consume for and invest in themselves, they were also faced with new challenges – competing in the corporate sphere, balancing work and life, and navigating shifting and uncertain gender norms in social and sexual relation-ships. These challenges have driven the advice industry, from fitness maga-zines to guides to parenting, home décor, career advancement, and power dressing (see, for example, Entwistle 1997; Kolbert 2004; McGee 2005).

Second, as suggested above, the editor's statement refers to the role of a particular class demographic in the growth of fitness publishing, and fitness goods more broadly: the middle class. Fitness magazines have especially tar-geted the upper professional/managerial echelon of the middle class, which makes up more than 33 per cent of the readers of the top-selling fitness magazines in 2005–6, as outlined in Table 4.2.

Not only do middle-class consumers have the economic means of con-sumption, but they are also assumed to be predisposed to investing in

Table 4.2 Audience profile, 2005–6

Publication	Paid circulation (000)	Average household income	% Professional/ managerial readers
Men's Health	1.78	$70,932	34.2
Shape	1.64	$75,137	37
Self	1.42	$71,975	37
Fitness	1.49	$60,296	26
Total percentage of professional/managerial			33.6

Source: Paid circulation figures for December 2005 from Mediamark Research Inc., MRI+ (http://www.mriplus.com [accessed January 2007]). Readership profiles available through online media kits at http://www.menshealth.com (Spring 2005 data), http://www.shape.com (Spring 2006 data), http://www.self.com (Spring 2006 data), and http://www.meredith.com (Fall 2006) respectively (accessed January 2007).

themselves through education and self-improvement, as routes to both social distinction and occupational success (Bourdieu 1984; Featherstone 1991). For the professional/managerial class and their clerical, sales, and personal service counterparts, who may work in the same industries but at lower (and less secure) levels, participation in the fitness field offers not only the cultivation of, but also the chance to display, the capacity to consume, and the particular forms of cultural knowledge that guide that consumption, including an attitude towards the body as a sign, status object, and vehicle for self-expression. Fitness magazines are a middle-class commodity in a triple sense: produced by the middle class (cultural intermediaries in publishing), for the middle class (especially the professional/managerial group and its aspirants), and of the middle class (the content of the magazines simultaneously representing and legitimating the tastes and lifestyles of the middle class).

Third, the editor's statement reflects the accepted marketing wisdom of the day: physical exercise was fashionable, and thus there was a ready demand for fitness-related goods such as a new monthly magazine. Indeed, the number of fitness and exercise products and services has risen dramatically since the early 1970s, none more visibly so than the athletic shoe, which has become a common staple of everyday fashion as well as an essential piece of fitness equipment. With hundreds of options within and between product categories (see Plate 4.1), how is a consumer to choose? Out of a morass of choices, there emerges a role and demand for product reviews and advice that apply a more concrete language of value to advertising's hyperbolic messages of need and desire (Zukin 2004). As such, *Self* was both a fitness product and a commentary about fitness products, contributing to the reproduction of the consumer market by linking readers to a fitness-oriented web of consumption.

Self was later followed by other fitness magazines, targeting both women (such as *Shape*, launched in 1981) and men (such as *Men's Health*, launched in 1988). Despite its pioneering hype, however, *Self* entered a marketplace in which fitness information and advice were already proven commodities. By the late 1970s, fitness was the subject of regular columns in women's magazines such as *Vogue* and *Mademoiselle*, and featured in general interest magazines as well. For example, *Time* and *House and Garden* in 1979 discussed the findings of the *Perrier Study* (Harris *et al.* 1984) about practices of, and attitudes to, fitness in the US.[3] The following year, various articles on fitness, exercise and health appeared in *Advertising Age*, *Marketing*, *Marketing News*, *National Underwriter*, *Business Quarterly*, *Business Insurance*, *Advanced*

Plate 4.1 How to choose? Shoes in shop window, New York.
(Source: Janet Mowat)

Management Journal, and *International Management*, suggesting that fitness was a matter of relevance to more than the devoted joggers and health club members. As a further indication of the cultural resonance of fitness and its associated connotations of status and the good life, advertising and promotional strategies used the language of fitness and health to sell a variety of products, such as Lincoln-Mercury cars: "the shape you want to be in" (Wallace 1986: 27).

Instructional guides to fitness, exercise and health have also been popular commodities. Jane Fonda's exercise videos, for example, sold in the millions in the 1980s, spurring on the nascent home video market; 23 per cent of the 15 million exercise videos sold by 1987 were by Fonda (Kagan and Morse 1988: 165). Bestseller lists[4] from the 1970s and early 1980s, for example, included fitness manuals such as Fonda's *Workout Book*, explicitly oriented towards women, and Charles Hix's *Working Out*, aimed at men (Justice 1998). The increased emphasis on market segmentation and niche publishing in the 1990s further intensified the production of lifestyle periodicals: between 1988 and 2000, the total number of magazine titles more than doubled, and the number of health, fitness and lifestyle magazines nearly tripled. Overall, the amount of press coverage devoted to physical fitness increased more than sixfold in the US between the mid-1980s and 2000.[5]

The publishing trade serial, *Publishers Weekly*, reviews hundreds of health and fitness titles each year. In a 2001 *Publishers Weekly* article, the marketing opportunities of fitness are spelled out for authors and editors:

> Consumers have a ferocious appetite for advice telling them what to do, how to act, what to eat and what to shun in order to feel good, spruce up their health and shed uncomely pounds. In fact, that hunger is so great that publishers scramble to sate it with books promising, if not the moon, at least a celestial body and mind.
>
> (Dahlin 2001: 24)

Recalling the *Self* editor's inaugural statement, the *Publishers Weekly* article makes clear reference to the role of, and demand for, such media as guides to everyday life. The increasing production of fitness advice is located within the general postwar expansion of "service" media, which address everyday life as a series of problems, and offer to audiences a range of suggestions and solutions (Eide and Knight 1999). This is not to suggest that such a genre did not exist prior to 1950; advice on navigating the difficulties of daily life could be found in early twentieth-century magazines such as Bernarr Macfadden's *Physical Culture*, and in self-improvement books dating back at least to Benjamin Franklin's eighteenth-century *Autobiography* (1970; see also McGee 2005). However, over the second half of the twentieth century there was a growth in the genres of lifestyle media and service journalism (Bell and Hollows 2005; Eide and Knight 1999).[6]

This growth is linked to an intensification of the problems of self and identity – the problem, in Bauman's phrase, "to *become* what one *is*" (2000: 32). The resulting mode of subjectivity, for which identity is a matter not of ascription (through a framework of rigid categories such as sex, class, and religion) but of achievement (through processes of choosing and consuming), has been characterized, variously, as a "do-it-yourself" self (Beck and Beck-Gernsheim 2002: 3), choosing self (Slater 1997: 59), commodity self (Ewen 1976: 47), performing self (Featherstone 1982: 27), and consuming self (Falk 1994: 136). Processes of industrialization, urbanization, migration, and globalization have all contributed to the weakening of traditional categories and authorities; this has brought with it a relative freedom to forge an identity based not on one's origins but on one's desires and aspirations.

However, this freedom is accompanied by both increased anxiety and risk (as the individual is held responsible for both good and bad choices, and their effects), and new modes of authority, recast in the therapeutic guise of the "helping hand" (Bauman 2000; Beck and Beck-Gernsheim 2002; Rose 1996, 1999).

Modernity's legacy is to render identity as a lifelong project of self-production and self-management; in short, identity becomes work. Lifestyle media bring to bear on identity an instrumental industriousness associated with the Protestant ethic (Weber 1992): self-improvement is to be achieved through rational and disciplined work. At the same time, like self-help literature more broadly (McGee 2005), this work ethic is accompanied in lifestyle media by an emphasis on self-actualization, expressivity, hedonism and aesthetics, associated with the Romantic ethic (Campbell 1987): self-improvement is to be achieved through indulging in new experiences. Identity is work, but more to the point, it is a work of art. The ethics of ascetic discipline and aesthetic indulgence have cut across modernity and driven the development of capitalism and consumer culture, complementing each other in their associated spheres of production and consumption, but also converging and, at times, conflicting.

Lifestyle media are not simply late twentieth-century commodities; they exemplify the contemporary condition, including the interconnections of ascetic and aesthetic ethics, the development of therapeutic expertise, and the problematization of the self and identity. Indeed, a glance at the self-help shelves at a major bookstore reveals the categories of problems faced by the contemporary individual: exercise and fitness, beauty and grooming, diet, and so forth (see Plate 4.2). The social function of lifestyle media, however, has a very long history. Looking back to the medieval period and the transition to modernity, lifestyle media are the contemporary manifestation of manners and etiquette manuals, through which Norbert Elias (1978) charts the gradual internalization of control over the emotions and bodily functions, as part of the emergence of a new personality structure suited to an increasingly complex, interdependent social structure. If the historical trajectory is extended back further still, the basic function of lifestyle media may be traced back to the prescriptive texts of antiquity, through which Michel Foucault (1985, 1986) examines the ways in which specific values and codes of conduct have been legitimated as the means by which individuals work on and produce themselves. Lifestyle media are repositories of, to use Foucault's phrase, "technologies of the self" (1988: 18):

Plate 4.2 Advice on the problematic self: fitness books.
(Source: Janet Mowat)

> which permit individuals to effect by their own means or with the help
> of others a certain number of operations on their own bodies and souls,
> thoughts, conduct, and way of being, so as to transform themselves in
> order to attain a certain state of happiness, purity, wisdom, perfection,
> or immortality.

Lifestyle media are implicated in identifying, codifying and legitimating not
only a "certain number of operations" by which individuals may work on
themselves, but also the ends (happiness, success, empowerment) to which
such work is directed, and the specific forms of expertise ("the help of
others") to which the self-managing individual can, and indeed should, turn.
They are a source of guidance as well as reassurance, confirming for the
reader that his or her anxieties and desires are recognized by experts and thus
rendered normal (Miller 2001: 16; see also Simonds 1992).

Fitness media can thus be understood as mechanisms for both educating
the consumer in the rules of the fitness field, and reproducing a self-managing,
self-improving subjectivity. The remaining two sections of the chapter use

the examples of fitness magazines and exercise manuals to examine how these "technologies of the self" are bound up with specific notions of lifestyle, a therapeutic mode of expertise, and particular techniques for disciplining the self.

MAGAZINES AND THE FITNESS LIFESTYLE

In the magazine section of a large bookstore such as Barnes & Noble, there are over a hundred health, sport, and exercise titles. In addition to the magazines focused on fitness, exercise and bodybuilding – aimed at men, at women and at both – there are titles specializing in individual sports and sport commentary, nutrition, alternative health methods, and "healthy" eating and cooking. The fitness magazine covers tend to feature the well-cut, glistening abdominal muscles of male and female models, accompanied by headlines promising the secrets to "Lose Those Love Handles!," "Get Ready for Bikini Season in Six Weeks!" and "Get This Guy's Abs!" – a comprehensive education in the problems and potentials of the body.

As lifestyle media, fitness magazines provide a useful lens through which to examine the different connotations of lifestyle in contemporary consumer culture. Mike Featherstone (1991) has noted the contemporary popularity of the term lifestyle, which is typically read off of a matrix of consumer choices of clothes, car, house, food, holidays, and so forth. The notion of choice is central to lifestyle's connotations of "individuality, self-expression, and a stylistic self-consciousness" (Featherstone 1991: 83), and to the pejorative use of the term, as in the label of "lifestyle disease," which implies individual culpability because of inappropriate life choices. In the popular imagination, lifestyle may be taken as the sum of its consumer parts and an expression of sovereign taste; however, its sociological formulation is quite different. Bourdieu (1984) understands lifestyle as an aesthetic or logical unity of practices and preferences, based not on consumer choices *per se* (wine or beer; opera or dog races; yoga or boxing) but on the logic behind such choices (a preference for the luxurious or the practical, the esoteric or the popular). From this perspective, lifestyle is the material outcome of habitus, a second-nature way of seeing and being in the world, which is shaped by individuals' conditions of existence – the type of society and their place within it, as defined through such categories as gender and class. The habitus shapes (but does not determine) tastes and preferences, such that consumer choice – which may be experienced as a manifestation of individual sovereignty – is in fact highly socially structured (Bourdieu 1984: 171, *passim*).

Perhaps the most straightforward manifestation of "lifestyle" is the way in which it is constructed in the marketing of cultural products. Since the mid-1960s, lifestyle has been the dominant framework for goods in advertising and marketing (Leiss, Kline and Jhally 1997; Zukin and Smith Maguire 2004). One of the best-known versions of this approach to marketing is the "values and lifestyles" (VALS) typology (Mitchell 1983), which attempts to explain consumer behavior through personality; thus, for example, inner-directed consumers could be more effectively targeted by appealing to their interest in new experiences, while outer-directed consumers would respond more to notions of belonging or prestige. According to the logic of lifestyle marketing, fitness magazines – and the larger body of lifestyle publishing to which they belong – differentiate themselves not on the basis of objective product qualities, but through appealing to the perceived qualities of the targeted consumers. The competition for readers and advertising revenue is fought not through scientific evidence concerning effective exercise techniques, but through the construction of an ideal reader who encapsulates the qualities of the magazine's target market.

Magazine advertising associates are central to the process of constructing the ideal reader. Intermediaries between readers and advertisers, advertising associates use circulation and reader demographic statistics and reader surveys as resources for constructing a plausible profile of their magazine's typical reader and that reader's imagined preferences for a universe of products. Daniel, for example, is the general advertising and sales director for a publisher of several fitness magazines for men and women, and he oversees three men's bodybuilding and fitness magazines. I asked him to describe his typical readers:

> *Grip* is for men who are heavily into bodybuilding, men who would love to compete. *Muscle Review*, I call that "*Grip for Wimps*" [*laughs*] because it's men who go to the gym a couple of days a week, but they've got other activities that they're into. I call them "vain-iacs" because they're very concerned with how they look, what other people think of them. *Fitness Forum* is "*Muscle Review for Wimps*" [*laughs*]. These are guys who go to the gym maybe two or three times a week, but they're interested in fitness because they're into other activities. Like, they'll be a runner, and will use fitness as a way to perform better. . . . The guys who are reading *Fitness Forum* aren't meatheads. You know, they go to the

gym, but when they're done they put their clothes on and they're doctors and lawyers.

In his hierarchical characterization of the magazines' readerships, Daniel draws on the demographic profile of his readership. For example, he knows that the average reader of *Fitness Forum* is approximately 34 years old and earns over $63,000 a year; hence the stereotype of the professional/ managerial occupations of medicine and law. The gap between these statistics and the character sketch of the readership, however, is bridged not by reader surveys but by the creative work and accepted wisdom of those in marketing and sales: fitness for inner-directed consumers is about overall performance; fitness for outer-directed consumers is about impressing others.

The ideal reader is employed to entice and retain readers and subscribers. Hilary is an advertising associate at *Total*, a women's fitness magazine; she highlights how appealing to actual readers requires that a balance be struck between personalization and inclusion:

> We try to create the magazine as a person. It is a woman. It is a woman you know. It's the woman you live next door to, so you feel like you know her. That's what we try to do. . . . She definitely doesn't have a face. You [the reader] create what she looks like. But she doesn't have a face. She could be a minority, for example. You read the magazine, and it's whatever it means to you.

Magazines must strike a balance between providing a narrow profile that speaks to readers and stands out from the competition, and a broad language of participation so as to include the largest possible population, without losing its aura of distinction. For Hilary, the ideal fitness reader is thus constructed as a generic persona rather than a particular body shape: a strategic choice, as the language of personality is more encompassing than the language of shape.

Besides a tool for increasing circulation, the ideal reader is also employed to sell a magazine's actual readership to advertisers. Jessica is an advertising associate at *Fit Life*, another women's fitness magazine. On the morning of our interview, she had been pitching her magazine to Volkswagen:

> We blew them away. They loved it. We match the age group, the characteristics and the personality – our readers match the people they want to reach.

When pressed about how she knows the readers' personality traits, Jessica highlights the gap between the uniform consumer she has pitched and the heterogeneous readership who will actually see the advertisements:

> The topic of fitness basically appeals to really outgoing people. People who want to get off their butt, get out there, be active, lose weight, make changes. It's a whole variety of people. There's obviously an overweight category, and they're looking for new ways to make changes. . . . For someone who's already active, we have detailed stories that they can follow each month.

Jessica uses the category of "outgoing" personality as the common denominator for the magazine's paid circulation of 1.2 million people (35 per cent of whom, according to their circulation statistics, are men, despite the dominance of advertising for women's toiletries and fashion), suggesting that the criterion for defining the ideal reader is not *what* they consume, but *why*. As with Hilary's faceless reader, the inclusiveness of the constructed ideal reader rests on notions of values, beliefs and attitudes (such as an interest in making changes and improving the self) rather than material qualities (such as ethnicity or body weight). For Jessica, the ideal reader of *Fit Life* has both the right attitude about life and the means to enact this attitude through consumption (be it of cars or exercise products).

Alexandra is an advertising associate at *Form*, a women's fitness magazine within the same publishing company as Daniel that attracts three times the size of the audience as their best-selling men's magazine. *Form* is also, of all of the company's titles, the least concerned with exercise *per se*. In an interview, Alexandra reveals the logic of marketing fitness as more than merely a matter of exercise:

> The person who reads *Form* is educated, they're into the lifestyle, but they're not as serious, as hard core. We're more fluffy, with articles that aren't just about exercise. You can't be that narrow, that hard core, and expect to get 1.6 million readers.

Despite Alexandra's suggestion that the lifestyle mix of *Form* is unusual, all of the popular fitness magazines employ to varying degrees this combination of exercise and health with information on fashion, beauty, food, relationships, sports, and travel.[7] The fitness lifestyle, writ broadly, attracts more readers than exercise alone, which in turn attracts more advertisers: a market logic of profitability that cements the link between fitness, lifestyle, and consumption.

Alexandra goes on to describe the psycho-demographic logic behind this wide variety of articles and diverse advertisers:

> If you're someone who's into fitness, then it's not just that you exercise. It might affect what kind of vacations you take. Maybe you'll go on a back roads bicycle trip, or you'll go skiing. If you're going skiing, you'll want to know about what kinds of equipment there are, and it affects what kind of car you take. It all sort of follows from your active lifestyle. . . . The demographics sell the magazine to advertisers. They know that they're reaching a young woman who's active. . . . So [advertisers are] reaching someone who isn't just interested in skiing, but who can afford it.

The fitness lifestyle is not just about the inclusion of physical activity, but about the ways in which each of those activities is affiliated with a chain of consumption options and choices that links together types of equipment, transportation, vacation and leisure, and so forth. As a result, the line between the advertising and editorial content of the magazines is often blurred. Fitness magazines include excerpts from new exercise manuals (sometimes written by their columnists), profile "celebrity" personal trainers, and illustrate exercise articles with photos "shot on location" at high-profile health clubs.

Echoing Jessica's category of the "outgoing" personality, Alexandra interprets an interest in fitness as a symptom of a more general attitude about life and consumption. This association of the fitness lifestyle with a particular mentality is made even more overtly by Hilary's colleague Sherry, who suggests how editorial and advertising content mutually reinforce each other at *Total*:

> The products that are advertised in the magazine are what can help [the readers]; they see them as tools to help them to maximize themselves. Like, if it's a lipstick, or a beauty product, it's about what can help you. So [advertisers] are reaching a women who really wants to look her best and *feel* her best. It's not just about looking good, but feeling good on the inside. . . . So [*Total*] is meant to inspire her to be her best self. And I think that the inspiration comes from the information.

For Sherry, *Total* is not simply publicizing fitness as a lifestyle; the magazine has a therapeutic role, advising the reader on how best to construct and "maximize" that lifestyle – particularly through the "tools" featured in the articles and advertisements. Sherry's construction of the ideal reader suggests how advertising associates, fitness magazine writers and editors (and lifestyle media and cultural intermediaries more broadly) are involved with the construction of the fitness lifestyle, and the reproduction of a mentality of self-responsibility and self-improvement, upon which are built consumer industries, health promotion policies, and contemporary social orders.

Characteristic of lifestyle media is their ordinariness: they are not only concerned with the mundane consumption of everyday life (cooking, cleaning, dressing, loving), but with ordinary people (Bell and Hollows 2005). In lifestyle print media such as fitness magazines, real readers are employed to complement the constructed ideal reader. One strategy for bringing ordinary people into the magazines is the selective inclusion of letters to the editor. For example:

> *Self* addresses me as a diversified, intelligent, contemporary female and offers reading that is guaranteed relevant to any woman who is trying to be her*self*: all that she is, all that she is trying to become and all that she is trying to overcome!
>
> (*Self*, February 1985: 42)

The real reader thus reinforces the ethic of self-improvement, which is implied both in the magazines and in the advertising associates' notions of the fitness reader.

Shape, the top-selling women's fitness magazine, provides two other examples of how ordinary people are brought into magazines that are otherwise populated by immaterial notions of the ideal reader, and images of the atypical fitness model. *Shape* offers its audience the opportunity to "see yourself in Shape," using readers as demonstration models in workout articles, and as the subjects of the long-running and popular "Success Stories." In the case of the former, the "fit, healthy reader" can apply to be a demonstration model by sending a photograph of both her face and her "full body in fitted workout gear" along with a description of her typical workout routine. Not surprisingly, these models typically embody the visual definition of fitness: more muscled than the razor-thin supermodels of fashion magazines and not so muscled as to put their femininity in question, these women have lean, tight bodies without bulging excesses, missing parts or skin discolorations. Furthermore, their representation is tied to an endorsement of fitness as a consuming activity – if nothing else, fitness requires the purchase of an appropriate outfit.

Readers featured in the Success Stories, on the other hand, are chosen more for their conformity with a fitness ethic than a fit look. These readers do not necessarily embody the slim, toned visual definition of fitness; rather, their biographies are regarded as evidence of taking up fitness as an ongoing way of life. Their stories of overcoming adversity – obesity, illness, debilitating relationships, lack of self-esteem – through fitness link to the ethos of individual responsibility and self-improvement characteristic of contemporary consumer culture: the "outgoing" personality that seeks to "maximize" itself. In the Success Stories, featured readers describe their transformation, and offer other readers their experience as inspiration and guidance. While reproducing the visual criteria of fitness (each story, for example, is accompanied by statistics on weight lost), Success Stories enlarge the terms of participation in fitness, from looking a certain way to thinking about and taking care of oneself in a certain way. At the same time that these stories personalize and individualize the magazine, they also, literally, associate the fitness lifestyle with success.

Thus, in the case of fitness magazines, lifestyle in the guise of target marketing is a question of engineering affinity: advertisers are encouraged to identify the ideal reader with their target market, and readers to identify the ideal reader with themselves, or at least an aspired-to self. In their descriptions of their work, however, the advertising associates reveal other, related connotations of lifestyle: as a consumer project, and a particular attitude about self-improvement. In addition, the advertising associates' accounts suggest how magazines attempt to position themselves as therapeutic guides and experts for readers' body work. For example, the editor of *Self* tells her audience, "We want to be a magazine and a friend" (Penney 1990a: 93). However, the construction of the magazine's role as a reader's confidant and counselor is problematic; it is difficult to be on the side of both readers and advertisers. This is especially pertinent with regard to the representations of bodies in the magazines.

In an era in which the critique of the media's role in the perpetuation of harmful body ideals for women (especially) has become common currency, there is often a conflict between fitness-as-look and fitness-as-ethic, as suggested above with regard to *Shape*. In article illustrations and advertising, models are overwhelmingly thin and able-bodied (albeit from a growing variety of age and ethnic groups), while at the same time magazines attempt to construct themselves as enlightened and trustworthy sources of information for women. This incongruity has not gone unnoticed by social researchers (see, for example, Duncan 1994; MacNeill 1994; Maguire and Mansfield

1998; Markula 2001; Real 1999; Smith Maguire 2006), who have commented on the discrepancy in fitness magazines and fitness culture more generally between the reproduction of traditional feminine forms and norms, and the feminist-friendly language about – and ambivalent potential for experiences of – empowerment, body acceptance, and control over health.

One way in which magazines negotiate this tension between a market demand for both "enlightened" expertise and aspirational (if unachievable) images is to simply pay lip-service to the critique of the media. For example, *Shape* declared in 1993: "we're rebelling against the pursuit of the perfect body" (May, 1993), thereby aligning the magazine with the reader, against the larger media industries and their role in women's body image disorders. Nevertheless, *Shape*'s headlines and features continued the perennial tradition of making May the month of bathing suit anxieties: "Summer Shape-Up Series" (May, 1993); "Your Best Body Ever" (April/May, 1994); "a get-ready-for-summer blitz!" (May, 1997); "Target Your Bikini Zones" (May, 1999).

Another strategy for mediating between selling unrealistic images and constructing an enlightened persona for the magazine is to identify with the reader's anxieties. For example, in 1990 the editor of *Self* responded to reader complaints about the use of "thinny-thin models" for the cover:

> You told me "get real!" . . . So yes, I'll get more real. As real as I can. But I can't deny that I have a fantasy quotient that I don't want to lose. I admit to an unrealistic notion that someday I will be truly svelte and perfectly fit. And I confess to fantasizing about appearing every day in absolutely gorgeous clothes. Is there anything wrong with having these dreams?
>
> (Penney 1990b: 151)

By claiming the fantasy of having a svelte body as her own, the *Self* editor legitimates the desire to see someone unlike oneself on the cover, and recasts fitness-as-look as a motivational tool for the fitness-as-ethic interest in self-improvement. The desire, here, is for day-dreams of a more perfect body (cf. Campbell 1987), not images of other imperfect bodies. In this way, the negative impact of media images is constructed as a problem of individual perception (Markula 2001) and the reproduction of those images as individual preference and desire. Moreover, the conversational tone of the editor's address is typical of the "voice" of lifestyle media and its construction of the role of the expert as advisory rather than dictatorial (Bell and Hollows 2005: 15).

Readers also comment upon the use of thin models as unrealistic and debilitating illustrations, in the letters-to-the-editor page. For example:

> Woman [*sic*] don't need another media image of an emaciated young woman to use as a sick role model. I've counseled anorexics and know that it is precisely these images which heighten their sense of shame and fear at having a woman's body emerging at adolescence. Your new cover depicts a very old attitude about women – that they should be anorectically thin and boyish. Please do the women and girls of America a service by not continuing to advertise this medically unsound, glossy depiction of unhealthy bodies.
>
> (*Self*, June, 1985: 42)

In this way, magazines employ real readers in the construction of their authority: publishing the letter is used to signal the magazine's reflexive awareness of the media's role in body image disorders. The use of reader letters suggests how magazines negotiate between using thin models and, at the same time, adopting a progressive tone in discussions of body image problems. In general, the commercial imperatives of magazine publishing create a tension between the content – which may, indeed, address issues of body image dysfunction and the complicit role of the media – and the cover and advertising images, which drive news-stand sales and revenue (Kuczynski 2001).

Both real and ideal readers feature in fitness magazines' construction of the fitness lifestyle. The ideal reader is deployed to attract both readers and advertisers, embodying a magazine's target market and differentiating it from competitors. In their discussion of ideal readers, advertising associates highlight the multidimensionality of the concept of lifestyle, from marketing assumptions about the link between personality and consumption choices to the cultural resonance of an ethic of self-improvement, the support for which enables magazines to position themselves as enlightened experts, despite their often retrograde imagery. In addition, the actual fitness reader is an important element in the construction of fitness as a legitimate style of life. In reader letters and *Shape*'s Success Stories, for example, reader participation helps to validate fitness as a respectable and responsible pursuit, legitimate the magazine as a therapeutic guide, and reproduce the affiliation of fitness with the good life. Both ideal and real readers are thus central to the magazines' construction of fitness as a "technology of the self" (Foucault 1988), associated with a particular formulation of expertise as authority that motivates, rather than directly intervenes.

MANUALS AND THE PROBLEM OF MOTIVATION

Without the "lifestyle" mix of content on fashion, travel and relationships, exercise manuals provide relatively more information than fitness magazines on the specifics of doing exercise. That said, like fitness magazines, exercise manuals are not only concerned with exercise *per se*; much more attention is directed at motivation. This is, in part, a reflection of the state of the consumer market: research suggests that 60 per cent of US adults do not get enough physical activity to achieve any health benefits, of which 25 per cent are not physically active at all (Roan 1996). Making a market for fitness thus requires encouraging people to take up fitness.

Exercise manuals construct fitness as a problematic project for the self. Consider the following three examples:

> Too many people drop out of fitness programs because they've gone into them with unrealistic goals. Don't expect immediate results. And don't get discouraged when you feel some aches and pains. They last, at most, a few weeks – the big question is: Can you?
>
> (Levy and Shafran 1986: 12)

> The current emphasis on and interest in fitness has brought many people (like you) into fitness programs. A major problem for you will be sticking with it, as in many programs up to 50% of participants quit within 6 months.
>
> (Franks and Howley 1989: 128)

> We don't want you to become a fitness statistic. The fact is, among people who start an exercise program, half quit within eight weeks. *Fitness for Dummies* will give you the knowledge to make sure that *you* stick with fitness for the rest of your life.
>
> (Schlosberg and Neporent 1996: 2)

Manuals utilize such information as a cautionary tale and a challenge to readers to succeed where others have failed. The problem – for fitness readers and for the consumer market more broadly – is viewed by the fitness industry as one of motivation.

The positioning of motivation as a central problem for the fitness field has two consequences for the education of the fitness consumer. First, to delimit something as a problem is to impose an essentializing framework upon a complex phenomenon, identifying who or what is a "problem" and thus casting what is outside the frame as unquestioned and unproblematic. By taking motivation as their problem, the authors of exercise manuals individualize the question of physical fitness, and thus take the social context of activity out of the equation. Second, problems are productive, in that they tend to imply solutions and thus a host of practices, benchmarks, and forms of assistance. By taking motivation as their problem, the authors of exercise manuals produce and legitimate their role as motivational experts. Before considering the motivational content of exercise manuals, it is important to place this notion of motivational expertise against a broader theoretical backdrop.

In his analyses of the historical shifts in the mode and exercise of power, Foucault (see especially 1991) characterizes the contemporary political economic order as "governmental"; that is, it is marked by a concern with the governing of personal conduct, so that individuals enact their capacity for self-management in ways that, more often than not, serve broader agendas. Governmentality is about the "conduct of conduct" (Dean 1999: 10): authority "softens" and rather than directly intervening in an individual's life, the governmental mode of power is concerned with indirectly managing the conduct of others (Burchell 1996). For example, to reduce individual risk and the social and economic costs of "lifestyle" diseases, health promotion campaigns stress the benefits of regular exercise with the aim of convincing people to become more physically active, rather than instituting mandatory physical exercise breaks during the workday (which, as an affront to the hallowed value of individual sovereignty, would surely be met with stiff opposition).

Rather than coercively shaping behavior, the governmental state relies upon individuals to manage themselves according to norms, rules and practices to which they have become habituated. The state is also thus reliant on the means of that habituation: disciplinary techniques such as rationalized, regimented training that produce specific capacities (both physical and mental), as well as the endorsed practices, goals, and experts of self-work (Foucault 1977, 1988; see also Smith Maguire 2002b). It is in this sense that disciplinary technologies intersect with technologies of the self in the reproduction of the social order (Foucault 1988: 19): the governmental state relies on individuals adopting particular habits of self-conduct (technologies of the self, which are themselves often self-disciplining), and encourages such adoption through – among other techniques – disciplinary mechanisms.

Self-managing subjects are required to care for themselves, and this involves an assessment of oneself as lacking (a general acknowledgment of the need to work on oneself), the identification of specific problems to be addressed, and the deployment of endorsed practices and strategies for the correction of such problems. For Foucault, care of the self requires the recognition of oneself "not simply as an imperfect, ignorant individual who requires correction, training, and instruction, but as one who suffers from certain ills and who needs to have them treated, either by oneself or by someone who has the necessary competence" (1986: 57). Self-management, therefore, does not mean that individuals are self-reliant; rather, it implies a particular relationship to therapeutic expertise. However, as the following excerpt from the *Fitness Facts* manual makes clear, the delegation of control to the expert is always partial:

> One major factor determines whether exercise will bring you its full benefits: *You*. You must decide to include exercise as a regular part of your life. . . . Decide that you are going to begin exercise now and continue it for the rest of your life.
>
> (Franks and Howley 1989: 156)

In other words, handing over aspects of self-management to an expert does not absolve one of self-responsibility: the individual ultimately is held accountable for the more or less competent use of experts. Within the framework of the problem of motivation, the failure to get fit is not only about a lack of will, knowledge, and dedication; it is also a failure to seek the right help – the right exercise manual, the right health club, the right personal trainer.

Exercise manuals, fitness magazines and lifestyle media more generally can thus be understood as governmental technologies, mediating between and knitting together individual anxieties and desires and their associated modes of self-work, and broader political, economic, and social agendas and goals. The "conduct of conduct" in exercise manuals works through a linear model of motivation: first, enticement; second, persistence; third, reward. To entice the reader to become a full fitness participant, manuals typically highlight the associated benefits of exercise, such as reduced health risk, and improved appearance and confidence. Persistence is addressed through techniques of self-discipline (thereby redirecting culpability for surveillance and control back to the individual). Finally, the rewards of participating in the fitness field are typically cast as instrumental forms of pleasure.

Enticement: fitness as panacea

Central to the workings of governmental power is the self-conduct of individuals, which cannot, in a modern liberal society, be determined in a top-down, oppressive fashion, but which can be mobilized through the promotion of "specific techniques of the self around such questions as . . . the development of habits of cleanliness, sobriety, fidelity, self-improvement, responsibility and so on" (Burchell 1996: 26). Thus, also central to the workings of governmental power are the various means by which individuals are enticed, encouraged and exhorted to take up those techniques of the self. In the case of exercise manuals, the enticements typically echo the problems of the body in contemporary consumer culture: the overlapping concerns with health and appearance. In both instances, fitness is prescribed as the ideal panacea – a construction found not only in fitness media but also in the promotion of health clubs (see Plate 4.3).

Consider the following example from an exercise manual from the publishers of *Men's Health* magazine, aimed at professional/managerial men:

> Fitness, as you know, touches on *every* aspect of your life. With exercise, you'll: Look and feel better; Cut your risk of deadly diseases . . . Have better sex and even prevent impotence; Meet new people, develop friendships, or maybe even find your future mate; Boost your self-confidence many times over.
>
> (Kaufman and Kirchheimer 1997: 2)

Long life, health and happiness are seemingly guaranteed for those who exercise. Fitness is employed as a floating signifier, making for an ideal marketing appeal: individuals are encouraged to project onto fitness whatever ills or deficiencies they detect in their lives.

Bolstered by medical research, manuals attempt to entice readers into becoming fit by highlighting the role of regular exercise in decreasing the risk of certain health-threatening conditions (such as heart disease, Type II diabetes, and some forms of cancer), managing the risks associated with other lifestyle habits (such as stress and smoking), and improving the overall quality of life (through improved self-esteem and weight control, for example). The following two excerpts are typical in this regard; the first comes from the already cited *Men's Health* manual, and the second from a manual by the American Heart Association (AHA):

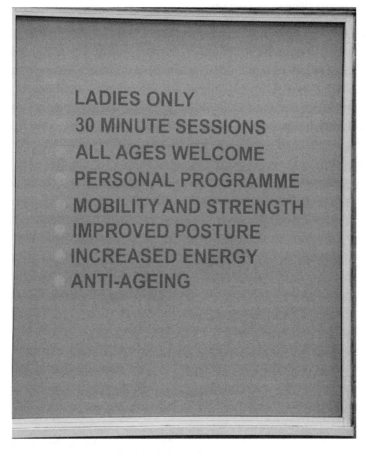

LADIES ONLY
30 MINUTE SESSIONS
ALL AGES WELCOME
PERSONAL PROGRAMME
MOBILITY AND STRENGTH
IMPROVED POSTURE
INCREASED ENERGY
ANTI-AGEING

Plate 4.3 Fitness as panacea: health club windows.
(Source: Joseph Maguire)

Unlike shortcuts that trim mere seconds or minutes from our crazed schedules, regular exercise . . . actually *adds* quality and years to your life. How much? If a 30-year-old, two-packs-a-day smoker with high cholesterol kicked the smoking habit, changed his diet, and started exercising regularly, he'd add 8 to 10 years to his life . . .

(Kaufman and Kirchheimer 1997: 24)

Whether you're twenty or sixty, physical activity is at least as important to your health as not smoking cigarettes and eating low-fat foods. In fact, some studies have shown that physically inactive people have the same risk of heart disease as people who smoke *two packs of cigarettes a day*.

(American Heart Association 1997: 5)

AMAZING RESULTS
WEIGHT LOSS
FIGURE SHAPING
TONING AND FIRMING
FREE DIETARY ADVICE
EASY, FUN AND FRIENDLY
NO WAITING

Plate 4.3 Continued.

At both ends of the lifestyle media spectrum, from the explicitly commercial exercise manual to the AHA manual's public service and health education orientation, health is presented as a quantifiable, calculable and predictable status. The language of risk is key to both this rationalization of health, and to the functioning of fitness as a panacea, anchoring the potential benefits from exercise to (seemingly) tangible probabilities. Participation in the fitness field offers both the reduction of risk, and the appeasement of anxiety about risk.

An unintended consequence of the rationalization of health, however, is the possibility for creative health accounting. In constructing all health-related behaviors as reducible to the same common denominator of risk, exercise manuals establish an illusory equivalence. For example, the AHA manual, quoted above, equates physical inactivity with heavy smoking; interpreted through the lens of equivalent risk, the corollary is that physical activity negates the risk of continuing to smoke. While such an interpretation may appear ridiculous, the dynamic of balancing vice and virtue, indulgence and restraint, is typical of both everyday behaviors, and the rationalizations people offer themselves about those behaviors (Nichter and Nichter 1991; Wilk 2001). Julie, the PhD student in her early 30s whom we met in chapter 3, and who works at a non-profit organization, provides a good example:

> I know I can get away with eating poached eggs and french fries every single morning because I run. And if I wasn't exercising, I would be really fat, eating that [*laughs*], and I would have to make a different choice.

Julie's logic may have some foundation in terms of energy input and expenditure, but what is at stake is rather that fitness activities both allow her to indulge, and absolve her from the associated guilt: running provides permission to indulge in the poached eggs and fries.

Fitness is also presented as a panacea with regard to the more nebulous (but no less real) risks associated with everyday life in an image- and performance-oriented service culture. Accordingly, the benefits of exercise are formulated in terms of assuaging anxieties about social presence – appearance, attitude, confidence – as in this manual from Gold's Gym (Dobbins and Sprague 1981: 7–8):

> Confidence in your body and a positive body-image are important elements in the make-up of your personality. It's hard to feel happy about yourself if you don't like your body. Weight-training helps give you the feeling that you *are* your body, not just *in* it. . . . Your body is no longer something you drag along or something that holds you back.

The assumption is that readers have already identified themselves as imperfect; the role of the manual is thus to specify the problem as the body (a root cause more readily available for intervention than, say, psychology or society), and identify weight-training as the solution. One aspect of the constructed problem is the disconnection between "having" a body and fully "being" in it, which draws from accepted wisdom about both the lack of corporeal engagement in everyday life (linked to the nature of work in service economies), and the body-consciousness of the middle class (Bourdieu 1984).

The Gold's Gym manual writers go on to observe:

> How you look doesn't just affect the way you feel, it also affects how other people treat you. Like it or not, people judge in large part on the basis of appearances. How you look is a basic part of your social identity and as you change and improve the look of your body you will see a change in the attitude of people you come into contact with. These days there aren't many things in life that an individual can control. You may not be able to lower your taxes or avoid the next rise in the price of gas, but you can become the master of your own body. You can change how you look and feel.
>
> (Dobbins and Sprague 1981: 8)

Again, the middle-class character of the fitness field is in evidence: an improved capacity for impression management is an enticement that resonates with those whose work involves managing interactions. More broadly, the expectation to assume responsibility for one's self-development cuts across class boundaries; with the intensification of such an expectation in times of social problems – such as with the energy crisis and stagflation in the 1970s – comes increasing attention to a shrinking sphere of influence: the body.

The Gold's Gym manual alludes to the psychological benefits of fitness, such as improved confidence. While such enticements make sense to the middle-class reader, they are also especially pertinent to women readers. The following comes from a 1983 weight-training manual for women:

> Expect to see physiological changes in three areas: strength, flexibility, and cardiovascular endurance. Don't be surprised if these change your entire life, though, because they add up to just one thing: improved self-image. Call it personal power, or self-worth, or self-actualization, or anything you want; you're going to feel an inner strength you haven't felt before.
>
> (Wolf 1983: 5)

A crude derivative of feminist ideals and self-help pop-psychology, the enticement is nonetheless alluring: building on the appeal of physical empowerment and its associations with political empowerment, fitness is presented as a route to self-competence and self-confidence.

A more nuanced, but similar, appeal is made in a 1998 manual from the publishers of *Self* magazine:

> What's a better body? It's a strong, healthy body in balance with a strong, healthy mind. Forget the notion that a better body is the "perfect body." It's not. There is no universal standard of physical perfection that we all can achieve. . . . All of us, however, have the capacity to tone, firm-up, slim-down, build stamina and cardio strength and live a happier, healthier life. We all have what it takes to be as strong, healthy and vital as we can be at every age and stage of our lives.
>
> (Billings 1998: 5)

Aimed at professional/managerial women, the manual addresses these readers as doubly predisposed to fitness as a mode of self-investment: through the filters of both class and gender, the perceived benefits of fitness are marketable and empowering. At the same time, the manual's author employs what Kathy Davis (2002) has called a "dubious" notion of equality, which threatens to disguise the historical and contemporary systemic inequalities (understood in terms of not only class and gender, but also ethnicity, age and physical ability) in access to physical culture, and erase the specificity of individual experiences of physical fitness.

In the *Self* manual, losing weight and improving one's figure are redeemed; no longer oppressive effects of the dominant patriarchal order (Bordo 1993; Wolf 1991), they are recast as expressions of an empowered woman's capacity for self-care and self-investment. However, the end result is, tellingly, the same: scrutiny, assessment and modification of the body relative to dominant norms. As Foucault (1980a: 57) observes of the emerging body culture of the 1970s, the body, seemingly liberated from earlier moral codes, provokes a response from the dominant social order:

> An economic (and perhaps also ideological) exploitation of eroticisation, from sun-tan products to pornographic films. Responding precisely to the revolt of the body, we find a new mode of investment which presents itself no longer in the form of control by repression but that of control by stimulation. "Get undressed – but be slim, good-looking, tanned!"

As with the attempts on the part of women's fitness magazines to position themselves as enlightened therapeutic experts, the *Self* manual demonstrates the ambivalence in consumer body culture around men's and (especially) women's bodies, which are both celebrated as the sovereign territory of the empowered individual, and scrutinized and criticized as imperfect clay to be molded through an endless array of products and services.

As governmental technologies, exercise manuals act at a distance, encouraging readers to adopt certain behaviors and practices through enticements rather than commands. Health risks are rationalized, social anxieties diagnosed, and bodily outcomes presented as calculable, predictable rewards, thereby positioning fitness as a prudent mode of self-investment. Getting fit is presented as in the individual's best interest, irrespective of the vested interests of the marketplace and social order, the ambivalent implications of the representation of rationalized outcomes, and the structural inequalities and collective risks that give the lie to the sentiment that "we all have what it takes."

Persistence: fitness as self-discipline

As much as exercise manuals attempt to convince readers of the benefits of becoming full fitness participants, enticement is not enough. The achievement of health outcomes and the cultivation of physical capital require regular and ongoing investment of time, money, and energy in the fitness field. As such, exercise manuals also provide strategies to assist readers in persisting with the fitness lifestyle. The American College of Sports Medicine (ACSM) is typical in highlighting the problem of perseverance for fitness participants:

> So now you're motivated to begin a fitness program to improve your fitness, be healthier and live longer. What's the ultimate secret of success? In a word, persistence! . . . Unfortunately, when it comes to lifestyle changes such as exercise, too many people think that it's an all-or-none phenomenon.
>
> (American College of Sports Medicine 1998: 13)

The problem of motivation extends to maintaining, not simply initiating, participation. Exercise manuals address the problem of persistence through a variety of techniques aimed at habituating in the individual the practice of regular exercise, but also self-discipline more generally.

Typical recommendations in exercise manuals include exercising at the same time each day, keeping an exercise log or diary, and charting one's progress as ways to "turn mere behavior into a good habit" (American College of Sports Medicine 1998: 17). Underlying these suggestions is a view of the individual as malleable and perfectible, a historically specific perspective, the origins of which Foucault (1977) locates in the early eighteenth century when population expansion and the increasingly complex societal division of labor necessitated the means of transforming bodies relative to the needs of production. Using the example of military training manuals, Foucault discusses a shift from a relatively passive view of bodies, their dimensions and capacities (one was either ready-made to be a soldier or not), to the active modification and training of bodies through deliberate, rational and repeated exercises.

Firmly entrenched in western culture over the modern era, the concept of a malleable self and its associated emphasis on body work are vital to service media and self-help literature. The link between body, self and perfectibility is exemplified in the primogenitor of self-help books, Franklin's 1791 *Autobiography*, the short second section of which set out a "bold and arduous project of arriving at moral perfection" (1970: 77). Franklin prescribed constant learning, routine, record-keeping, and self-reflection in the habituation of 13 moral virtues, the first of which – and thus the precondition for the rest, including order, industry and cleanliness – was the prudent treatment of the body: "temperance: eat not to dullness; drink not to elevation" (1970: 78). Franklin focused on one virtue per week and kept a daily log, in which his transgressions against each of the virtues could be recorded and, at the end of the day, reflected upon. Following the rational model of progress, Franklin thus believed that if he could avoid transgressions against a virtue for an entire week, the virtue would become a habit, thus requiring no conscious attention to ensure its persistence. A Presbyterian, Franklin epitomizes the Protestant work ethic, not only with regard to the specific virtue of industry but also, more importantly, to the application of such a work ethic to the project of self-improvement.

Of particular interest with regard to the parallel with exercise manuals is Franklin's discussion of the virtue of order (1970: 78, 84) and the necessity – but also the difficulty – of strict time keeping. As was discussed in Chapter 3, time is a central issue for the fitness field: health clubs must compete with other leisure businesses for consumers' discretionary time. Rather than question the social structures that pattern and constrain work and non-work time, the AHA exercise manual promises readers: "you can simply 'fit in fitness' with your current existing lifestyle" (1997: xv–xvi). Similarly, the

Men's Health manual informs time-pressed professional/managerial male readers that fitness requires the disciplining of time: "The issue [of time for fitness] really boils down to time management. . . . It's a matter of setting priorities. . . . Being in great shape is something that we'd love to do . . . if we had the time" (Kaufman and Kirchheimer 1997: 28). The authors include several time management suggestions, including laying out clothes the night before, hiring help for chores to create time for exercise, and waking up earlier. Here, the assumed character of the occupational class of reader mediates how time is constructed: a taken-for-granted work ethic is extended into the domain of leisure (cf. Parker 1976).

The *Self* manual encourages its intended female readership to "make a date" with fitness:

> On your calendar, book fitness appointments with your gym, park or playing field then record what you accomplished during your date. (When you feel like standing up your Stairmaster, looking back on weeks' worth of good workouts will make you less likely to break your winning streak.)
>
> (Billings 1998: 42)

Charting progress, as a motivational technique, is also a bureaucratization of self-discipline, reducing self-control to data entry. A similar suggestion is found in *Gym Psych*, a manual geared towards men:

> When you're starting out with a fitness program, self-discipline is often one of your highest hurdles. Many people find that devising a schedule is the easiest way around that. In the beginning, you may want to schedule your workouts at the same time each day. . . . Making specific appointments and keeping them is something you're used to in life. If you can do it for the dentist, you can do it for your sense of well-being.
>
> (Levy and Shafran 1986: 19–20)

Thus, readers are encouraged to use existing time-management skills – capacities formed through a lifetime of regimentation and scheduling in schools and workplaces. In general, the management of time is central to self-discipline (Foucault 1977): the control of movements through time (such as with schedules, logs and timetables) facilitates the observation, measurement and training of bodies relative to established norms. Furthermore, repeated patterns of exercises, schedules and routines encourage the internalization of rules and habituation of behavior, such that the habit of exercise (for example) persists once the exercise manual is read and discarded.

In addition to the regulation of time, self-discipline requires, more broadly, the production of a self-knowledge that identifies and acknowledges both specific problems and the need to address them, either on one's own or with the help of others (Foucault 1986: 57). A key element, then, in the production of persistence is educating readers to know their bodies in particular ways. Exercise manuals include tables and equations to allow readers to measure and assess their bodies against accepted norms. In addition to a superficial introduction to anatomy – being able to tell pectorals from deltoids, for example – exercise manuals instruct readers in how to measure their Body Mass Index (BMI), resting and target heart rates, and caloric expenditure for their rates of physical activity. For example, a 110-pound (50-kg) person can burn 300 to 500 calories over an hour of fencing (Franks and Howley 1989: 122–3), while a 130-pound person can expect to lose 6 pounds (2.7 kg) over the course of a year from playing with children (while standing) for 20 minutes each day (American Heart Association 1997: 134). A 170-pound (70-kg) man should be consuming 123 grams (4.3 ounces) of protein each day, and a 3-ounce (85-g) chicken breast contains 26.7 grams (0.93 ounces) of protein (Kaufman and Kirchheimer 1997: 8). These mundane measurements not only furnish readers with a knowledge of their body once reserved for medical and sport professionals; they also encourage in individuals an attitude of self-monitoring and calculation. Furthermore, they are presented as motivational tools in themselves: "Any tool that can contribute to your sense of accomplishment is a tool worth having" (Billings 1998: 57).

Self-examination is not only accomplished against objective benchmarks. Readers are also encouraged to assess themselves relative to other fitness participants. This comparison may be cautionary (as when manuals encourage readers to avoid becoming "yet another fitness drop out") or inspirational. For example:

> Find a hero. Model yourself after someone who's been a fitness success. . . . Your hero can be your grandma who walks a mile in the park every day. It can be some guy in the office who wears size 42 pants but has started going to the gym four times a week. . . . Just find someone about whom you can say, "If *that* person can do it, I sure as heck can."
>
> (Schlosberg and Neporent 1996: 35)

Like the Success Stories of *Shape* magazine, a fitness "hero" is one who has adopted an ethic of self-improvement through exercise. The recommendation to compare oneself with other fitness participants is reinforced in the health club, through the spatial structuring of visibility: mirrors and the position of equipment and exercise areas facilitate surveillance of, and by others, encouraging the individual to adopt a permanent attitude of self-surveillance (Foucault 1977).

One of the tools of self-assessment is confession. The *Fitness Facts* authors, for example, suggest that the chance of fitness success – or failure – depends on the individual's self-critique:

> One of the most difficult skills in dealing with yourself is being able to differentiate between the real reasons for your behavior and rationalizations that often sound better than the real reasons. It is impossible to progress with exercise or other health behaviors until you acknowledge the real reasons for your current behaviors. *Being completely honest with yourself* and the fitness leader is an important step in increasing healthy behaviors.
>
> (Franks and Howley 1989: 83; emphasis added)

Knowing oneself requires reflection, confession and a commitment to truth (cf. Foucault 1985, 1986, 1988). This is not to posit a single truth with regard to an individual's fitness, but to acknowledge that such truth is produced *through* the fitness field: exercise manuals not only provide the terms of that truth (psychological motivation rather than structural inequality, for example), but also endorse the means by which that truth is made available, such as introspection, and disclosure to a therapeutic expert or its proxy, such as a diary.

Self-knowledge also involves adopting a learning attitude more generally. The following from the ACSM manual is typical of this endorsement of an educational outlook:

> Learn all you can about the whys and hows of exercise. If you thoroughly understand the benefits . . . you'll be more likely to stick with it. Good instruction provided by qualified exercise leaders, such as those certified by the American College of Sports Medicine, will give you the knowledge.
>
> (American College of Sports Medicine 1998:14)

While such messages might be expected in the health education-oriented ACSM manual, similar content appears in the more overtly commercial manuals, such as the following from *Fitness for Dummies* and the *Men's Health* manual:

> Any subject is less intimidating if you know something about it. . . . Our ignorance makes us feel a bit foolish. . . . [I]t always pays to educate yourself. . . . You'll have more confidence and more fun with your workouts if you read about fitness in magazines, newsletters, and books – even on the Internet.
>
> (Schlosberg and Neporent 1996: 37)

> Fight the feeling. Your training results are just a few weeks away, but you feel like your motivation is flagging. What to do? Educate yourself. Go to a bookstore and study fitness magazines or books, or talk to others in the gym who look like they know what they're doing. It may go against every Y chromosome that you have, but you'll probably learn something.
>
> (Kaufman and Kirchheimer 1997: 34)

Lessons about fitness – learning about the body, one's motivations and limitations, the benefits of exercise, and the disciplinary means to "fit in fitness" – are presented as motivational devices, thereby reinforcing the manuals' role as therapeutic aids.

Self-knowledge, through techniques of measurement, examination and confession, must be accompanied by the regular and rational inculcation of behaviors if fitness activities and self-disciplining more generally are to become habits. Such lessons are central to the construction of self-responsibility, equipping individuals with (some) expertise and thus charging them with the duty to apply that expertise, if only in the form of an educated choice of therapeutic aids. The self-improving, lifelong-learning attitude that is being endorsed is not only relevant to participation in the fitness field; it also perpetuates both an ideological climate of individual responsibility, and a consumer market reliant on constructing the self as an inexhaustible problem.

Reward: fitness as pleasure

The material practices of the fitness field correspond in key ways with the social, political and economic context of contemporary life: participation offers reduced health risks and health costs, improved social presence, and opportunities for social interaction and status display. Nevertheless, fitness is an awkward commodity in a consumer culture organized around indulgence and instantaneous gratification, especially when diet and weight-loss commodities promise an easy alternative to the hard work of exercise (see Plate 4.4). Set against a cultural imaginary of leisure as a time of freedom, relaxation and the absence of work, the fitness media must invest considerable attention to convincing individuals to participate in the fitness lifestyle, and disciplining that participation.

The problems of motivation, and the fitness field more generally, are shaped by this tension between leisure and work, indulgence and discipline, the aesthetic Romantic ethic and the ascetic Protestant ethic (Featherstone 1982; McGee 2005). This tension is revealed in the exercise manuals:

> It takes work and time. You are about to begin something that I hope will become a permanent part of your life. It is important to understand that you will only get out of it what you put into it. Toning and firming can begin to show within days, but for a deep, total and lasting effect, you need to work hard and regularly.
>
> (Fonda 1981: 73)

Plate 4.4 The promise of instant results: weight loss products.
(Source: Janet Mowat)

> Realize that building a new body takes time and patience – a fact that we
> don't consider depressing. Stick with exercise for a while and you'll find
> that the process of getting in shape can be just as fun and rewarding as the
> results. You sleep better, you feel less stress, and you have more energy.
>
> (Schlosberg and Neporent 1996: 283)

The conversational tone of these excerpts is typical of lifestyle media. The
acknowledgment of a tension between expectations of instant results and
the reality of physical training is intended both to motivate the reader and
to establish the credentials of the authors as reliable experts and honest
brokers. However, the acknowledgment then presents the dilemmatic tension
between fitness-as-leisure and the work of fitness-as-self-improvement. This
dilemma is negotiated – if not resolved – through the promise of pleasure as
the reward for self-discipline. Pleasure takes on different forms in the exercise manuals, shaped by the particular dynamic between the aesthetic and
ascetic ethics.

The first mode of reconciling the tension between aesthetic indulgence
and ascetic discipline is to position them as separate, but sequential, logics.
In this vein, the hard work of fitness and the cultural imaginary of indulgent
leisure are presented as complementary, the former making permissible the
latter. Take the following advice, offered in *Fitness for Dummies*:

> Be nice to yourself. . . . Attach an appropriate reward to each of your
> long-term, short-term and immediate goals. If you lose the 15 pounds
> [7 kg] over 6 months, buy yourself that watch you've been wanting. . . .
> Sure, it's bribery, but it works.
>
> (Schlosberg and Neporent 1996: 28)

Here, pleasure is constructed in the exercise manuals as a motivational device
by offering an indulgent reward after the hard work of exercise. This
endorsement of shopping as the reward for self-discipline and self-denial
contributes to the naturalization of consumption as the taken-for-granted
domain for fitness: not only is shopping one's due reward, but it is also an
endorsed motivational device.

The authors of the *Men's Health* manual also recommend reward shopping as a means of motivation:

> It makes . . . sense to wear clothes that reveal some of your progress.
> That will serve as a visible reminder that your hard work is paying

off. . . . Remember when you used to fill out your letterman jacket in all the right places? Striving to repeat that pleasant past can help motivate you to keep exercising. Or promise to buy yourself a new Armani suit when the shoulders and chest on this one get too small.

(Kaufman and Kirchheimer 1997: 32–3)

Confirming the enticement of improved social presence, one of the promised rewards of self-discipline is the pleasure of showing off one's newly fit body. The new body necessarily requires new accessories to facilitate its display, and thus pleasure in the body is amplified through pleasure in shopping for it. Both of these manuals present the aesthetic ethic as the legitimate reward for working out, thereby offsetting the long-term discipline of persisting with fitness with immediate consumer gratifications of different types.

Unlike *Fitness for Dummies* and the *Men's Health* manual, the AHA manual makes an explicit attempt to downplay the need for consumption as part of its attempt to broaden access to and participation in fitness activities. The AHA manual reassures readers that fitness does not require a "personal trainer, fancy gym, or strict diet" (1997: 135). Nevertheless, the manual also acknowledges the role of consumption as a motivational device:

We'll say it again: All you need to fit in fitness is a comfortable pair of walking shoes. So why spend money on fitness equipment? In a word, *variety*. Variety is not only the spice of life, it's what keeps physical activity *fun*. Boredom, on the other hand, is one of the most common reasons people give for quitting regular exercise.

(American Heart Association 1997: 96)

Even fitness advocates present exercise as tainted by the tedium of the pro- ductive sphere: exercise is hard work, repetitive, boring. Rather than examin- ing the potential for intrinsic and spontaneous pleasure within the exercise activity itself, the solution is located externally in the novelty of fitness products, or the indulgence in commodities for the newly fit body. All three manuals present a guilt-free notion of shopping: just as the creative health accounting discussed earlier in the chapter allowed Julie to absolve her guilt over french fries through the discipline of running, the self-denial of working out is taken as legitimation for indulgence in the consumer market (Wilk 2001).

The second mode of reconciliation involves a fusion of the ethics of aesthetic indulgence and ascetic discipline. The authors of *Fitness Facts*, for example, suggest: "Many regular exercisers know how good it feels to have the discipline to complete a workout even on busy days" (Franks and Howley 1989: 155). Similarly, Jane Fonda writes:

> You will always have a good reason to skip your workout. You could be cleaning the house, baking, watching a movie, going straight home from work or sleeping late. But when you make yourself exercise and after-wards feel that tingle through your body, the *sense of exhilaration and your own pleasure in your discipline*, you'll agree it was worth it.
>
> (Fonda 1981: 56; emphasis added)

One of the promised rewards of persisting with the fitness lifestyle is a feeling of virtuousness, which rests on the representation of the exer-ciser as triumphing over the obstacles presented by everyday life. As such, the responsibilities of everyday life (going to work, cleaning the house, caring for one's family) are presented as problems, standing in the way of doing the "right" thing. The reward of virtuousness reinforces the con-struction of fitness as a socially esteemed means of enacting one's self-responsibility.

In addition to the pleasure of virtuousness, the ethics of self-denial and indulgence come together in the pleasure of embodiment. A comprehensive awareness of and engagement with the body, its presence and capacities are aspects of life made less common by the sedentary nature of work-ing and commuting; the physicality of fitness activities thus presents the opportunity to engage with the body in a more complete fashion. For example, bodybuilding offers the "weight-trainer's bonus":

> When you work your muscles strenuously with weights, you can actu-ally feel the extra blood rushing into them and swelling them up. This feeling is called a "pump" and it's one of the extra rewards of weight-training. It's a strong feeling of well-being in the right use of the body. It's the "high" of weight-training.
>
> (Dobbins and Sprague 1981: 7)

The experiential benefits of exercise are formulated differently, depending on the exercise in question. For aerobics, for example:

> From this point on, I will often mention the "burn" and exhort you to "go for the burn." This burn is a unique sensation that you get when you

have used a muscle very strenuously. . . . When I first did the buttocks exercise . . . my muscles burned so much I had to stop three or four times during the exercise. Now the burn comes later and I don't have to stop. I've even come to look forward to it. It lets me know that I'm really working hard.

(Fonda 1981: 68)

These vivid descriptions of feelings of embodiment are reminiscent of what psychologist Mihaly Csikszentmihalyi (1990) refers to as "flow" experiences, in which one is so absorbed in the activity that there ceases to be a conscious awareness of a separation of the self from the activity, allowing an enjoyable loss of self (see also Maguire 1992).

Fitness flow experiences are represented in the manuals as rewards in a triple sense: in themselves through the immediate feelings of gratification; in their associated feelings of authenticity and self-actualization; and in their instrumental function as pleasurable memories, to be drawn on at a later date when self-discipline flags. The corporeal experience of fitness can thus reaffirm other pleasures, as well as self-discipline: both during exercise and afterwards, muscle fatigue and tenderness, and improved levels of strength, endurance, and flexibility, serve as embodied reminders of the virtuous work done, and reinforce one's resolve to remain physically active. Even when pleasure is explicitly represented as something intrinsic to the fitness activity, it remains yoked to the problem of motivation.

Common across these different forms of rewards is an instrumentality that harks back to the physical culture of the nineteenth century: pleasure is a means to an end – the reproduction of participation in the fitness field – rather than an end in itself. When the ethics of self-discipline and indulgence are treated as separate, pleasure is found externally and extrinsically in the effect one's body has on others, and the permission that working out provides for guilt-free consumption. Located at the intersection of the two ethics, the pleasures of virtuousness and fitness flow experiences are nevertheless instrumentalized, thus privileging self-discipline: pleasure is to be found *in* and *through* discipline, and is subsequently enlisted in the service of perpetuating that discipline.

The embodied, non-instrumental enjoyment of movement is largely absent from exercise manuals, in part because of the nature of the genre. The fitness flow experiences of the manuals' authors may be included as proof of authority and authenticity, but the one-way mode of address in lifestyle print media (as opposed to lifestyle television, for example; see Bell and

Hollows 2005) means that the flow experiences of readers are, necessarily, unavailable. Furthermore, a decline in physical education and physical activity more generally may mean that readers cannot identify with the notion of radical, pleasurable embodiment and kinesthetic awareness via physical exercise; they can, however, identify with the instrumental logic of reducing health risks, losing weight, improving appearance, and the pleasures of shopping for a slimmer, younger-looking body.

Fitness media filter the practices and potential benefits of working-out through their vested interests in market expansion, profitability and their legitimation as therapeutic experts. This chapter's focus on the ideal texts of fitness magazines and exercise manuals is intended neither to ascribe experiences to fitness participants as if these were unproblematically distilled into the content of fitness media, nor to suggest a complete disconnect between commercial discourse and actual experience. Thus, it is useful to consider a few examples of how fitness participants understand the rewards and pleasures of fitness. All of the women interviewed raised issues of competence, control or concreteness as part of their experience of fitness and exercise activities, and their motivation for continuing. The sample size does not permit the making of claims about how gender and class mediate both the subjective experience and the articulation of the experience of embodiment; rather, these examples are offered anecdotally to illustrate how the enticements and rewards promised in fitness media are resonant with the actual experiences of participants.

Teri (whom we met in Chapter 3) is a retired teacher in her early 50s. Her reflections on fitness echo the enticements made in the manuals regarding health and overall feelings of well-being:

> For me, being fit is about feeling strong, and empowered. And I like the fact that I can lift heavy weights, and it just makes me feel good and healthy and strong. I think it spills over into other areas. You know, other areas of my life are maybe here or there, but I come to the gym and I feel like, "I'm *good* at this. I can *do* this." Yeah. So, and it's very concrete.

Teri highlights how the experience of physical competence may be particularly satisfying when in the context of a life that is felt to be chaotic, changing or lacking in structure. This point was made in different ways by several of the respondents, who juxtaposed their sense of concrete accomplishment in working out with their work lives. For example, Fiona is a doctoral student in her early 30s:

There's a very concrete sense of accomplishment because you can measure what you've done, and you can measure yourself getting stronger. . . .
And especially when I feel like, being in graduate school, spending all
this time thinking about concepts and ideas that are so abstract, it's a
very concrete sense of accomplishment. In a weird way, you can sort of
be proud of it. . . . And yeah, the sense of getting better than you were a
week ago, a month ago, whatever, there is this real progress that you can
see being made that you can't often see being made in other areas of your
life [*laughs*].

Comments from both Teri and Fiona suggest the complementarity between
the physical work of fitness and the nature of middle-class occupations, the
roots of which may be located in the late nineteenth century's middle-class
problem of neurasthenia (Green 1986), as discussed in Chapter 2. In addition
to cultivating the physical capital that counts in middle-class work (Bourdieu
1984), and proactively working on one's health as part of one's middle-class
identity (Crawford 1994), fitness field participants can also recapture feelings
of physical competence and authenticity, which have diminished with the
increasingly abstract, immaterial nature of middle-class occupations (Lash
and Urry 1987; Slater 1997).

Meredith, in her mid-30s, works in publishing. Her reflections on her
favorite fitness activity of swimming, and the experience of being overweight, bring together Teri's feelings of physical competence and Fiona's
sense of accomplishment:

Swimming is one of the only times when I feel powerful and strong. . . .
Being in the pool, it's very personal, you have some space. You
can think. And also . . . if you walk around with a hundred extra pounds
[45 extra kg] on your body, you feel heavy, no matter what you do.
Whereas in the pool, the buoyancy factor . . . you feel light. Which is
not something you ever get to experience when you are heavy, because
you're *always* heavy. . . . So, I get a couple things out of swimming. . . .
I feel like I've done something, I feel like I've participated . . . which is
good, because . . . I've never felt like I really can participate.

Meredith's feelings of virtuousness and physical competence suggest how
the experiences of accomplishment and embodiment are mediated by physicality, shaped by factors such as body shape, weight, age, and disability. Just
as the commercial nature of the fitness field constrains the way in which

exercise manuals represent non-instrumental pleasure (such that pleasure is enlisted as a means to an end – creating and expanding the fitness consumer market), the cultural emphasis on the health risks and diminished market value of being overweight constrains Meredith's subjective experience of the non-instrumental aspects of fitness. While the pleasure of feeling light may be an end in itself, it is located within Meredith's overall goal: "My fitness agenda is really quite strictly just to lose weight."

For Liz, a financial analyst in her early 30s, running and doing yoga provide not only a feeling of accomplishment, but also a sense of control:

> It's like you're taking control, it's something that you control. You can go out, you can do it well, you take control of yourself, and every-thing. . . . You can go to work, and everything can go wrong, and you can't control that, it might have nothing to do with you. But this, you can do. You can do it right, you can finish it, you can do it.

In addition to working-out at health clubs, Julie is also an avid runner and roller-blader. Like Liz, she highlights the experience of control over oneself, explicitly linking this to external circumstances:

> There's also . . . a *freedom* in being able to hop on your roller-blades and just *soar*, you know. And to be able to have the strength and the ability to just do it. . . . After September 11th . . . I realized I could walk home [to Canada]. I'm strong, and fit enough, that if I had to make the trip, *I could*. I mean, that was a big relief. It would take me a couple weeks, but it's a great gift to *know* that that's an absolutely doable thing.

Julie was not alone in having negotiated the events of September 2001 via the fitness field. Health clubs around the US reported a surge in club member-ships and club use in the months after the attacks (Buckley 2001; Forman 2001; Levine 2001; Stobbe 2001). Especially against the backdrop of social crisis, the body provides a refuge: working on the body offers the possibility to be feel proactive, to seek reassurance that the world is not entirely out of control, and to feel safe, if only in one's physical capacity to move about in the world.

CONCLUSION

As mechanisms of consumer education, fitness texts broadcast the field's practices and values to an audience that is defined by readership rather than exercise, presenting the opportunity for both vicarious, spectator fitness and the development of popular expertise in the body's machinations. Fitness magazines and exercise manuals transcend the short-lived experience of working out, transforming fitness from an immediate activity into a gradual course of instruction, and an intellectual, critical and aesthetic issue (Ferguson 1998: 610). It is through such texts that fitness is produced as a consumer lifestyle, the ideal consumer is represented, and the role of lifestyle media as therapeutic guides more generally affirmed.

Fitness is but one field in which the consumer is educated in the necessity and strategies of negotiating the double bind of contemporary culture: the seemingly opposed duties of diligent work and self-actualization, and conflicting demands to treat the body as a site of work and a vehicle for gratification. The endorsement of consumption as the parallel indulgence to the self-denial of working-out, and the location of the pleasure of working-out external to the fitness activities themselves, however, construct an instrumental notion of pleasure. Pleasure is not to be found intrinsically in the exercise itself, but in the ensuing effects: a better body for consumption – to be consumed by others (improved impression management), and to be consumed for (guilt-free shopping). Locating pleasure in the discipline of working-out is less instrumental and offers an embodied reconciliation of the ascetic and aesthetic ethics in the fitness "flow" (Csikszentmihalyi 1990) experience. Nonetheless, such a synthesis still involves the rationalization of pleasure as a motivational device – ultimately, rationality and instrumentality are privileged over spontaneity and embodiment, in that the intrinsic pleasure is then coopted as a motivational device – by both the individual exerciser and the manual author on behalf of other readers.

5   Personal trainers
In the service of fitness

In addition to the culturally specific site of the health club, and the fitness media's lessons in the practices and rewards of the fitness lifestyle, the fitness field is further consolidated by the emergence of a "cadre of experienced producers" (Ferguson 1998: 603): personal trainers, who serve as instructors, motivators and status symbols for their clients. These elements – place, media, consumer, producer – converge in the entrenchment of the definition and function of fitness as commercial leisure, and as a consumer lifestyle that requires particular products and services. As the frontline service workers of the fitness field (Smith Maguire 2001), personal trainers are key figures in both the production of fitness services, and the promotion and consumption of the fitness field more broadly. Through the occupation of personal training, the practices of the fitness field are institutionalized as the specialized skills and knowledge of a select corps of experts. Furthermore, the personal trainer embodies the ethos of the fitness field; the body's status as a site of investment, a form of capital, and an expression of self is nowhere better illustrated than in the figure of the personal trainer.

The chapter proceeds with an overview of the occupation of personal training. Of particular interest are the conditions for its expansion and transition from an elite personal service for the wealthy, to a mass-market, middle-class service. The expansion of personal training has been bound up with a process of professionalization, which includes an increasing emphasis on training and qualifications. Professionalization has also given rise to a growing number of producer texts: specialized journals, manuals, and newsletters addressing the professional practitioner (cf. Ferguson 1998: 630). Like the consumer texts examined in Chapter 4, occupational texts attempt to educate personal trainers in the practices and criteria of fitness field expertise.

Drawing on an analysis of the content of the personal training occupational journal, *IDEA Personal Trainer* (*IPT*), from 1990 to 2000, and interviews with those involved in the occupation, this chapter explores the ideal construction and subjective experience of personal training. The second section of the chapter discusses the cultivation of personal trainers' credibility as fitness experts through different forms of capital, many of which stand in awkward relation to their professional credentials. The final section examines how such forms of capital, and the tension between the professional and entrepreneurial aspects of the occupation, shape the work of personal trainers as cultural intermediaries. Linking together their roles as motivators and promoters is the status of the personal trainer as the perfect fitness field participant, who not only sells, but also embodies, the fitness lifestyle.

FROM ELITE TO MASS-MARKET SERVICE

Paid to design and facilitate individual fitness programs on a one-to-one basis, personal trainers have become a common feature in the fitness field. With the service available in 94 per cent of commercial health clubs in 2002,[1] personal training has become a standard denominator by which clubs attempt to distinguish themselves, along with specific classes, location and décor, and so on (see Plate 5.1). Typically, personal training is not included in membership

Plate 5.1 Services for sale: health club window ads.
(Source: the author)

fees, and trainers are paid on an hourly basis[2] rather than a flat salary, meaning that the recruitment and retention of clients are essential both to the trainer's livelihood and to the club's revenue base. While the chapter is predominantly focused on health-club-based personal trainers, it is important to note that the need to recruit and retain clients is even more pressing for self-employed trainers (approximately one-third of the occupation[3]), who often work in clients' homes and thus do not have the exposure of working in a health club to help generate a client base.

Health clubs often offer members a complementary personal trainer session as a bonus upon joining; this session provides the member with an introduction to the facilities, and allows the trainer an opportunity to attract clients. Typically during their first meeting, the personal trainer will conduct a "fitness assessment" of the client, using measures of fitness (such as Body Mass Index) to outline an exercise program based on such factors as the client's health concerns, lifestyle issues, and personal goals. Following the assessment and program design stage, personal trainers then "coach" the client through a workout, correcting technique, adjusting equipment, and providing guidance on the pace and progression of the exercises. Most importantly, the trainer provides motivation, talking to the client about fitness and non-fitness issues, and offering positive feedback and encouragement. In subsequent sessions, the trainer will update and adjust the exercise program to match the client's physical progress and to counter boredom. Repeated sessions often give rise to a quasi-personal relationship in which fitness instruction blurs with gossip, cheerleading, and coaching as the trainer continues to motivate the client to pursue his or her fitness goals.

The scope and organization of personal training are difficult to assess because there is no single organizational body through which to audit the occupation. Nevertheless, the International Dance-Exercise Association (IDEA), the major occupational association for fitness professionals, estimates that there were over 100,000 personal trainers active in the US in 2006.[4] IDEA surveys of their members have found that nearly three-quarters of both trainers and their clients are female, suggesting (in the case of trainers) the continuation of well-established patterns of the feminization of service work (and the added benefit such organizations offer to women practitioners in terms of credibility); and (in the case of clients) the role of personal trainers in helping women negotiate access to the fitness field. Using education and occupation as indices of socio-economic status, IDEA survey results also confirm the middle-class character of the fitness field already discussed with regard to health clubs and fitness media: 49 per cent of trainers hold a bachelor's degree and an additional 20 per cent have more advanced degrees; and the largest groups of clients are professionals (28 per cent), homemakers (20 per cent), and business owners (13 per cent). Finally, 63 per cent of all personal trainers work part-time, highlighting the flexibility of the work, as well as its tenuousness: only 35 per cent of full-time trainers and 3 per cent of part-time trainers receive full health coverage; 30 per cent of full-time trainers and 57 per cent of part-time trainers receive no employment benefits at all.

Personal trainers are subsumed within the US Bureau of Labor Statistics (BLS) occupational category of "fitness trainers and aerobics instructors." This occupational group totaled 189,220 in 2005, representing approximately 6 per cent of all personal care service occupations; however, this does not include the self-employed, making this a low estimate of the total.[5] The BLS also reports that approximately 64 per cent were employed in fitness and recreation centers in 2005, and that fitness trainers and aerobics instructors constitute the largest group of employees (25.1 per cent) within fitness and recreation sports centers – reinforcing both the primacy of the health club as the stage upon which fitness experiences are constructed, and the role of personal trainers as key frontline service workers in the fitness field. Reflecting the occupational split between full- and part-time trainers, annual income ranged from $14,540 to $55,020, with a mean annual income of $31,060. Relative to other personal care and service occupations, fitness trainers, and aerobics instructors fall near the middle of the category with, for example, manicurists and pedicurists earning approximately $20,000 and flight attendants approximately $54,000 per year in 2005.

However, to fully understand the current scope and role of personal training in the fitness field, it is important to appreciate the development of the occupation from an elite to a mass-market, middle-class service. While personal training may be commonplace today, the occupation was relatively new in 1991, when the American Council on Exercise (ACE) published its first personal trainer manual, which outlined the context and state of the occupation:

> Exercise enthusiasts are becoming more educated about fitness and health, more insistent on an exercise regimen that caters to their schedules, and more adventurous and versatile in the activities in which they participate. Emerging from the demands of these individuals is the need for fitness instructors conversant with a variety of sports and activities and willing to meet clients at the fitness center, in the home, or elsewhere

to personally guide them through an exercise program designed specifically for them. This has generated a new fitness niche, and we are witness
to a new breed of fitness instructor – the personal trainer.

(Marks 1991: xix)

This "new breed" of instructor, however, was built upon the much older foundation of the provision of instruction in the practices of physical exercise.
Physical educators, sport and athletic coaches, drill instructors, and military
trainers are all examples of long-standing occupations focused on exercise
instruction.

Examples of famous exercise instructors are found throughout the history
of physical culture. In the late nineteenth century, for instance, Madame
Bergman Österberg led British children in the Swedish system of gymnastics
(McIntosh 1968: 114–45); in the US, James Naismith worked as a physical
educator and coach at a Massachusetts YMCA (famously inventing basketball in 1892 in the process).[6] In the twentieth century, each of the businesses
that sold exercise space – the executive club, boxing gym, exercise salon and
YMCA – also had its version of instructors, paid either by the club or the
client to coach, teach, lead and guide. Outside of the immediate physical
space of the gym, salon or club, exercise instruction was also available in
books and on television. For example, Charles Atlas began selling his mail-
order exercise manual in 1928 (Gaines 1982: 65), and Jack La Lanne began
broadcasting his exercise television show in the 1950s. In New York exercise
studios between the 1950s and 1970s, Marjorie Craig taught exercise to
women at the Elizabeth Arden "Body Department" (Bender 1968: 52), while
Lotte Berk and Nicholas Kounovsky taught their methods of movement at
their studios (Taylor 1972, 1974).

However, these are examples of group exercise instructors – whether
the group was defined by readership, viewership, or membership. Personal
trainers, as their name implies, are defined by the personal, one-on-one nature
of their instruction. Historical examples of personal exercise instructors
are typically associated with an elite stratum of consumers. In the 1930s, for
example, Artie McGovern[7] operated a lavish and exclusive gymnasium on
Wall Street for a clientele of "leading financiers, lawyers, architects, and
bankers of New York" (Smith 1931: 68). In addition to his club, McGovern
offered a special service, in his words: "pushing the big shots out of bed"
(Smith 1931: 68). McGovern and his staff of trainers would wake some of
New York's millionaires each morning with their dose of physical exercise.
According to McGovern:

It's not as easy as you would think. It takes as much diplomacy as any ambassador to get some of them out of bed. You mustn't make them too mad, but you've got to get them up. You've got to give them orders. . . . You have to just shove them out of bed and order them around if you want to get any results at all.

(Smith 1931: 68)

McGovern's clients included Babe Ruth, John Philip Sousa and John Muir, "the oldest member of the Stock Exchange" – men whose daily responsibilities often kept them from exercise (Smith 1931: 168).

In the 1980s, as the growing health club industry intersected with the Zeitgeist of competitive consumption, elite personal fitness services became more common. Magazines targeting the professional/managerial "Yuppie" class, such as *Business Week*, *Working Woman* and *Black Enterprise*, highlighted the trend of busy corporate executives hiring personal trainers to shape their bodies (Dunn and Segal 1988; Frons 1989; Lee 1989; Siegel 1991). In a 1988 article in *Business Week*, for example, one New York personal trainer observed: "If you have custom-designed suits, why not a custom-designed body?" (Dunn and Segal 1988: 166). Journalistic accounts of personal training services were not only offered as market reports on the growing fitness industry; they were also lifestyle advice for time-pressed and body-conscious corporate executives and business people.

Top athletes and Hollywood stars also made use of personal trainers. The physical development of celebrities – particularly emblematic strong bodies such as Sylvester Stallone (Muir 1995) or Linda Hamilton in *Terminator 2* (Jordan 1992) – was publicly attributed to the help of trainers, raising the public profile of the occupation as well as the cachet of particular trainers. These "star" trainers often became celebrities in their own right, parlaying the status of their clientele into sales for their own books, videos and clubs. For example, in the 1980s, personal trainer Jake Steinfeld's client list of Steven Spielberg, Harrison Ford, Morgan Fairchild and Priscilla Presley helped launch his own exercise studio (Body by Jake), fitness show on ESPN, and motivational book (Burggraf 1986; Hellmich 1993).

In the late 1980s and early 1990s, economic recessions and declines in discretionary income created the conditions for marketing personal training to a broader audience. Eight New York health clubs closed in 1991 (Gault 1991), and the overall number of health clubs in the US dropped from 13,854 in 1990 to 12,146 in 1991.[8] In an effort to preserve their businesses, many health club owners began to offer new services such as personal training to make their clubs more attractive investments for consumers' shrinking discretionary income (Gault 1991). This strategy built on the commercial clubs' existing ranks of exercise instructors, and incorporated the niche business strategy of a small group of elite competitors: personal training-only studios.[9] As well, health clubs incorporated into their staff (or excluded from their spaces, through non-competition agreements) those self-employed personal trainers who were training their own clients in commercial facilities.

Not only were clubs competing amongst themselves, but also against an exercise video market that expanded as part of a shift towards home-based leisure (MacNeill 1998: 165). That health club owners turned to service workers as the key to a competitive edge should come as no surprise. Following the post–1960s expansion of the service economy, consumer industries – fitness included – have placed a growing emphasis on frontline service work and its direct interaction with the customer (something lacking in videos and other home-based options) to add value to their products (Pine and Gilmore 1998; Sherry 1998; Watkins 1993; Wharton 1993). This emphasis on service has been reinforced through the construction of retention-based clubs as the "good" business model, in which professional staff and service-oriented programs (such as personal training) are strategies to generate customer loyalty and revenue.

IDEA estimated that the number of personal trainers increased tenfold between 1990 and 1995 (Davis and Davis 1996: 2). As the number of personal trainers increased, market competition generated more affordable rates. In the late 1980s, personal trainer rates ranged from $50 to $200 an hour (Dunn and Segal 1988); a half-hour session at Body by Jake, for example, cost $60 (Burggraf 1986). By 1992, many trainers were charging only $35 to $50 per hour, promising "fitness trainers for the masses" (Clark 1992: 107; see also Muir 1995).[10] Although high-priced celebrity trainers continued to feature in media reports (Nasatir 1996; Snowden 1994), and the market's notion of the "masses" was narrowly defined by the means of consumption, the expansion of the occupation meant that personal fitness service was no longer simply for the elite: personal trainers became a service for the middle class. The middle-class appeal of the service, however, lay not only in the exercise instruction itself, but also in personal training's connotations of status, which are derived both from its past existence as an exclusive personal service and present construction as an "extra" (the consumption of which thus demonstrating not only a client's capacity to consume, but also his or her responsible self-production); and from the fact that its practitioners are themselves stratified by price and (as the following section examines) other forms of capital.

The growth of personal training can thus be linked to a public awareness of fitness products and services, and their associated rewards and connotations of status, which helped to create a market for one-on-one exercise instruction; and, at the same time, increasing health club market competition emphasized the importance of personal service workers such as personal trainers in recruiting and retaining members and generating revenue through the sale of ancillary services. Also facilitating the expansion of the ranks of personal trainers was a lack of regulation: there were no formal requirements as to who could practice, no state regulation, and few start-up costs for offering personal training services at a health club.

The issues of certification and regulation have been central to the emergence of fitness instructors' occupational organizations. The leading organization, IDEA, began in 1982 as part of the growth of aerobics instruction. Through its conventions and publications, IDEA has promoted itself as "The Health and Fitness Association,"[11] providing information on such topics as exercise science research, questions of professional ethics, liability insurance, and marketing strategies. In 1985, IDEA created a separate organization, the IDEA Foundation, to oversee questions of professional training and certification; this was renamed the American Council on Exercise (ACE) in 1991, a year after the organization began offering its Personal Trainer Exam. The ACE exam was accompanied in 1991 by the publication of ACE's *Personal Trainer Manual* (Sudy 1991), the official companion text to the exam; a third edition was published in 2003. IDEA also began publishing a six-page monthly newsletter, *IDEA Personal Trainer* (*IPT*), in 1990; it became a 40-page, full-color magazine in 1994, and in 2004 was re-launched as *IDEA Fitness Journal*. Shortly after the start of ACE, in 1993, a personal trainer organization emerged in Canada (the Canadian Personal Trainer Network);[12] a similar organization emerged in the UK (the National Register of Personal Fitness Trainers) in 1992.

While there continues to be no standardization for certifications (trainers have dozens of options, from universities and organizations such as ACE, to dubious diploma companies), and calls for mandatory certification are opposed by the trainers themselves, many of whom would be put out of business given their own lack of standard credentials (Ryan 1995: 30), there has nevertheless been a gradual move towards certification as a standard occupational expectation. In 1989, only 2,500 people had been certified by ACSM as health/fitness instructors – the most relevant certification at the time for personal training (Calistro 1989). By 1996, an IDEA survey found that 94 per cent of trainers had been certified; by 2000, ACE had certified 44,000 personal trainers.[13]

The development of occupational organizations such as ACE and IDEA, and the increasing prevalence of certifications, are key features of the ongoing professionalization of personal training. Several factors differentiate professions from other occupations (Abbott 1988; Caplow 1954; Larson 1977; Pavalko 1971; Wilensky 1964). First, a profession is typically defined by mastery of a distinct body of abstract knowledge, the techniques for application of that knowledge, and the course of training through which mastery is produced and tested. The emergence of various certifying bodies and training programs for personal trainers is significant in the establishment of a purportedly objective measure of skill and thus professional credibility, even in the absence of external regulation. Second, professions are character-ized by normative codes that place service before self-interest and tend to justify the prestige of the profession by reference to a larger social need or value. Such professional ideology is written into codes of ethics, such as the one devised by IDEA in 1988 and updated in 1997 (Davis and Davis 1997: 2). Third, in comparison with other occupations, professions have a relatively high level of autonomy, in that professionals tend to regulate themselves. The development of IDEA and ACE referral services is one example of internal regulation and monitoring of the quality of service and qualifications.[14]

Certifications, codes of ethics, the internal regulation of occupational standards, and the cultivation of an overall professional identity have been promoted by occupational organizations such as ACE and IDEA as strategies to improve personal trainers' levels of remuneration and possibilities for career advancement, as well as to improve public confidence in the expertise of trainers, all of which are key elements in the construction of personal training as a mass-market, middle-class service. Certifications, however, are a necessary but not sufficient form of capital in the construction of profes-sional credibility and the pursuit of occupational success as a personal trainer.

CREDIBILITY AND CAPITAL

Organizations such as ACE and IDEA, in conjunction with occupational texts (many produced by these organizations, such as *IPT*), are central to the standardization and dissemination of a professionalized occupational identity, associated with a particular code of conduct, and a set of work practices and strategies that serve as "marks of distinction" (Bourdieu 1993: 117) setting personal trainers apart from, and above, other fitness service workers. Despite claims to professional status, however, a fundamental aspect of personal training is the need to recruit and retain clients. The entrepreneurial aspects of the occupation are made clear in *IPT*, in which articles consider four major issues: the technical skills and specialized knowledge utilized in designing the service; the question of legitimacy and credibility in determining relative positions of status within the occupation (linked but not reducible to qualifications based on technical skills and specialized knowledge); the entrepreneurial skills required to sell the service; and the interpersonal skills in delivering and customizing the service, particularly to address the problem of motivation. Clearly, these issues are interrelated, as in the following example:

> [C]onsider that in this business, selling knowledge is a given. The difference between trainers is service. . . . Outstanding service means that you: remember a client's particular health concern, and bring an article addressing that issue . . .; provide wake-up calls . . .; meet with a client and physician or physical therapist . . .; develop a strong resource support system for your clients . . .; take clients to look at and test exercise equipment that you recommend.
>
> (*IPT* 1992, 3 [September]: 2)

Selling, motivation and specialized knowledge intersect in the work roles of personal trainers.

Similarly, other *IPT* authors suggest service strategies such as sending clients birthday and thank-you cards, leaving motivational messages on clients' answering machines, or faxing clients workout instructions when they are away on business trips (e.g. *IPT* 1993, 4 [January]: 1–3; *IPT* 1992, 3 [July/August]: 6; *IPT* 2001, 12 [February]: 28–37). These client recruitment and retention strategies are not presented as expressions of an organic, professional care for others, but as instrumental means to making a living. Thus, in addition to those work roles and duties that affirm their professional identity, personal trainers must also perform forms of work – soliciting clients, setting fee rates, negotiating contracts, maintaining client loyalty – that undermine or contradict an ethic of service.

The credibility of personal trainers is therefore problematic, in large part due to the tension between claims to professional status and the instrumental, market-driven nature of the work. This is not only the case for personal trainers; the status of professionals more broadly is changing (Cohen *et al.* 2005; Dent and Whitehead 2002; Leicht and Fennell 1997, 2001). Increasingly, professionals are managed relative to the expectation that they achieve financial viability if not profits, as with the emphasis on billable hours for doctors and lawyers, and grant income for academic researchers. This undermines traditional claims to professional autonomy; complicates the service-oriented professional ethic with an instrumentalist ethic; and challenges the conventional assumption that professionals and entrepreneurs inhabit mutually exclusive spheres of knowledge and practice.

Furthermore, Foucault's work (1986, 1991) on the historical shifts in the modes and exercise of power would suggest that the authority of all professionals – like the authority of lifestyle media – must be understood within the contemporary governmental context, in which authorities work at a distance by indirectly managing the conduct of others (Burchell 1996). In such a context, professionals must find ways to influence, instruct and motivate (rather than intervene, dictate and punish): tasks that call upon forms of performative and emotional labor that are increasingly common in consumer culture (Bryman 2004; Hochschild 1983), but which contradict traditional notions of professional credibility because of their emphasis on appearance, demeanor and personality.

The tension between the traditional norms of professionals and an instrumental market-driven logic is thus not restricted to, but is particularly salient for, new or quasi-professional occupations such as personal training that cannot draw upon the conventional status conferred on established professions such as medicine and law in order to accomplish credibility and influence. Rather, credibility is constructed through the mobilization of different forms of capital. In the ideal constructions of the occupation and subjective experiences of the work, personal training involves three forms of capital in particular, emphasizing the resources that are at stake in the fitness field (Bourdieu and Wacquant 1992: 98): certifications; social networks; and embodied resources. These are introduced below before considering, in the following section, how they come into play in the personal trainer cultural intermediary roles of motivator and promoter.

Certifications from established organizations such as ACE and ACSM represent important investments in the credibility of a personal trainer. Examinations for personal training qualifications borrow from academic disciplines such as exercise physiology, anatomy, kinesiology and biomechanics, reinforcing claims to professional status through the mastery of an abstract body of knowledge. Certification as a personal trainer is not simply "proof" of occupational membership, but serves as evidence of professional expertise, which separates the personal trainers from the *poseurs*, and the high-priced, better-qualified trainers from the low-priced services of trainers with fewer certifications. This is made clear in the ways in which professional bodies such as ACE promote their particular certifications:

> The decision to pursue professional certification is an important step in being recognized as a competent practitioner in one's discipline. By becoming ACE certified, you will be better equipped to empower, motivate, challenge and retain your clients. . . . The ACE Personal Trainer Certification Curriculum is continually evaluated and updated to ensure that it includes the most current exercise science information and keeps today's fitness professionals ahead of the competition.
>
> (http://www.acefitness.org/getcertified/certification_pt.aspx
> [accessed January 2007])

In addition to legitimacy in the eyes of consumers, benefits such as improved market competition and occupational performance help to sell certifications to personal trainers. Certifications provide a measure of quality, and are thus linked not only to credibility (as a professional fitness service provider) but also to status (the stratification of the personal service market); as the editor of *IPT* writes: "quality is a market issue as well as a service issue" (*IPT* 1995, 6 [July/August]: 34).

Certification thus represents an important form of capital for the personal trainer, not only providing the technical knowledge to design and deliver fitness programs, but also serving as a positional good (Hirsch 1977) that allows trainers to locate themselves relative to other trainers as better qualified and more credible. The link between certification and credibility was noted by long-time trainers, such as Frank and Maureen, who have worked in the fitness industry since the mid-1980s as personal trainers. Frank is the director of personal training at a branch of Apple Fitness, a large chain of New York health clubs:

> Personal training has changed drastically. About 15 years ago, personal trainers were all muscle-bound, muscle heads. He knew how to train himself to get really big, but he was taking some kind of stuff, steroids or whatever. So people would look at him, and see what he looked like, and think he was great: "He must really know what he's doing." But he

didn't! Now, we go into the details, the exercise physiology, the anatomy, and we learn how to train individuals, not just training *yourself*, like 15 years ago.

Maureen is the director of recreation programs (including personal training) at a Manhattan YMCA; she began working as a personal trainer in the early 1980s at a training-only studio in New York, and later ran her own one-on-one business. Reflecting on her experiences, she recalls:

> In 1985, I started working as a weight room monitor in one of the New York gyms, and I was doing my MA at the same time [in physical education and fitness management]. There were *not* a lot of women working in fitness then. I'd see these women come in from schools, and they would last maybe six weeks. You'd see the "chunky monkey" boys just hover around them, waiting for them to do something wrong. I learned to be one of the boys. I learned the correct spotting procedures, so they took me seriously. . . . But the philosophy, the dogma, really turned me off. Basically, their philosophy was "train them 'til they puke."

Such observations as those of Frank and Maureen highlight how the increasing emphasis on certifications has entailed a rationalization (however partial and ambiguous) of personal training, in that technical knowledge supplements – if not altogether replaces – the charisma and physique of the trainer as the ostensible basis of expertise.

Furthermore, Maureen's comments suggest the gendered nature of the cultivation of expertise. In the "male preserves" (Dunning 1986) of weight rooms, a woman's outsider status means that she would not be taken seriously. Other female trainers mentioned similar issues in interviews with regard to gender and credibility. For example, June, a self-employed trainer, discussed gendered constraints in her work:

> I try not to get males as clients because I prefer training women. I don't think men take it seriously if you're a woman trainer. I'll be at a bar, hanging out and I'll be talking to some guy. I'll say, "I teach exercise." And they'll be like [*in a sexually suggestive tone*], "Oh, I'd like to work out with you." I'm cautious about that, and that's pretty typical for other female trainers I know.

The possession of specialized, technical knowledge provides women trainers with the basis for claiming competence and expertise, and combating gendered stereotypes and the trivialization of women's physical culture (MacNeill 1999). Bourdieu (1986: 248) makes this point more generally about academic qualifications, the legitimacy and cultural value of which are relatively independent of their bearer because of their standardization and rationalization; as such, certifications confer guaranteed value irrespective of the other forms of capital possessed by (or lacking in) the individual.

Despite their importance, the limitations of certifications as guarantors of credibility and tools of distinction are acknowledged by the very organizations promoting certifications. In the absence of mandatory qualifications, I asked Dean, a senior representative of ACE, what advantage certification offered to personal trainers. He responds: "The asset is credibility." Nevertheless, Dean emphasizes that certification establishes a "minimum competence" for personal training:

> Certification is not the be all and end all. . . . Personal training isn't just expertise in designing an exercise program; it's people skills. You want someone who is approachable, someone who can speak knowledgeably, who has good speaking skills, who can tactfully deal with issues, who has good problem-solving skills, and can deal with personalities.

As Dean's comment suggests, certification does not address those interpersonal skills that determine the quality of service. Certifications may facilitate a standardization of the service, but ultimately the accomplishment of credibility and achievement of occupational success rest on forms of capital – including interpersonal skills and performative flexibility – that are largely exempt from the rationalization of expertise. Despite the increasing standardization of qualifications, the nature of the work thus resists rationalization, which has the benefit of shielding personal trainers from the most alienating forms of top-down scripting, de-skilling, and external management directed at some forms of emotional labor and service work (Hochschild 1983; Leidner 1999; Smith Maguire 2001; Steinberg and Figart 1999; Wharton 1993, 1999).

In addition to certifications, the construction of credibility also involves social capital. *IPT* articles, for example, address the advantages of forming a referral network with links between personal trainers and doctors, nutritionists and physical therapists. Such social networks allow personal trainers to benefit from the more established credibility of other health and fitness occupations. The author of one such article suggests:

Being associated with a physician instantly provided my company with credibility. . . . If you want to work with the medical community, however, you must have the appropriate knowledge base. In my company, contacts with physicians are handled by a trainer who is a kinesiologist. You must be able to speak the physician's language to establish credibility.

(*IPT* 1992, 3 [July/August]: 6)

Thus, capital in the form of academic qualifications stratifies trainers within the same social network: the kinesiologist personal trainer is deemed to be more professional than his or her colleagues. Fluency in the scientific vocabulary of medical practitioners reproduces the exclusivity of health professions, legitimates fitness as a scientific domain (MacNeill 1999: 218–19), and provides personal trainers with authority in the eyes both of consumers and of other health professionals.

Establishing a social network with health care providers helps to legitimate personal training's connotations of professionalism; it also offers the possibility of following the referral structure of health care provision. The editor of *IPT* writes:

Since most trainers firmly believe in exercise as preventive medicine, they want to have clients referred to them by physicians (which would coincidentally supply a client base) and/or to have insurance companies reimburse trainer services (which would eliminate the possibility of clients saying they can't afford training).

(*IPT* 1995, 6 [July/August]: 28)

Referrals from health professionals thus offer a more stable income, and absolve the trainer of the need to be an entrepreneur, thereby reinforcing the professionalization of the occupation. However, the goal of entering a referral network is in part blocked by competition from within the health field: the need to sell one's services separates the personal trainer from the physical therapist, who has already cornered the market in prescribed personal exercise.

The social capital of networks is also cultivated through the pursuit of a prestigious clientele. Famous clients, for example, elevate the value of a personal trainer; a celebrity endorsement signals the trainer's distinction relative to other equally fit, qualified and enthusiastic trainers. For Dom, a personal trainer and the owner of Areté, an elite health club with celebrity clientele, the relationship between certification and credibility is not clear-cut:

I think certifications are pretty much bullshit. . . . We have a pretty malleable set of requirements. If they have an academic background, it's got
to be grounded in practical experience. If they've got a practical background, then it needs to be backed up with some academic experience.
But that's supplemented by two or three very important aspects of
the person. One, they've got to have a sense of humor. Two, they've got
to want to teach. That's what we primarily do. And three, this has to be
their career. They're not actors, who are just "doing this."

Dom has a vested interest in dismissing standard certifications; he is selling
an expensive and exclusive service to affluent and influential clients, who
demand not standard qualifications, but exceptional credentials. Mediated
by his social capital, Dom's construction of credibility involves downplaying
standard certifications while privileging a professional ethic and a particular
personality (interpersonal skills, and a commitment to fitness as pedagogy
and a career).

The social capital of clientele is not reserved for celebrity trainers such as
Dom. Occupational success rests on client recruitment and retention and
thus the maintenance of an active network of clients is fundamental to the
work of all personal trainers. As such, interpersonal skills are emphasized
repeatedly in *IPT* with regard to the requirements for occupational success.
For example:

As a personal trainer, your ability to establish rapport with others is
essential if you're to facilitate a working relationship that maximizes
your effectiveness and your client's productivity. Lack of this ability will
eventually hinder your business, regardless of your knowledge and
teaching skills.

(*IPT* 1993, 4 [October]: 1)

Similarly in interviews, personal trainers remarked on the importance of a
particular kind of personality: someone who is extroverted and enthusiastic,
enjoys talking to and helping people, and in general is a "people person,"
echoing the advertising associates' construction of the "outgoing" personality
as the ideal fitness magazine reader.

For example, Olivia is a founding member of the Canadian Personal
Trainer Network and has been involved in the training of personal trainers
for over ten years. In addition to knowledge of exercise and anatomy, Olivia
suggests that trainers require an (innate) attitude:

If you care about people as well as can be enthusiastic about what you do: if that energy, that enthusiasm is there, then you're halfway there. That is when you come to the courses, the teachable material . . . it is not easy, but you just have to memorize and go through it. . . . Of course they still have to get through the certification, but if people come in with such an attitude – friendly people and they care, they love it – then they're halfway there.

Technical knowledge, like the equipment at the health club, is a necessary but not sufficient resource in fitness market competition; like the clubs that have increasingly focused on décor and personality to attract and retain members, the personal trainer requires interpersonal skills to achieve a stable client network (and with it, a more secure occupational status). The work of personal training thus involves not only the training *per se*, but also the work of cultivating and displaying an appropriate, "fit" persona.

The ACE personal training manual explicitly links credibility and professionalism to affective resources: empathy, warmth, and genuineness. Being "genuine," however, is a reference not to being faithful to one's authentic feelings, but to cultivating an authentic-seeming persona:

> *Genuineness* can be defined as authenticity or being honest and open without putting up a front or façade. It is a state in which the helper's words and actions are congruent. . . . Genuineness is the ability to relate to people without hiding behind a clipboard or a white coat. It is not necessarily being self-revealing, but rather being committed to a responsible honesty with others.
>
> (Sudy 1991: 375)

Like sales representatives and flight attendants, personal trainers are coached in the (paradoxical) cultivation of authenticity, in which the service provider's sincerity and enthusiasm are testaments to the truth and value of what he or she is saying and selling (Hochschild 1983: 24). Genuineness is a question of performance, and the convincing management of verbal and body language in the delivery of the service. It is not that personal training is a form of charlatanism, but that success as a personal trainer requires the ability to cultivate an appropriate presentation of self, which conveys the desire to do a good job and a belief in fitness as a mode of self-work.

Thus, although certifications and social networks are forms of capital that explicitly reference traditional notions of professional credibility – be it in the form of specialized personal training knowledge, or connections to the specialized knowledge of other health professionals – they are also dependent on other, embodied forms of capital: "long-lasting dispositions of the mind and body" (Bourdieu 1986: 243) including a "fit" personality, performance and appearance. Such forms of embodied capital are typical of the resources required for emotional labor: the ways in which workers manage their own feelings in order to create a specific bodily display (such as a welcoming, smiling persona) that will then evoke an appropriate emotional response in another person (Hochschild 1983). Indeed, the service provider's body type, appearance and communication abilities are often more important to a customer's feelings of satisfaction than traditional factors such as price (Solomon 1998). Furthermore, such forms of embodied capital are central to credibility for the governmental, therapeutic expert: the personal trainer's ability to exert interpersonal influence in the management and motivation of others requires that he or she acts and looks the part (cf. Goffman 1959; Hochschild 1983).

For example, Krista, a manager of a health club's personal training program, insists that credibility as a personal trainer requires a fit body:

> You have to be fit, because you have to look the part. You have to at least try to look the part. You have to show people that you work out, you have to show people that you like being in the club, you have to go in with a good attitude, you have to leave with a good attitude.

Possessing and investing in a fit physique are visual demonstrations of a commitment to health and fitness, and thus assets in constructing credibility. Despite Frank's perception of changes since the 1980s, noted earlier, the construction of credibility still rests to a large extent on the trainer's own physique, a theme to which the remainder of the chapter will repeatedly return: the fit body is mobilized as both a badge of authority, a motivational device, and a promotional object, serving to market the trainer's services.

In western cultures facing population-wide problems of overweight and obesity, the fit physique has a scarcity value that increases a personal trainer's overall exchange value. As such, personal trainers understandably exemplify the cultural concern with beauty as a form of capital (Baudrillard 1998) through their investments in physique, be they made through physical exercise or other modes of body work. According to an article in the lifestyle publication *New York*, for example, the clientele of Manhattan plastic surgeons includes a significant portion of personal trainers (20 per cent according to one doctor):

> Doctors say trainers are among the best candidates for liposuction –
> since usually they have good cardiovascular health, need the least fat
> extraction, and recover most quickly. And plastic surgeons love them as
> clients, since they're the most likely to maintain their bodies.
>
> (Colman 2000: 46)

This is not to suggest that all personal trainers exemplify the tight and toned fit physique. The same logic of embodied capital and credibility creates a market value for the less-than-perfect body: personal trainers who do not match the "fitness look" can create niche markets for themselves by virtue of their embodied credentials, which help to convince clients that they are "normal" and thus credible (Higginbottom 2006). For most personal trainers, however, being fit is synonymous with being successful.

The emphasis on embodied capital exists at the awkward intersection of the different aspects of personal training work. On the one hand, physique and a particular attitude make the trainer's expert knowledge more market-able, helping to recruit and retain clients. On the other hand, an overt emphasis on physique undermines claims to professional credibility. As an *IPT* article suggests:

> Present yourself as a professional, not as a "meathead" with bulging
> biceps or a "bimbo" with a tight bottom. You want to make clients feel
> comfortable, not intimidated. This doesn't mean you can't have a good
> body – just that you stress the knowledge that gave you this result.
>
> (IPT 1994, 5 [October]: 8)

Personal trainers are placed in a double bind: an overt emphasis on their body shape will undermine their professionalism by perpetuating unhealthy body attitudes and contradicting traditional professional criteria such as cer-tifications; but at the same time, their occupational credibility is literally embodied, and thus must be self-consciously performed in order to achieve the desired effect. Embodied capital thus takes the form of not only a fit physique, an enthusiasm about fitness, and an interest in caring for others, but also a promotional subjectivity (Wernick 1991: 193): an awareness of the continual need to produce oneself for competitive exchange. Part of the "fit" personality – that is, what "fits" a personality for personal training work – is a promotional disposition, the capacity to appear and perform appropriately in order to convince people of one's credibility, and sell one's services.

In summary, the cultivation of personal trainers' credibility involves the mobilization of a range of different forms of capital – the intellectual capital of certifications and technical expertise, the social capital and prestige of relationships with other health and fitness professionals and clients, and the embodied capital of a fit physique and a "fit" personality. As such, personal training is implicated in the valorization of particular forms of capital for field participants more generally; the field-specific value of a tight and toned physique, for example, is standardized and institutionalized in the occupational texts and opinions of practitioners, thereby encouraging in clients an investment in their own physical capital. Reflecting their quasi-professional role as fitness experts, the performative and emotional labor elements of their service work, and the larger context of governmental authority, credibility for personal trainers is not ascribed but must be achieved through a process that is inseparable from notions of status and stratification. What distinguishes personal trainers as credible also ranks them relative to their competitors.

The case of personal trainers chimes with Bourdieu's account of the authority of cultural field producers:

> [T]he more [a] field is capable of functioning as a field of competition for cultural legitimacy, the more individual production must be oriented towards the search for culturally pertinent features endowed with value in the field's own economy. This confers . . . cultural value on the producers by endowing them with marks of distinction (a speciality, a manner, a style) recognized as such within the historically available cultural taxonomies.
>
> (Bourdieu 1993: 117)

The authority and credibility of cultural field producers and therapeutic experts in contemporary consumer culture are as much a matter of performance and disposition, as of technical skill and specialized knowledge. Personal trainers must negotiate the tension between their different resources: investing in social and embodied capital can both reinforce their intellectual capital in the production of authority, and undermine their claims to professional status. These forms of capital intersect and interact in the work of personal trainers as cultural intermediaries.

CULTURAL INTERMEDIARIES AND THE PROBLEMS OF FITNESS

Personal trainers embody the fitness lifestyle; they provide consumers with a primary "public face" for, and point of entry into, the fitness field; the quality of their services is utilized as a principal means of competition between health clubs; their own physical development is mobilized as a sign of credibility; their clients are educated in both the practices of the fit body and its exchange value; their services blur the line between professional authority and entrepreneurial instrumentality: in these respects and more, personal trainers provide an ideal case study of the work of cultural intermediaries (Bourdieu 1984; du Gay and Pryke 2002; Featherstone 1991; Negus 2002; Nixon and du Gay 2002). Cultural intermediaries perform the "relational work" (du Gay 2004: 100 [citing Cochoy, "On the captation of publics", 2003]) that takes place between the spheres of consumption and production. Personal trainers do not simply stand between the consumer and the fitness field; they actively weave the two together through their own commitment to the field. They are thus a particular brand of service workers, involved in both the production of the fitness lifestyle and its consumption – for it is their own lifestyle that they are selling (Bourdieu 1984).

The central problem of the fitness field – as dictated by its commercial agenda and market logic – is its own reproduction, which requires both the enticement and retention of participants to particular nodes in the field, and the broader incorporation of participants into the field's web of consumption linking health clubs, fitness media and exercise goods and services. Thus, the commercial nature of the fitness field is central to the way in which the service of personal training is constructed and experienced. As the following section explores, personal trainers address both of the field's needs through their dual roles as motivators and promoters: their work is centered around the motivation of clients to take up and maintain a fitness regime, while at the same time fulfilling an entrepreneurial role of promoting their personal training services, as well as the fitness site in which they work, and the broader fitness industry.

The problem of motivation

The problem of motivation cuts across the fitness field. As Chapters 3 and 4 have explored, health clubs are positioned as motivational spaces, in which amenities, décor and social ambience assist members in maintaining their participation; and fitness magazines and exercise manuals warn readers of the rates of fitness attrition and provide lessons in the means of self-discipline. Exercise manuals, for example, endorse personal trainers as a motivational device. Trainers' expertise makes them ideal fitness role models, and their added expense creates an intensified commitment to exercising: "Sagging motivation can often be propped up by a professional. Nothing will get the blood pumping like the thought of an $80-an-hour missed appointment fee" (Billings 1998: 77). Personal trainers are thus also shaped by the problem of motivation: charged with instructing and inspiring clients through a personalized service, their therapeutic expertise is framed as a matter of interpersonal influence.

Regarding the problem of motivation, what differs between the education of consumers in fitness magazines and manuals, and that of personal trainers in their occupational texts, is that, for trainers, motivation is both a job task and an occupational responsibility, as the ACE manual makes clear:

> Rather than simply placing the blame for non-adherence on the client, the personal trainer must view motivation as a joint responsibility shared with the client. . . . Because motivating the client is one of the trainer's most important and most difficult responsibilities, the ability to address the motivational needs of the client in an ongoing, effective fashion may well be the single largest measure of a trainer's success.
>
> (Sudy 1991: 363)

The professional legitimacy of personal trainers is inextricably linked to the problem of motivation: helping clients to maintain their commitment to physical fitness is central to the occupation's service ethic and civic virtue. The "solutions" to the problem of motivation that arise in the occupational texts and reflections of practitioners and clients suggest that success as a motivator ultimately rests less on the specialized knowledge and rationalized skills afforded through certifications, and more on forms of embodied capital: physique, interpersonal skills, and enthusiasm.

First, the personal trainer's physique is a key motivational tool. As June, the self-employed trainer, remarked: "You should look at a trainer and say, 'That's the body I want.'" Embodied capital in the form of a fit physique is not only important to the cultivation of credibility as a fitness expert; it is also a means of motivation (a reminder to the client of the end goal) as well as enticement (a billboard that attracts new clients). Kerry, for example, regards her body as central to her capacity as a personal trainer to motivate clients:

If I let myself go, everybody thinks they can let themselves go. So it's an image. It's an image because if I don't show them that I can do this, then what makes them think they can do it? I practice what I preach . . . well, most of the time. It's a lot easier talking about it than doing it! [*Laughs.*]

Even fitness experts have difficulty adhering to a fit lifestyle at all times. Nevertheless, Kerry's motivation lies in the notion that being fit is part of her professional credibility and service ethic: working out benefits Kerry as well as the client. Typical of the governmental therapeutic expert who influences and mobilizes rather than directly intervenes, personal trainers lead by example – here, in the case of having and working on a fit physique.

The emphasis on physique implies a mandatory investment in physical capital for the personal trainer. Maureen makes clear that this can pose obstacles to those who regard personal training as a long-term career:

I knew I was getting to the end of working only as a personal trainer when I was no longer willing to maintain my own looks in order to maintain my business. I still train a few clients, because I can draw on my experience, my education. I have a lot to offer. But most trainers have to rely on their body, their appearance, to get clients.

The implicit obligation of taking up a particular lifestyle organized around the maintenance of a fit physique places constraints on personal trainers (cf. McFall 2004). Despite Maureen's negotiation of such constraints by mobilizing different forms of capital (education and experience), the personal trainer's body remains a promotional object, advertising the trainer's embodied capital. For Maureen, the body is a promotional object to be overcome; for Kerry, it is to be relied upon.

The second motivational tool is interpersonal flexibility. The ability to modulate one's performance to suit individual clients is a significant skill as a personal trainer. Frank, for example, refers to his "fitness psychic skills" that help him to manage clients' egos as well as bodies:

You are making sure that the training is being done correctly. . . . But you also have to know when to approach them, and when *not* to approach them. You don't walk up to them and say, "You're doing that wrong." You have to approach them, with [*in friendly voice*] "Hi. My name is so-and-so. I'm a fitness trainer here. If you have any questions, you can always ask me. What exercise are you doing today?" And then you come back to them later, when they're *not* doing the exercise, and that's when you get to talk to them. Nobody likes to be told if they're doing something wrong. They get very aggressive. What makes you ashamed is what makes you mad.

Such modulation of emotional labor on a case-by-case basis requires job autonomy for the personal trainer; top-down management of service interactions (through scripts and strict procedures) leads to inauthentic service. Occupational texts such as *IPT* offer articles and scenarios on the issue of motivation, in an attempt to impart the skills of emotional management. However, the mutability of the trainer–client service interaction means that formulaic scripts are impossible for management to impose (except perhaps in the first "fitness assessment" meeting). Formulas – if they are imposed – are reserved for the exercise programs, and the service of motivation is largely left to the trainer's discretion. The "problem" of emotional labor arises not from the management of emotions *per se* – which is part of everyday life – but from the regulation and bureaucratization of emotional management. Thus, at least in terms of interpersonal interaction in the role of motivator, personal trainers' emotional labor is conducive to job autonomy and satisfaction (Leidner 1999; Smith Maguire 2001; Steinberg and Figart 1999; Wharton 1993, 1999).

Rob works at a training-only studio. Like Frank, his description of his work as a personal trainer foregrounds the importance of managing people's emotions in order to motivate them to work out:

> You become their coach. You are their teacher. You become their coach, their shrink, and their slave driver [*laughs*]. You have to stay on top of them. If they come in, and they're whining that they're tired and don't want to work out, you have to know how to cope with that. You're dealing with people's personalities. They come in, they've had a bad day, their boss yelled at them, and they don't want to work out. You have to know what to do to make sure they have a good workout. I'm their mentor. I'm Yoda! [*Laughs.*] I tell them, "You want to be a Jedi? You have to listen to Yoda."

Motivating clients thus involves a range of performative modes. This requires particular skills to create an impression of genuineness and authenticity, and a relatively high degree of autonomy in order to work effectively with the clients' emotions.

In his cataloguing of motivational personae, Rob's inclusion of "slave driver" is not unusual. Indeed, the majority of personal trainers interviewed mentioned a rendition of this persona, which they used with some of their clients. For example, Krista recalled how one of her clients gleefully called her "Hitler," and Mark referred to training clients as "putting them to torture":

> That's what they pay for. I'll train my clients till they are sore, they can't walk the next day. But they like that. Because then they feel like they've worked hard. There's a lot of people, they want to feel a soreness or else they feel like they haven't worked hard enough.

Soreness provides a tangible result, and the pleasure of both virtuous discipline and engaged embodiment – themes also mobilized as motivational devices in the fitness magazines and exercise manuals.

More generally, Kerry suggests that the disciplinarian mode of motivation is effective even without an overt "drill sergeant" performance:

> I push you. I can stand behind you, not even tell you what to do, and you're going to work three times harder. It's me being there that pushes them, because it's like they want to prove something to me, saying "OK, yeah, I can do this." They think, "If you say I can do it, I can do it. I'm going to prove it to you." That's where my mind games come in, because sometimes I won't even watch them. I'll turn my back on them and they'll *still* do it.

Personal trainers exemplify the governmental mode of authority, by acting on the attitudes of clients rather than directly coercing physical exercise. This is not to suggest that a more interventionist mode of disciplinary power disappears in governmental social orders (Foucault 1991: 102); rather, the disciplinary mode of power is reconfigured and held in abeyance. Discipline can then be targeted at those who fail to enact their self-management in an appropriate fashion; or, as Kerry's comments suggest, it can be solicited by those for whom the burden of self-management gives rise to an ambivalent nostalgia for discipline.

This point is made by Meredith, a fitness consumer in her 30s who works in publishing:

I think that there's something good about the enthusiasm that comes from the trainer. Because I can drum up some enthusiasm, but I don't actually really like gyms all that much. So I think that it's partially a camaraderie thing. Because then it becomes a social activity as opposed to a duty that I have to do. Because then, to me, it shifts the responsibility of, "OK, I've got to do this, and I've got to do that," and it makes it enjoyable.

Thus, whether in the guise of the drill sergeant or some other motivational persona, the personal trainer offers to the client the possibility of deferring or displacing some of the responsibility for accomplishing the exercise, and for self-responsibility more broadly. Meredith's comments also bring to light the third motivational tool, closely linked to interpersonal flexibility: the personal trainer's energetic performance, which is offered to the client as a template of the appropriate attitude towards fitness.

However, as with the emphasis on maintaining a fit physique, the need to be upbeat at all times poses challenges and constraints for personal trainers. As Krista suggests:

You are always on the go and you've got to be exciting, you've got to be energized and you've got to show people that they can do it and you have to be working with them and, oh, by the end of six hours, "Hello! I can't do that any more!" You have to be supersonic all the time.

There is a blurring of embodied and social capital in the "supersonic" performance, which involves both a disposition that lends itself to the construction of an extroverted, animated persona, and "an unceasing effort at sociability" (Bourdieu 1986: 250) that forges connections to clients. The cultivation of credibility and the effective accomplishment of the role of motivator both require personal trainers to adopt an ongoing attitude of self-investment: work on one's physique, persona and affective relationships with clients is never done.

A personal trainer's emotional investment in the role of motivator is an occupational necessity and hazard. Feelings may be a resource to be used for social and occupational ends (Hochschild 1983: 55), but they are an exhaustible resource. Thus, personal trainers face the threat of burnout, as *IPT* articles make clear:

How can you serve your clients if you are not mentally, emotionally and physically prepared? People in our industry give and give and give and then give some more. We have to be positive and upbeat at all times. At the end of the day, we can be exhausted.

(IPT 2001, 12 [February]: 35)

To cultivate a convincing, genuine service persona, many personal trainers forgo surface acting (simply pretending to care for and listen to the client) and instead often rely on "deep acting" to cultivate empathy for the client whom they sincerely want to achieve a healthy lifestyle (cf. Goffman 1959; Hochschild 1983: 33). However, this then poses particular challenges to their claims for professional credibility. Personal trainers fulfill many of the same roles as other therapeutic experts – listening, counseling, and advising, providing support – but within the context of a fee-based, paid service relationship. Thus, a sincere interest in helping the client becomes entangled with the need to regard the client as an income source. A "fit" personality, deep acting strategies, and emotional investment in one's work may be occupational requirements, but they also leave the personal trainer vulnerable to emotional burnout.

According to Dean, the senior ACE representative, the risk of emotional exhaustion is mediated by different employment patterns, and by a particular disposition:

> Burnout is very easy. Imagine if you have seven clients that you see, one after another, every day for seven days in a row. Obviously, the opportunity for burnout is high, so a lot of them work part-time. For example, some will work as group exercise instructors. But I also notice that a lot of them are what I call "blue." They have a health care worker mentality. They wouldn't be doing this if they weren't interested in helping people.

Similarly, June links the energetic performance to a therapeutic professional service ethic in her criteria for success as a personal trainer:

> It's how you look, it's enthusiasm, how aware you are, and what you know. That all comes across. It has a lot to do with your spirit. It's something that lends itself to wanting to train in the first place; you can't hate talking, advising, teaching, being gentle, dealing with people.

The risk of emotional exhaustion is balanced against not only the monetary rewards of occupational success, but also the satisfaction arising from a deep-seated disposition towards helping others. Such a "helping" disposition, however, is a double-edged sword: it may facilitate the cultivation of credibility and an effective performance as a therapeutic expert, but it also increases the risk of emotional burnout, because it is placed in the paid service of the client (and, for the majority of trainers, the health club).

The risk of emotional exhaustion is thus shaped by the conditions of employment and the general tension between the professional and entrepreneurial aspects of personal training. No matter how sincere the helping disposition, it is the instrumentalization of the disposition as the means to sell the trainer's services that poses the risk of emotional alienation. This is all the more pressing an issue with the move of lower-status, sales-driven health clubs to include personal training as a service, which results in lower-status, sales-driven personal training. Trainers in such clubs are paid less, and tend to have less intellectual capital (with fewer, if any, certifications beyond the club's own "training" program) and less control over client appointments. In the absence of good pay and good working conditions, the quality of service declines, raising issues for the experience both of personal trainers, and of their clients. The "slowdown" of emotional labor (a brief smile, a half-hearted hello) is a form of self-protection for the worker against emotional exhaustion, and a type of resistance against poor working conditions (Hochschild 1983: 126–8); it is also an obstacle to those clients who look to personal trainers as a source of motivation and find them wanting.

In summary, the problem of motivation is twofold for personal trainers. On the one hand, motivation is a job task and thus a technical matter of the unceasing investment in particular modes of appearance, performance, and attitude in order to effectively motivate clients. On the other hand, motivating clients is a professional responsibility and an issue of negotiating between a service ethic mentality and the conditions of employment. Claims to professional status are reinforced through the helping disposition invoked by occupational representatives, practitioners and texts, but at the same time undermined by the entrepreneurial aspects of the personal trainer's work: the need to sell one's services, and the goods and services of the fitness industry more generally. In short, the problem of motivation runs up against the problem of promotion.

The problem of promotion

The problem of promotion bears upon personal trainers in three ways. First, the commercial nature of the service means that personal trainers must find ways to promote themselves if they are to recruit and retain clients. Second, for the majority of personal trainers employed by health clubs, the work of training also includes being a frontline service worker, representing and promoting the employer. Finally, as a corps of professional fitness producers, personal trainers are also implicated in the promotion of the goods and services of the fitness industry more generally.

The strategic device in each of these three modes of promotion is the personal trainer's own investment in the fitness field. As is the case for cultural intermediaries more generally, personal lives, bodies, attitudes, and tastes are crucial occupational resources. Personal lifestyle bestows legitimacy not only on the cultural intermediary's products, but also on his or her authority as an arbiter of taste and lifestyle: for example, the personal styles of fashion designers are mobilized to add symbolic value to their clothing designs (Rocamora 2002: 350); the clothing choices of sales assistants are displayed as symbols of their "fashion competency" (Pettinger 2004: 179); and the cosmopolitan lifestyles of advertising creatives are used to define their occupational identity (McFall 2004). The physical bodies and private lives of personal trainers – their exercise and diet habits, especially – are central to their cultivation of professional credibility, motivation of clients, and promotion of their services and the commercial fitness industry more generally.

To address the first promotional problem of recruiting clients, personal trainers rely heavily on their bodies. Mark makes this point explicitly when asked why being fit is important for his work as a personal trainer: "A lot of it is a form of self-advertising. If people look at you and say, 'Oh, well he can do this, he obviously knows what he's doing.' " Similarly, Shane is a personal trainer and program director at a health club; he comments on the role of physique in attracting clients:

> Exposure on the floor as an exercise trainer is one of the best ways to get a client without making a heavy sell. And when you work out here during your time off, people are looking at you, seeing what kind of body you have. People look really different out of uniform, and so if you're working out in a tank top, and you're really working and getting sweaty, people see that you have a good body. So they put one and one together [and hire you].

Thus, a personal trainer's physique is not the only promotional resource in question. Trainers must also be conspicuous consumers of the fitness lifestyle, working out during non-paid time to demonstrate their credibility, and display their physical capital (all the better displayed because trainers are not required to wear the standard health club uniform during their non-paid time). Like cultural intermediaries more generally, personal trainers thus disrupt notions of a distinct boundary between work and leisure (Nixon and Crewe 2004: 131; McFall 2004: 74): exercising during one's "free" time is an investment in physical development; doing so in the "work" setting of the health club is a means of target-marketing one's services.

If professional credibility and entrepreneurial success rest on physique, then working out is an obligation for personal trainers – fitness becomes a mandatory lifestyle, and not simply a deep-seated disposition towards physical activity. In fact, the promotional benefits of working out during non-paid time have not been lost on the health clubs, some of which require their personal trainers to work out at the club for a certain number of hours per week, in addition to their client hours. This mandatory fit lifestyle helps trainers to distinguish themselves from other fitness instruction services, from other trainers who are competing for the same clients, and from the clients themselves who supposedly look to trainers' general lifestyle as an indicator of their reliability and authority. A personal trainer may regard the occupational necessity of working out during non-paid hours as a negative encroachment of work into leisure time, but may also experience it as an advantage of his or her chosen occupation, and an opportunity to extract added value from one's leisure pursuits.

The second promotional problem – representing the health club and retaining health club members – also draws heavily on the personal trainer's embodied capital, with the emphasis placed more on a "fit" personality than a fit body. For example, *IPT* articles counsel personal trainers (many of whom own, or hope to own, training studios and businesses) in the market value of attitude:

> As a personal trainer, you are the most valuable commodity a client or a health club will ever see. In a club setting, the personal trainer is the one who can help close a sale with a guest or who will leave a new member with a very positive attitude about the club's member service program.
>
> (*IPT* 1996, 7 [October]: 33)

As was discussed in Chapter 3, the symbolic value of health clubs is largely dependent on the personality of the staff, foremost of which are the personal trainers. As with the expansion of the occupation in the early 1990s, personal training remains a key strategy for health clubs' market competitiveness: personal trainers offer instruction, efficiency, status, and the added value of customized service, thereby addressing a variety of obstacles to the recruitment and retention of health club members.

According to Kimberly, the head of personal training for the Apple Fitness chain of health clubs, personal trainers are instrumental in the retention of club members:

> A personal trainer can help a lot. And if members are happier, and feel more comfortable, they're more likely to stay members. You don't want them feeling frustrated because they don't know how to use some piece of equipment, and can't find anyone to help them, so they feel confused and ignored.

Like other frontline service workers, personal trainers occupy a "boundary-spanning" position that combines the emotional labor roles of customer service and company representation (Wharton 1993, 1999). Unlike in their role as motivators, which involves interpersonal flexibility, this promotional dimension of the work presents personal trainers with an explicit challenge to their claims to professional status, in that job autonomy is constrained by the demand from the employer (the health club) for compliance to a company image. Furthermore, as income generators for health clubs, personal trainers often find themselves subject to targets: failure to sell a sufficient number of training sessions can result in termination, highlighting the tenuousness of the professional autonomy of trainers.

Finally, the third promotional problem – advocating for the fitness industry – utilizes the trainer's embodied capital as an endorsement of a whole web of related goods and services. The role of personal trainers as brokers has not gone unnoticed in the fitness industry, leaders of which credit personal trainers with facilitating sales of home exercise equipment (Sporting Goods Manufacturers Association 2000: 22). IDEA's annual convention for fitness professionals includes a "fitness expo" by equipment manufacturers, which is presented as yet another aspect of trainers' continuing education – not as exercise instructors, but as consumer advisors. Some companies will provide trainers with discounts or free products in return for referrals, but in most cases, the broker role is largely an unpaid part of the service work of personal trainers.

Trainers exert influence on clients' purchasing behavior both implicitly – through their credibility as fitness producers and personal choices of equipment – and explicitly, through recommendations and endorsements of the fitness industry's other goods and services, such as apparel, diet and exercise books, massage therapy sessions, and nutritional supplements. For example, Dom, the owner of the elite health club mentioned above, remarks:

> It's very seductive being a trainer. You give out opinions on things you're not qualified to be giving out opinions on. Because you've had a good run with a client, they'll trust you and so of course they're going to ask you questions and assume you know what you're talking about.

More generally, an IDEA survey of its personal trainer members found that 77 per cent of trainers recommended or discussed sports and exercise equipment with their clients. In addition, 70 per cent felt that their suggestions were acted on most of the time;[15] whether correct or not, it suggests the level of self-belief and self-promotion apparent in the occupation.

Given their position as therapeutic experts, personal trainers must monitor the conflict between such forms of promotion and their claims to professionalism. This tension is manifest in the IDEA code of ethics,[16] the first principle of which is "always be guided by the best interests of the client":

a   Remember that a personal trainer's primary responsibility is to the client's safety, health and welfare; never compromise this responsibility for your own self-interest, personal advantage or monetary gain.
b   Recommend products or services only if they will benefit the client's health and well-being, not because they will benefit you financially or occupationally.
c   If recommending products or services will result in financial gain for you or your employer, be aware that disclosure to the client may be appropriate.
d   Base the number of training sessions on the client's needs, not your financial requirements.

It is telling that all three promotional modes are referenced in the code of ethics: recommendations of training sessions, products and services (including health club membership) must be weighed against the client's best interests. The underlying assumption is that the client's best interests and the trainer's self-interest are not necessarily congruent.

Furthermore, the trainer's self-interest is itself ambivalent, in that promotion can impede effective motivation. Mark, for example, reflects on this conflict:

> It kind of messes with the rapport with the client. It is hard to be a sales person and a friend at the same time, because they don't know if you are going to be sincere. They'll think, "Are you selling because I need personal training, or because you need to sell the package?"

Similar observations were made by Fiona, an academic in her early 30s. After receiving 10 personal training sessions as a birthday gift, Fiona found that she developed an awkward relationship with the trainer, which was part professional and part personal:

> So after the ten sessions were up, it was sort of like breaking up with the trainer, that whole problem of, "Oh my God, what am I going to say? If I say I don't want to do this any more, is he going to feel bad?" I mean, it was horrible. So I said, all right, I'll keep doing this, once a week. And then it got to twice a week. I mean, it was *crazy*. It *really* wasn't a friendship. That's what was so weird about it. It was certainly closer than the person who cuts your hair, you know, who many people become friendly with, that kind of a service person. It was definitely more than that. But it was very hard to know because you always had this feeling: how much of this is a constant sales pitch, or how much are they being friends with you because they want your business?

The recurring conflicts between promotionalism and professionalism, reflected in occupational texts as well as the accounts of practitioners and clients, suggest that the problem of selling is not peripheral but fundamental to the development of an occupational disposition (du Gay 2004). This disposition is captured in the following three examples.

In an *IPT* article on "the ethics of selling products," personal trainers are reminded of the code of ethics and their pledge to put the client's interest ahead of their own financial gain. Nonetheless:

> In addition to being fitness professionals dedicated to helping individuals lead healthier lives, many of us are also small-business owners.

We're always looking for better ways to serve our clients, but we want to grow our businesses as well. . . . Most trainers would agree that there is a distinct difference between selling yourself and selling products.

(*IPT* 2000, 11 [October]: 26)

After reviewing five different scenarios (including selling no products at all, and selling as many products as possible), the author concludes, "After considering all of these factors, you are the one who has to feel comfortable with the idea of selling products" (*IPT* 2000, 11 [October]: 33).

In the same way, another *IPT* article blurs the work of selling with personal belief:

The word "sales" has a bad reputation in the fitness industry. However, selling personal training is something that many of you are doing daily without even knowing it! Most of you truly love your work. You represent a healthy lifestyle, a fit mind and body, and a positive self-image. Selling often becomes second nature when you present the concept of personal training to someone else. Your own personal commitment generates enthusiasm and sparks an interest.

(*IPT* 1993, 4 [June]: 1)

In commenting on how personal training services are sold, Tony – a general manager of a health club – similarly suggests how a trainer's personal lifestyle resolves the problem of selling:

Over the last five years, we have asked trainers to be sales people. But you have to explain to them that they're selling their services, their skills. Many of them are uncomfortable when you first suggest it, because they have this image of selling as selling used cars. You have to explain to them that they're selling health and fitness. You're selling something you believe in.

The significant lesson for personal trainers is not whether they should or should not sell products, but that trainers can – and should – sell themselves and their personal attitudes towards fitness. The resolution to the tension between the professional and entrepreneurial aspects of the work thus lies in a vocational disposition (Weber 1946): selling what you believe in. Nevertheless, the problem of selling intensifies as the promotional chain lengthens: recruiting clients is largely regarded as an unavoidable (if awkward) aspect of the occupation, whereas marketing health clubs and, even more so, endorsing fitness goods explicitly pitches an instrumental market logic against a professional concern with the client's well-being, testing the robustness of the vocational disposition.

In his observations on cultural intermediaries, Bourdieu (1984: 359–71) raises two issues of particular interest for an understanding of personal training: the tension between promotionalism and professionalism, and the importance of an endorsed vocational disposition. First, cultural intermediaries – particularly those in the "new" professions associated with consumer lifestyles – have an ambivalent relationship to their occupational status, which is steeped in the therapeutic morality of the teaching and medical professions (the established middle class to whose status they aspire), while at the same time involving the entrepreneurial work of the shopkeeper (representative of the working class from which they work to distance themselves). This tension between professionalism and entrepreneurialism is embedded within the stock of capital required of the personal trainer: the intellectual capital of the health-care provider and the embodied capital and emotional labor of the service worker are both complementary and conflicting in the trainer's accomplishment of credibility.

Second, arising from this tension, cultural intermediaries are personally invested in their occupations. As such, Bourdieu (1984: 365) suggests that cultural intermediaries are ideal need merchants:

> sellers of symbolic goods and services who always sell themselves as models and as guarantors of the value of their products, and who sell so well because they believe in what they sell . . . [T]he honest, trustworthy vendor . . . deceives the customer only insofar as he deceives himself and is sincerely "sold" on the value of what he sells.

The apparent conflict between a professional ethic that places clients' interests first, and the self-interested, instrumental labor of the entrepreneur, is resolved through a personal belief in the field. Personal trainers are not simply service workers in the fitness field; their work is in the service of a cause in which they believe – selling is thus reconfigured as an altruistic calling.

The vocational disposition represents a further and fundamental form of embodied capital that draws upon and complements the trainer's physical capital and "fit" personality. Personal trainers not only enact a repertoire of emotional labor strategies in order to get the work done, but their belief in the fitness field is itself a tool for accomplishing interpersonal influence. Surface and deep acting are pragmatic strategies for delivering the service, but the more fundamental resource for personal trainers is a vocational interest in converting others to their fit way of life. Indeed, the conversion stories from sickly childhood to robust (and long-lived) manhood of Charles Atlas and Jack La Lanne, or from self-loathing teenager to empowered woman of Jane Fonda, suggest that the evangelical and the entrepreneurial are inseparable in the fitness producer.

Trainers are thus encouraged to identify wholly with their occupation, blurring their personal lifestyle and professional image. For example, an *IPT* article suggests:

> The first step toward capitalizing on the potential for referral success is to scrutinize your public persona and image. You communicate your energy and intentions through your demeanor, through your honest enthusiasm for helping others improve their lifestyles and reach their fitness goals, and through the activities you pursue to develop yourself personally and professionally. When people meet you, they should feel your competence, enthusiasm and values.
>
> (*IPT* 1994, 5 [November/December]: 33)

As the "honest vendors" (Bourdieu 1984; see also Zukin 2004) selling their own beliefs, personal trainers not only reconcile but also accomplish both facets of the work: personal belief in the fitness lifestyle is not only a sign of professional dedication, but also a means for cultivating referrals from clients (thereby decreasing the pressure on selling their services). The trainer is encouraged to wholly identify with the professional role, scrutinizing his or her personal life as an occupational resource, thus interconnecting personal lifestyle with professionalism, and blurring the lines between work and non-work time.

In similar fashion, and in marked contrast to the consumer exercise manuals that attempt to *convince* readers of the benefits of exercise, the ACE manual addresses a community of the converted:

> Those of us working in exercise or physical fitness find physical activity to be an integral part of our lives. . . . For such persons, regular exercise remains a high priority regardless of what life may bring. Unfortunately, only a relatively small percentage of people in the US and other Western countries share this attitude. While many acknowledge the importance

of physical activity to health and well-being, surprisingly few are regularly active enough to receive significant health benefits.

(Sudy 1991: 359)

The role of personal trainers, as constructed for them in their occupational texts and professional socialization, is inherently missionary: they are to help reshape those for whom daily exercise seems an unattainable – even unthinkable – goal, thereby justifying an instrumental promotional disposition and reinforcing a vocational disposition through reference to larger social problems (an overweight and inactive population) and ideals (individual responsibility for health and self-care).

Reviewing the problem of promotion, it becomes clear that trainers are not only implicated in the endorsement and marketing of their services, health clubs and the wider fitness industry. In their work, personal trainers position themselves as role models, their personal way of life offered as a recommended template for clients. They are thus promoters in a fourth sense as well: personal trainers are advocates for the fitness field and its associated lifestyle, making them consummate fitness producers and consumers.

The perfect field participant

Cultural intermediaries are, for Bourdieu, the "perfect consumers" (1984: 371; see also Featherstone 1991: 91): not only involved in the production of cultural goods and lifestyles, cultural intermediaries are also both their most committed consumers, for they are selling their own tastes and ways of life, and their most ardent advocates, for the legitimation of such tastes and ways of life is also the legitimation of their class position. Personal trainers can thus be understood as the perfect fitness field participants. They are ideal producers and consumers of the fitness field because they are selling their own lifestyle. The professionalization of personal training is thus not only a question of career stability and the cultivation of credibility; it is part of a larger cultural process of making legitimate the anxieties, aspirations, tastes, and lifestyles of the post-industrial middle class, and lending to them an aura of distinction and objective cultural value.

Through their professional socialization, personal trainers internalize the structures of the fitness field, acquiring a feel for the fitness "game":

The habitus as the feel for the game is the social game embodied and turned into second nature. Nothing is simultaneously freer and more constrained than the action of a good player. . . . [T]he constraints and demands of the game . . . impose themselves on those people – and those people alone – who, because they have a feel for the game, a feel, that is, for the immanent necessity of the game, are prepared to perceive them and carry them out.

(Bourdieu 1990: 63)

That is, the rules of a field, like the rules of a game, have the greatest consequences for those who recognize themselves and their social position in the game. Some participants have more "at stake" in the field, depending on their relative investment in the field's logic and capital. Personal trainers are the model fitness participant: their professional identity is at stake in the social recognition of fitness as a legitimate field of expertise. Occupational success requires developing fitness-specific capital – a fit physique and persona – but also a "genuine" commitment to fitness as a way of life. In the blurring of personal and professional identities, personal trainers are encouraged to believe in what they are selling. The implication for personal trainers, and fitness field participants generally, is that the inscription of the field's structures – such that they become second nature – not only generates tastes for particular lifestyle activities, but also "fits" the body for specific kinds of interactions – in the case of the personal trainer, for service interactions (cf. Shilling 1993: 135). Personal trainers have an embodied feel for the service game and the means for gaining a competitive edge – to influence, attract and motivate others, one requires the cultivation of intellectual, social and embodied capital, of which a vocational disposition is fundamental.

The vocational disposition of personal trainers is central to the accomplishment of professional status in an occupation characterized by instrumental, entrepreneurial work. Beliefs in physical fitness as a key to quality of life, the value of an outgoing and caring persona, and the importance of participating in fitness activities and investing in physical capital in one's private, non-paid time are expressed and endorsed by both occupational texts and practitioners (if less problematically in the former than the latter). This vocational disposition mediates the challenges posed by the work of personal trainers – selling themselves, health clubs and the fitness industry, and the blurring of paid and non-paid time in their body work and lifestyle choices – to notions of a professional service ethic, occupational autonomy, and rationalized intellectual capital. Personal trainers are encouraged to view their work as promoters – and especially the problem of selling – as part of the virtuous task of espousing a way of life that they believe in and follow themselves.

The personal trainer is thus positioned as the ideal central figure through which the individual nodes of the fitness field are connected as a web of consumer fitness, as captured in Figure 5.1. Beginning with the most obvious connection to the fitness field, personal trainers are a primary producer of fitness services. However, personal trainers are not only service producers; they are also fitness service consumers, using the services of other producers (such as exercise instructors, massage therapists, and other personal trainers) as part of their physical development in their non-work time. More closely linked to their professional status is the emphasis on certification and ongoing recertification; personal trainers consume the services of occupational conventions and training courses, such as those offered by IDEA and ACE.

Second, personal trainers are consumers of fitness goods. Working out during their non-paid time involves the use of exercise equipment, as a personal exercise preference and/or occupational necessity, as their work

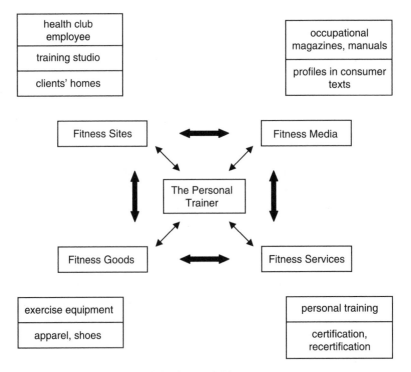

Figure 5.1 Personal trainers and the fitness field.

requires that they are familiar with the range of equipment on offer in health clubs. In addition, personal trainers consume fitness gear such as athletic shoes and sport clothing for their workouts during non-paid time, and their work during paid time (despite health club uniforms, personal trainers typically use their own shoes, for example). Furthermore, as was discussed with regard to their role as promoters, personal trainers are producers of the fitness goods industry, in the sense that they (implicitly or explicitly) endorse such products for their clients.

Third, personal trainers take part in both the production and consumption of fitness sites. Whether in a health club or personal training studio, personal trainers are frontline service workers, involved in the production of the fitness site's symbolic value and personality. Personal trainers are also frequent consumers of health clubs as the site for their own physical development and, like health club members more generally, as a positional good: the status and clientele of a trainer's health club (be it their employer club or not) can then be converted into occupational social capital. For those who work in clients' homes, the personal trainer produces an *ad hoc* fitness site in the domestic sphere of the client, transforming that private space into a node, however temporarily, of the larger fitness field.

Fourth, in terms of fitness media, occupational texts such as *IPT* and the ACE manual are produced both by and for personal trainers; consumption of such texts has become mandatory in the sense that they are integral to the process of certification. Personal trainers also read consumer texts such as popular fitness magazines and exercise manuals, as an expression of a general, personal interest in fitness and/or an occupational strategy to ensure that the trainer stays one step ahead of the client. Furthermore, personal training provides content for consumer texts: exercise manuals by celebrity personal trainers, and fitness magazine profiles of, and advice columns by, personal trainers, promote the public image and credibility of personal training.

Finally, the various nodes of the fitness field interconnect through the figure of the personal trainer to form a web of consumption. As both producers and consumers of the fitness field, personal trainers constitute significant links in the promotional chain of fitness, not simply drawing clients together with other fitness professionals, health clubs, fitness commodities, and consumer and occupational texts, but also galvanizing such connections through fervent belief, and girding them through professional credibility. As such, they are promoters in the widest sense of the term (Wernick 1991: 16): the figure of the personal trainer – and especially the embodied capital of a fit body and "fit" personality – advertises both the trainer and, more significantly, everything to which it is imagistically and ideologically linked.

Personal trainers, and cultural intermediaries more broadly, are involved not only in the *production of consumption* – creating and managing images, experiences, and lifestyles in service interactions – but also, crucially, in the *consumption of production* – investing in, and internalizing, work identities and occupational resources as part of one's non-work life. The vocational disposition, which places the personal trainer in the service of the fitness field, mediates the blurring of work and non-work time and behavior in the construction of professional credibility; encourages the investment of personal belief, attitude and appearance in occupational identity as an expression of authenticity rather than instrumentality; and neutralizes the challenge that selling poses to claims of professionalism by transforming a market logic of client recruitment and retention into a matter of health- and wellness-oriented "good works."

CONCLUSION

Over the 1990s, personal training developed from an elite service for the wealthy to an occupation serving a mass, middle-class fitness market. The growing number of and the increasing competition between trainers, and the efforts of occupational organizations such as IDEA and ACE, have produced personal training as professional service work, rationally stratified by intellectual capital in the form of certifications. However, certifications are a necessary but not sufficient form of capital for personal trainers. The stratification and credibility of personal trainers also rest on less objective, if no less rational, grounds: the social capital of affiliations with health professionals and a stable network of clients; and the embodied capital of a fit physique, promotional subjectivity, and vocational disposition. These other forms of capital are crucial to a personal trainer's ability to motivate clients, and thus fulfill – and reconcile, however imperfectly, the tension between – both their entrepreneurial agenda and their professional mission.

Personal trainers provide insight into the ways in which cultural inter- mediaries mobilize their personal lives as occupational resources, blurring work and leisure time through their embodiment of, and investment in, the rules, practices and stakes of the fields of which they are producers. The trainer's body, especially, is called upon as a symbol of credibility and professional commitment, a tool of motivation and influence, and a promotional object that advertises both the trainer and the broader fitness field within which the exchange value of the fit physique is affirmed. Personal trainers are thus the perfect fitness field consumers and producers; they are both buying into and selling their own lifestyle, and their claims to professional status help to legitimate fitness as the field within which to negotiate the status of the body as a form of capital, a site of investment, and a means of self-expression.

6   Lessons from the fitness field

Changing cultural, political and economic conditions have posed new challenges for the individual body, and these have been reflected in shifting notions of an individual's fitness for social life. Notions of fitness in the early twenty-first century are shaped, first and foremost, by the tenets of individualization, which take identity, health, and social mobility as individual duties and responsibilities. Ultimately, "being fit" is about possessing the appropriate capacities and resources to undertake the project of the self in a competent fashion, minimizing health risks, and maximizing market value. Fitness is a measure of aptitude for life in consumer culture and a service economy.

Participation in the fitness field is thus an education – for producers and consumers – in the skills and resources necessary for competent self-production in consumer service culture. Evan Watkins (1993: 5–6) has suggested that we should understand

> these fields – service economy and consumer culture – as indeed *educative*, which means more than identifying ideological agendas or manipulation.... Like public education, [consumer culture's] payoffs always involve the differentiations and distinctions of social position; ... it speaks to and with the languages of rising social expectations; ... it promises the positional rewards of mastering crucial lessons across an elaborately structured "curriculum" of subject areas ...

Mastering the lessons of the fitness field may offer gains in physical and mental strength, flexibility and endurance, the reduction of health risks, and an improvement in appearance. However, underlying these and other motivations is the larger issue at stake: the production of bodies and selves that are fit for consumption – fit to consume; fit to be consumed.

What can we learn from the fitness field in the US? The chapter looks back over the historical and contemporary roots and institutional elements of place, media, producer, and consumer in order to review the themes that cut across the different nodes and webs of the fitness field: lessons regarding the negotiation of competing and often conflicting social pressures on the body to be a focus of both work and leisure, that its function and form – its health and appearance – be maintained and improved, and that it be both disciplined and enjoyed as a source of pleasure. The final section of the book returns to the connections between fitness and the field of health, which has lent scientific credibility and political-economic urgency to commercial fitness. Given the contemporaneous rise in commercial fitness industries and population rates of overweight and inactivity on a global scale, we must ask if, and to what extent, fitness can be said to be "good" for us.

FIT FOR CONSUMPTION

The contemporary construction of fitness as a consumer lifestyle, to be undertaken during one's leisure time with the help of a range of therapeutic goods and services, has become – along with achievement sport and media sport (Maguire 2005) – a dominant form of physical culture today. This is not to suggest that fitness has reached a final, static state; as the history of physical culture demonstrates, the objectives of fitness, claims to fitness expertise, and exchange value of particular corporeal resources will change in time with shifting social conditions. Today's dominant forms may become tomorrow's residuals (Williams 1977), just as the nineteenth-century function of fitness as social improvement has receded, and been recast as the ethic of self-improvement. With the US currently engaged in a prolonged and unpopular foreign military engagement and facing economic uncertainty, there may yet be a resurgence of fitness articulated primarily in terms of national and moral strength; certainly, this theme is apparent in political rhetoric around personal responsibility for choosing healthy lifestyles (Bush 2003). However, over the past three decades, the dominant articulation of the purpose of fitness has been at the scale of the individual, in terms of the problems of, and rewards for, bodies and selves in a consumer service economy.

A consumer culture rests on individuals locating meaning – and not simply use-value – in processes of acquisition, use and appropriation of goods and services; consumption is a necessary – indeed, primary – sphere in and through which relationships, identities and interactions are forged (Douglas and Isherwood 1996; Ilmonen 2004; Miller 1998, 2001). At the same time, a service economy requires a workforce that is finely attuned to the strategic value of social interaction; body and face work are necessary – indeed, vital – elements in shaping performances and interactions (Bryman 2004; Dent and Whitehead 2002; Hochschild 1983). The material and symbolic practices and consequences of participation in the fitness field align with the anxieties and aspirations associated with a life – particularly a middle-class life – in which the disposition to consume, and to perform oneself for the consumption by others, is central to the reproduction of the social order and economy.

The fit individual is a competent consumer, who understands of his or her choices not only the criteria (notions of value, credibility, status), but also the context (the consumer market), and the ends (self-improvement, self-responsibility). Refusing the obligation of self-production through consumption is not an available choice (Rose 1990, 1996): we are *obliged* to consume in order to become ourselves. The fit individual is also a competent service actor. Both production and consumption in the post-industrial economy of the US increasingly take place through service interactions. Service competence, for producers and consumers alike, involves adopting strategic forms of self-presentation and performance in order to succeed: to get the desired quality of service from the service worker; to manage the emotions and ensure the satisfaction of the client; to promote oneself and influence others. Participation in the fitness field is bound up with producing subjectivities that are fit to consume, in that they locate the production of meaning, identity and relationships with others in the processes of consumption; and producing bodies that are fit to be consumed by others as visual representations of an individual's identity, social position, and subjectivity. These capacities are addressed in the following three lessons from the fitness field, regarding the tensions between work and leisure, form and function, and discipline and pleasure.

Work and leisure

It is within the sphere of leisure time, using leisure products, guided by new ranks of leisure professionals, that individuals engage with fitness. Consumer leisure has become the dominant form of fitness; this has crystallized most clearly in the setting of the commercial health club. Health clubs have constructed themselves as leisure businesses, shaping fitness in the mold of other leisure services with an emphasis on status, convenience, entertainment, and the symbolic added value from the personality of the space, staff and clientele. In general, health clubs, fitness media and personal trainers all contribute to the naturalization of the association between fitness and discretionary leisure time, and thus expenditure on fitness with discretionary income. These associations are important in terms of the status rewards possible through field participation, as leisure and lifestyle choices are the primary stakes in competitions for distinction and prestige in consumer culture (Bourdieu 1984; Featherstone 1991; Slater 1997).

Leisure is imagined as a time of relaxation, making working out (a sweaty, strenuous activity even for those who intrinsically enjoy it) difficult to market as a "downtime" pursuit. Thus, the problem of motivation is a thread that runs throughout the elements of the fitness field. Exercise manuals attempt to educate readers to "fit in" fitness and discipline their leisure time, extending a middle-class work ethic into the sphere of leisure (Parker 1976) through the application of devices such as time schedules and appointments and a rational logic of efficiency, investment, and reward. The tension between work and leisure is especially apparent in the work of personal trainers, who epitomize the blurring of work and leisure that characterizes cultural intermediaries (Nixon and Crewe 2004; McFall 2004). For personal trainers, the health club is a site both of work and of leisure, paid work involves the application of a rational work ethic to the client's leisure time, and the nature of occupational resources (especially physique) implies a mandatory use of leisure time to work on one's embodied capital. The personal trainer's resolution of the tension between work and leisure through a vocational disposition is instructive for field participants more widely: to regard working out as a good use of leisure time fulfils the tenets of responsible self-production.

The fitness field represents an institutional and discursive mode by which individuals are educated in how to yield more value from available time and corporeal resources. The duty at the core of consumer leisure and lifestyles must be the "production of *value* – distinctive value, status value, prestige value" (Baudrillard 1998: 157). Thus, the cultural imaginary of leisure as a time of freedom *from* work and responsibility is accompanied by a parallel construction of leisure as a time of freedom *to* take up the work and responsibility of self-production. In his observations of the *nouveaux riches* in the US at the turn of the twentieth century, Thorstein Veblen commented upon the "work" required to display and defend their new class position, such that social mobility for the gentleman tends "to change his life of leisure into a more or less arduous application to the business of learning how to live a life of ostensible leisure in a becoming way" (1959: 34). With the expansion of consumer culture has come the expansion of the obligation of productive leisure, from the *nouveaux riches* to the post-industrial middle class more generally.

Locating participation in the fitness field within discretionary time reproduces notions of fitness as an individual's choice and responsibility, as it is over leisure time that individuals are assumed (if incorrectly) to exercise control. What this ignores and obscures is the degree to which discretionary time is structured and constrained by factors beyond the individual's control, such as patterns of work and commuting, and issues of life stage and gender. If fitness is a choice about how to spend one's discretionary time, then not everyone is equally capable of choosing.

Form and function

Form and function intersect in the fitness field in different ways. Appearance and health are valuable embodied resources in an image-driven service economy organized around the individual's responsibility for self-improvement and a healthy lifestyle. This is clearly illustrated in the enticements that exercise manuals offer as the means to motivate readers to discipline their leisure time appropriately (that is, by making time for fitness). Fitness is constructed as a panacea for all of the ills – individual and collective – of contemporary life: exercise is the means to reduce health risks, improve energy levels, cope with stress, lose weight, improve appearance, feel younger, and so forth. Thus, the body's form and function are represented as modes of physical capital, and complementary objectives in the motivation behind participation in fitness. Nevertheless, the representation of health in fitness media – and personal training – blurs function and form, with health often reduced to appearance. For example, the actual health of a personal trainer is not what is at stake in the cultivation of credibility; it is the appearance of health that serves as the promotional signifier.

Form and function are also juxtaposed in the broader construction of value in the fitness field, such that symbolic value is largely privileged over use-value (cf. Ewen 1999). Lessons in the economic value of symbolic capital permeate the production and consumption of health clubs, fitness media, and personal training services. The consolidation of health clubs, expansion of lifestyle publishing, and standardization of personal training certification have all contributed to a flattening of material differences in use-value between different fitness goods and services. By and large, health clubs offer much the same equipment, fitness magazines and exercise manuals have similar content, and personal trainers possess the same basic principles of exercise science. Consequently, both fitness producers and consumers are encouraged to differentiate between products – and to differentiate themselves – based on less tangible, but no less valid, measures of worth. Health clubs, fitness media, and personal trainers cultivate prestige and distinction through the personalities of producers and imagined, ideal consumers, associations with the affluence of a professional/managerial core of consumers, and the legitimacy of the health and therapeutic fields with which they are associated. Consumers are encouraged to identify with and buy into the health club's personality, the magazine's reader profile, and the personal trainer's lifestyle, thereby producing and affirming their own sense of identity and personality through the consumer market.

At the same time, fitness texts and personal trainers also represent the function of the body *as* form – that is, the function of the body in consumer service economies is as an expressive and positional good. This is especially pronounced for personal trainers, for whom the body is a promotional object – a billboard upon which is displayed their credibility and vocational disposition. Form trumps function in three respects: health is reduced to appearance, symbolic value is privileged over use-value, and the body's most valued function is its capacity to serve as a sign. Fitness is marketed as a way to gain control over, and invest in, one's sign value. In an era of uncertainty and risk, the scope of control that individuals expect and demand increasingly narrows to their own bodies.

What is problematic about the construction of fitness as a cure-all and mode of control over one's sign value is that collective sources of risk (geopolitical instability, pollution) and other risks beyond individual control (inherited predisposition for diseases, accidents) are obscured by the focus on individual responsibility (Beck 1992). The form of control on offer in the fitness discourse is inherently unstable and tenuous. Control over one's life is reduced to a command of the body, which is often disrupted by impositions from a disorderly social world – highlighting the limits of the individual's control. Bodies are inherently fluid – the body ages, falls ill, erupts and diminishes despite our best intentions or fervent desires; thus, attempts to control them inherently carry also the possibility of upheaval, resistance, and disorder (cf. Crawford 1984).

Discipline and pleasure

The problem of motivation touches health clubs, fitness media and personal trainers, and each field element is marked by the intersections of an ascetic ethic of discipline and an aesthetic ethic of indulgence. Exercise manuals and health clubs construct fitness as a leisure activity in keeping with the broader cultural imaginary of fitness as a time of fun and pleasure. However, there is a particularly narrow vision of pleasure on offer in the fitness field: exercise itself is not pleasurable, but is a matter of discipline; pleasure comes from the effect one's fitter body has upon others, the satisfaction in having made "good" use of one's leisure time, the distractions provided through the amenities and status rewards of the health club. Even when fitness activities are represented as enjoyable, they are rarely constructed as ends in themselves. Exercise is instrumentally rationalized as the means to other ends: reduced health risks, improved appearance, or both (see Plate 6.1).

Discipline and pleasure are configured as separate and parallel ethics (as in: working out legitimating an indulgence), or as a hybrid, when pleasure is found through discipline (as in: feelings of virtuousness, or the flow experiences of embodiment; Csikszentmihalyi 1990). For example, personal trainers utilize a drill sergeant mode of performance, which compels the client to work out, but also offers both pleasurable pain (as when sore muscles the day after confirm one's virtuous exercise) and the pleasure of a reprieve (however temporarily) from the responsibility of self-discipline.

Consumption plays a crucial role in the resolution of the tension between restraint and indulgence: the prospect of shopping for a newly fit body is a means to reward discipline with pleasure; the buying of a health club membership, new sports equipment or personal trainer services is represented as a "necessary" indulgence in order to accomplish self-discipline. Reconciling the hedonism of consumer culture with the asceticism of exercise by linking them as cause and effect (work out now; shop later) serves as an engine for consumption, and perpetuates the double bind of indulgence and restraint characteristic of consumer culture (Campbell 1987; Featherstone 1982; McGee 2005; Weber 1992).

Despite the emphasis in fitness media (especially) on the instrumentalization of exercise and pleasure, the narratives both of personal trainers and consumers reveal the possibilities for the non-instrumental pleasure of exercise for its own sake: feelings of freedom, competence and strength in doing the activity itself. In contrast to the increasingly sedentary patterns of work and everyday life, it is little wonder that fitness activities can offer intense

Plate 6.1 The means to many ends: health club ad.
(Source: Joseph Maguire)

experiences of embodiment; what is striking is the relative absence of emphasis on such benefits in the exercise manuals. In the fitness field, control over the body is prioritized over pleasure in the body, and instrumental pleasure over spontaneous, non-directed play (Huizinga 1955), raising questions as to its suitability as a field within which to pursue health.

FIT FOR HEALTH?

A fundamental precondition of the fitness field is the increasingly sedentary way of life in western consumer cultures, and around the world. Such a context makes possible the construction of physical exercise as an individual choice (rather than an integral part of everyday life), and the accumulation of worth in the fit body, in its scarcity value (amidst an overweight and inactive general population), political-economic value (in light of preventive health economics and the rhetoric of individual responsibility), and symbolic value (as a visible statement of the means and disposition to invest in oneself).

Over recent decades, many western countries have experienced a strange paradox, with sport, exercise, and leisure industries expanding alongside problems of inactivity and obesity. This juxtaposition is imprinted on the fabric of everyday life, with health clubs sitting alongside fast food restaurants as part of the urban environment of global cities (see Plate 6.2). It is thus important to ask: is fitness good for us? This is not a "yes or no" question. Over the past three decades, medical research has continued to substantiate the role of exercise in decreasing the risks of various diseases and ailments, including arthritis pain, breast cancer, colon cancer, osteoporosis, stroke, type 2 diabetes, and congestive heart failure (Hardman and Stensel 2003; Krupa 2001). However, when exercise is taken to be an unproblematic "good,"

Plate 6.2 Fit and fat: street scene in Hong Kong.
(Source: the author)

the vested interests and unintended consequences associated with the current construction of fitness are exempt from questioning. Thus, posing the question in a polemical fashion facilitates a questioning of the taken-for-granted, in order to underline how the commercial fitness field benefits from, but is poorly equipped to address, population-level health issues such as inactivity and obesity.

Cultural fields establish themselves and operate in relation to other fields, from which they have relative autonomy (Jenkins 1992; cf. Becker 1982). The fitness field exists in a dynamic relationship with the health field. Cultivating the difference between fitness-as-leisure and fitness-as-prescription – and thus emphasizing the distance between the fitness and health fields – has allowed health clubs, for example, to compete through the criteria of pleasure, convenience and status, rather than health *per se*. At the same time, the commercial fitness field has benefited through associations with the health field; for example, media attention generated by Surgeon General warnings, direct referrals through physician-prescribed exercise, and the legitimacy from scientific findings on the benefits of exercise, reinforce the fitness field's construction of exercise as a panacea and a morally good use of leisure time. More broadly, patterns of disease, sedentariness and so forth not only give rise to the social problems of inactivity and obesity, but also create a need for purposive physical exercise, which is filled by the commercial fitness industry, which in turn benefits from the legitimacy that the health field has bestowed upon the problems of inactivity and obesity.

Advances in medical science have largely controlled the major causes of death in the nineteenth century – communicable diseases such as tuberculosis – at least in developed countries at a collective level through immunization and curative pharmaceuticals. With these advances has come a changing context of health and disease, such that non-communicable diseases – especially cardiovascular disease, type 2 diabetes, and some types of cancers – accounted for 60 per cent of global deaths in 2001 (WHO 2004). According to the World Health Organization (WHO), five of the major risk factors for non-communicable diseases are closely linked to diet and exercise – poor habits of which contribute to global patterns of rising obesity and inactivity (2004). These are intertwined problems, giving rise to interconnected agendas, including the WHO Global Strategy on Diet, Physical Activity and Health (2004), the Move for Health programme (WHO 2002), and the UN's 2005: Year of Sport and Physical Education campaign. Of the two problems, obesity has received the greatest attention in the popular media; this is further reinforced in government policies and health promotion strategies, which tend to subsume a multitude of initiatives (including those addressing inactivity) under the banner of a "war on obesity."

To understand the growth, success and limitations of commercial fitness, it is important to consider the issues of obesity and inactivity. Obesity and inactivity are global problems. Though linked in the media and popular imagination with the developed world, obesity and inactivity rates are rising across the globe, resulting in the coexistence of obesity and under-nutrition in some countries (WHO 2000). Global statistics on obesity are difficult to compare because of irregular definitions of the surveyed population, definitions of obesity itself, and survey periods. The most comprehensive analysis is the WHO MONICA (MONItoring of trends and determinants in CArdiovascular diseases) Study that compared specific cities from 48 different, but mostly European, countries, and used the Body Mass Index (BMI) scale to compare populations (such that a BMI of greater than 25 qualifies as overweight; greater than 30 as obese). The data from a city cannot be generalized to a country as a whole; nevertheless, the data provide an indication of overall patterns, particularly as the study is longitudinal. The results show that in all but one case, between 50 and 75 per cent of adults were overweight or obese between 1983 and 1986 (WHO 2003b), and that these proportions are increasing over time. Despite similar problems with global measures of inactivity, statistics are largely consistent: around the world, 60 to 85 per cent of adults are not physically active enough to achieve any health benefits (WHO 2002).

It is important here to note – as does the WHO (2000: 7) – that BMI is a crude but useful measure of population trends of overweight and obesity. Because it does not account for variations in body fat distribution, it is not a particularly good assessment of an individual's status as overweight and obese. While it is important to question the moral panics around obesity and inactivity, especially with regard to the unstated moral agendas and vested interests at play in the focus in the media, government policy and everyday lives on these health issues (Campos 2004; Gard and Wright 2005; Oliver 2006), the complaint that BMI is an arbitrary fiction (e.g. Bee 2006) reflects a misunderstanding of population measures. The imperfect nature of BMI as a measurement of *individual* weight does not discount its utility in assessing *populations* over time – its application in the WHO MONICA Study.

Obesity is not only a global, but also an escalating, problem. Rates have risen in particular during the past 20 years. In the past ten years, the United Kingdom's rate of obesity has doubled, and in general, European countries have seen an increase of between 10 and 40 per cent (WHO 2000). In the US, obesity rates increased by two-thirds between 1960 and 1990, and increased another two-thirds over the 1990s alone (Farley and Cohen 2001). In roughly the same time period that the number of US commercial health clubs more than doubled and the number of fitness magazines tripled, consumption of fast food tripled and the consumption of soft drinks increased by 131 per cent (Farley and Cohen 2001).

Significantly, obesity and inactivity are stratified by gender and class (National Center for Health Statistics 2005; WHO 2000, 2002; YWCA 2001). Women have higher rates of obesity than men, men have higher rates of overweight, and in both instances, rates of obesity increase as socio-economic class decreases. Similarly for inactivity: physical inactivity is higher for women and girls, and worse in poor urban areas (WHO 2003a). Among other things, poverty means a lack of access to safe recreation areas and high-quality, low-cost foods – contributing factors in inactivity and obesity (Critser 2001, 2003; WHO 2000, 2002). But socioeconomic class is not only about economic capital; food and activity choices reflect cultural and social capital – for example, having the knowledge of and preferences for certain activities and foods such that the "healthy" option takes on the appearance of being the "natural" preference rather than the difficult choice. Rising socio-economic levels on a population scale create the conditions for obesity and inactivity – eating too much becomes a possibility, rather than under-nourishment, while technology, changing modes of production, and urban development make physical inactivity a likelihood for increasing portions of the population. However, obesity and inactivity are then stratified individually by class – choosing to be fit then becomes a sign of status.

At bottom, it is the class dimension of obesity and inactivity that is the key to the fat/fit paradox, just as it is to understanding the fitness field. In the US, 73 per cent of commercial health club members have a household income of at least $50,000; similarly, professional/managerial individuals constitute approximately a third of personal trainer clients and the readership of the top three fitness magazine titles.[1] The fitness field is middle-class in a triple sense: produced by the middle class (cultural intermediaries in publishing, personal training), for the middle class (especially the professional/managerial group and its aspirants that constitute the core consumers), and of the middle class (the lessons of the fitness field affirming and legitimating the valued forms of capital and the leisure projects of the middle class).

Like the problems of obesity and inactivity, the "problem" of fitness is also global in reach. There is a further relevant lesson that can be drawn here from the fitness field, by broadening the focus from the US to fitness industries in other cultures, regarding the standardization of physical culture. Mediated by local conditions, including long-term patterns of privatization and the growth of the middle class, commercial fitness industries are developing in countries around the world. Without substantive research to indicate how such industries function as cultural fields (cf. Ginsberg 2000; Spielvogel 2003), the global traveler will nonetheless note a marked similarity in the way in which health clubs in the US, Singapore (Plate 6.3), Malaysia (Plate 6.4), and Japan (Plate 6.5), for example, reflect similar associations between fitness and the good life, be it signified through references to a desired lifestyle or standardized images of the ideal body. Similarly, the interiors of health clubs also bespeak the global homogenization of fitness cultures, be it through the ubiquitous banks of treadmills and televisions (as in Hong Kong, Plate 6.6), or the global reach of pre-fabricated, patented exercise classes. The range of

Plate 6.3 Health club, Singapore.
(Source: the author)

Plate 6.4 Health club, Malaysia.
(Source: the author)

Plate 6.5 Health club, Japan.
(Source: the author)

Plate 6.6 "Health Club, Hong Kong".
(Source: the author)

possibilities for participation in a physically active life is thus narrowing along the axis of body cultures as well as class cultures.

Is fitness good for us? For the majority – and in particular for those lower down the socioeconomic ladder who are more likely to be inactive and overweight – the answer is no, both because a lack of capital and suitable consumption preferences make participation unlikely, and because the private provision of fitness services facilitates the ongoing withdrawal of their public provision. The commercial fitness field represents the commodification and reproduction of the problem: the already deeply entrenched class-based stratification of health and health risks. For a much smaller group of people, the answer is a qualified yes: the fitness field provides goods and services that may facilitate the accomplishment of regular physical exercise for individuals, but in such a way that is deeply restrictive at a collective level. Some individuals, as the interviews make clear, locate in the fitness field a space for significant sociality, a rewarding career, the ability to assuage or control anxieties, or an opportunity to fully engage with the body without reference to an instrumental end; this is no bad thing. However, the "lessons" of the fitness field involve the promotion of an individualized notion of exercise (as a disciplined use of one's own time rather than addressing collective patterns of space and time use; and as an individualized cure-all for what are, at bottom, collective problems and patterns), an instrumental view of pleasure through exercise (rather than a non-instrumental "play" ethic, which remains under threat if not altogether absent from daily life; see Huizinga 1955), and the narrowing of the parameters of participation to those provided by the consumer market.

In his book *The Sociological Imagination* (1959: 8–9), C. Wright Mills uses the example of unemployment to illustrate the difference between personal troubles and public issues. Both the source and solution to personal troubles lie within the character and relations of the individual. If one individual in a population of 100,000 is unemployed, then the problem should be defined as a personal trouble, and the resolution sought in the individual's character, skills and immediate opportunities. Public issues, on the other hand, stem from structures, and the interrelations between different social milieux. Thus, when 15 million are unemployed in a nation of 50 million, neither the problem nor the solution lies in the capacities of any one individual. Mills (1959: 9) writes:

> The very structure of opportunities has collapsed. Both the correct statement of the problem and the range of possible solutions require us to consider the economic and political institutions of the society, and not merely the personal situation and character of a scatter of individuals.

Obesity and inactivity are the contemporary equivalent of Mills' example of unemployment.

Drawing on Mills (1959), the fat/fit paradox of the past three decades, in which fitness industries have boomed alongside increasing rates of population inactivity and obesity, can be understood as the rational outcome of addressing a social, structural problem with an individualized solution. The result has been a further entrenchment of the existing class divide in health, and the rationalization of health and exercise as matters of appearance management and status consumption. Individual sovereignty, so prized in consumer culture, is "healthy" only insofar as it is accompanied by collective responsibility to tackle social problems through collective solutions: for example, more funding for public provision of recreation services accessible across class divides; a commitment to the sort of urban planning that makes active living the easy, not the difficult, choice; and compulsory childhood physical education (PE) that produces an appreciation of the joy of movement and the habit of physical activity.

In conclusion, I highlight four ways in which the fitness field – sometimes at cross-purposes to, sometimes in conjunction with, the health-care and health-promotion fields – is unsuitable for addressing population health problems such as inactivity and obesity. This is not an exhaustive list, but illustrates the larger conflicts facing population health and fitness, and provides four starting points for further discussion – among and between government policy makers, health professionals and promoters, leisure and recreation professionals, and physical educationalists as well as those involved in the commercial provision of fitness goods and services.

First, the fitness field in conjunction with the health promotion field encourages individual solutions to collective problems. Since the 1970s, health promotion has focused on individualized "active" strategies (including those – like higher taxes on fatty foods – that masquerade as collective strategies), which assume that, given the appropriate information, the rational actor will make "good choices." Fitness and health experts construct the problems of the body and self – fatness, weakness, inactivity, boredom, laziness, poor time management – as personal failings, requiring the investment of individual time and effort. Obscured by this narrow focus on individual responsibility for healthy behavior are the deeply social causes of obesity and inactivity. What is required is an acknowledgment that the problems of obesity and inactivity are collective problems, which require collective solutions. This is not simply a matter of putting more funding into collective provision of recreation services that are accessible across class divides (or into the development of a pill to kill appetite, annihilate fat, and cure obesity). A fundamental transformation is required in how the state regards itself relative to its citizens, and how citizens understand their rights and responsibilities relative to the state, themselves and each other, so that – if individuals are truly to bear the responsibility for their lives – there is greater equity in the capacity of individuals to control the context of choice.

Second, the fitness field's naturalization of exercise as a leisure time activity to take place within designated and specialized sites reinforces the lack of attention given to the environment and its impact on population health. Contemporary consumer society is an "obesogenic" environment (Lang 2004), from the auto-centric configuration of daily life to the differential accessibility of fast food and its healthier alternatives. A shift in urban land use is required, despite the seemingly insurmountable inertia of infrastructure. Health promoters may recommend walking to work, but they do not address the patterns of suburbanization and the lack of government funding for mass transit and bicycle lanes in the US and elsewhere that spatially segregate work and home life and make sedentary commuting (i.e. car or train rather than walking or bicycling) an inevitability for many. Of course, making long-term policy and funding commitments to an activity-friendly environment requires an accompanying ideological shift, as outlined in the first point, as these collective solutions impose a collective burden as much as they offer collective opportunities.

Third, the commercial provision of fitness facilities and services has the unintended consequence of facilitating the ongoing decline of their collective provision, particularly for the disenfranchised. Population inactivity and obesity stem in part from the decline of childhood PE, a central element in the collective provision of exercise and recreation opportunities. Given the general decline in the US and elsewhere of institutional childhood socialization into physical activity, the production of new adult habits requires a complex web of motivational techniques – exercise logs, entertaining workout classes, inspiring magazine stories, personal training sessions, messages of guilt, hope and encouragement. But motivation comes at a cost, and is directed at a middle-class market, reinforcing the economic and cultural capital boundaries that surround the fitness lifestyle.

Health benefits, such as decreased risk of heart disease, diabetes and colon cancer, are associated with *regular* (ideally, daily) exercise. Thus, to improve the health of the population, physical activity has to be ingrained as part of everyday behavior, and this is most effective if it is accomplished as part of childhood socialization. Childhood PE, however, does not simply require more funding; childhood education more broadly requires improved and sustained funding in order to improve health at school by, for example, removing the reliance on income from vending machines, and redesigning schools' interiors, exteriors and access routes to encourage physical exercise. Reinvestment needs to be accompanied by reinvention: PE's focus on competitive, performance-oriented sports has excluded many from participation because of cultural backgrounds, body culture interests and physical capacities. Hence, not only is the *provision* of PE declining, but so too are levels of *participation*, especially among young women (YWCA 2001).

Fourth and finally, the fitness field reproduces the tension – typical of consumer culture more broadly – between indulgence and restraint. This cultural ambivalence is expressed in the simultaneous increase of consumption of both fatty and diet foods (Nestle 2002), exercise classes and television, miles spent on the treadmill and in the car. The problem with fitness, from the point of view of health, is that the field's prescribed negotiation of denial and pleasure produces not healthy but *consuming* behaviour. The work of the workout is rationalized as a means to earn rewards – a thinner and more toned body, a chance to buy smaller-sized clothes, the status credit of belonging to the right gym or hiring a personal trainer. Such an instrumental attitude undermines the potential benefits of exercise for improved body image and self-esteem by focusing attention on changing, rather than enjoying, the body's capacities. Physical activity *can* provide a sense of control, pleasure and joy. But these benefits are undercut by the promotion of exercise as a rationalized instrument of appearance and health management. As Johan Huizinga (1955) has suggested, the need for and enjoyment of movement – of the body as a whole – is deeply embedded within us, but this play element of culture is increasingly subsumed within the rationalization of movement.

Fitness producers and consumers construct the status of the body through negotiations of the tensions between work and leisure, form and function, and discipline and pleasure. The body is constructed as a status object, a site of investment, and a means of self-production, but often to paradoxical effect as the rationalization of the body's exchange-value strips physical culture of the potential for spontaneous enjoyment of our capacities as embodied selves. What makes us fit is not necessarily what makes us healthy or happy. In summary, the fitness field illustrates the intended and unintended consequences of the body's place as a status object in contemporary consumer culture, in which occupation is privileged over recreation, form over function, and control over enjoyment. That is, for bodies that are fit for consumption, leisure is work, health is an appearance, and pleasure lies in discipline.

Appendix
Suggested research tasks for students

Fitness, as the history of physical culture makes clear, is neither monolithic nor static. Definitions of what counts as fitness – its associated visual ideals, social goals and bodily rewards – and who counts as the legitimate therapeutic experts and service providers change over time, relative to local contexts. This book is thus intended not as the final word on the culture of fitness, but as one part of a growing body of knowledge on the roles that fitness plays in different societies around the world in relation to people's everyday lives, the social and political-economic order, problems of obesity, inactivity and class stratification, cultures of consumption and the privatization and commercialization of leisure, and broad patterns of individualization.

Below are five suggested research tasks for each of the main chapters of the book, picking up on the main themes and findings contained therein. This is by no means an exhaustive list, and leaves aside those avenues of inquiry not taken up in the present study – including other nodes in the fitness field, other factors (such as age, ethnicity, sexuality, or disability) shaping participants' access to and experiences of the fitness field, and comparisons between fitness fields in other cultures. As such, these suggestions, and the book as a whole, should be seen as an invitation to others to continue the exploration of the fitness field.

THE ROOTS OF FITNESS

1   Using newspaper archives, examine the different ways in which fitness has been constructed as a problem over time. Try to sample from time periods that present a range of external conditions, such as war, economic recession, and peace and prosperity.

2   Conduct interviews with fitness participants regarding their motivations or reasons for working out, with special focus on the role of gender in shaping how concerns about health, appearance, and other bodily capacities are articulated.

3   Conduct interviews with fitness participants, with special focus on the role of occupation and class position in shaping how the expected rewards of working out are articulated.

4   Examine the content of official health policy documents and media coverage of health issues, paying close attention to the ways in which individual responsibility is constructed and promoted.

5   Analyze the different ways in which appearance is constructed as an essential resource for social and occupational success, comparing the content of media such as fitness and health magazines, lifestyle magazines, and self-help books on topics such as relationship and career success.

HEALTH CLUBS

1   Evaluate how the provision of health and fitness spaces has changed over time by conducting "fitness biography" life history interviews. One might also consult past telephone directories in the local library to trace how the number and type of clubs has changed over time.

2   Compile a "map" of the health clubs in the local area, using the "Field of Choice" diagram from Chapter 3. Try to identify what factors differentiate clubs from each other in the vertical and horizontal bands.

3   Conduct a personal assessment of a health club's clientele by visiting the club at different times during the week and the day. Note differences in who is using the club when, and compare this to the official "personality" the club constructs in its advertising.

4   Compare two different health clubs and the ways in which they construct their symbolic capital. Draw from as many sources of data as possible, including visiting the clubs, reading consumer reviews in the newspaper, and talking to staff members.

5   Compare a commercial health club with another type of health and exercise space, such as a recreation centre, physiotherapy clinic, or physical education facility, and note their similarities and differences with regard to membership, equipment, staff, connotations of leisure and status, and so forth.

FITNESS MEDIA

1 Using circulation and readership statistics (such as can be found in media kit information for advertisers on fitness magazine websites), analyze the similarities and differences between several magazines' ideal target readers.

2 Carry out a content analysis of a fitness magazine with regard to the editorial content: how much of the magazine is about exercise *per se*? Use the findings to construct a "map" of the fitness lifestyle, identifying the main elements and their relative prominence in the magazine.

3 Looking at both the advertising and editorial content of several different fitness magazines, identify the linkages between fitness magazines, other elements of the fitness field (such as endorsements of exercise equipment, promotions of exercise manuals, and profiles of specific health clubs), and the broader consumer market.

4 Analyze the ways in which gender mediates the framing of bodily rewards (such as reduced health risks, weight loss, stamina, and so forth) by comparing the content of an exercise manual aimed predominantly at men with one aimed predominantly at women.

5 Compare the content of an explicitly commercial exercise manual and one from a health education perspective, with specific attention to the similarities and differences in the ways in which commercial products and services are discussed and endorsed.

PERSONAL TRAINERS

1 Conduct archival research on the representation of personal training in the popular media to see how the occupation's connotations of exclusivity, status and professionalism have changed over time.

2 Examine how kinesiology textbooks present personal training as a potential occupation, with specific attention to issues of academic qualifications and professionalization.

3 Comparing sales-driven and retention-driven health clubs, investigate the different ways in which personal training services and the personal trainers themselves are promoted.

4 Explore the similarities and differences between physical exercise instruction as a consumer service and as a health care service, by

interviewing a personal trainer and a physiotherapist with regard to their relationship with clients and work experiences.

5   Analyze the concept of physical capital by interviewing personal trainers about the different roles of their bodies in their work.

Notes

1 Making sense of fitness

1 Data on the health club industry are taken from the IHRSA website (http://www.ihrsa.org [accessed January 2007]).
2 Google is a search engine of online content (http://www.google.com [accessed January 2007]).
3 Given Wolfe's profuse use of the ellipse, I have enclosed in square brackets those ellipses that I have inserted in place of text.

2 The roots of fitness

1 These changes were felt first and most acutely in the Northeast; as such, it is little wonder that physical culture movements began there (Adelman 1986; Green 1986). With the closing of the frontier at the end of the nineteenth century, it is likely that the physical culture of the West came to exhibit a character of its own.
2 Not coincidentally, the leadership of the Playground Association of America included renowned settlement house worker Jane Addams, Luther Gulick of the YMCA, and Theodore Roosevelt (Green 1986).
3 Luther Gulick, like Theodore Roosevelt, had studied at Harvard University under Dudley Sargent, a leader in physical education since the late 1870s who promoted athletic training, sportsmanship, and the will to win, coupled with forms of exercise that included pulleys and weight machines (Green 1986: 202–4).
4 For example, US Steel-South Works in Chicago paid for at least half of the construction costs for a nearby YMCA building, and Wisconsin Steel supported a full-time YMCA office on its grounds (Cohen 1990: 180).
5 The Olympic Games, revived in 1896, were another important connection between athleticism and nationalism (Green 1986: 237; see also Maguire 2005). For a wider discussion of the connection between the internationalization of sport and the rise of nationalism in the late nineteenth century, see Hobsbawm (1990).
6 Elizabeth Arden, "The Miracle of Susan" advertisement, from the *New Yorker*, 1942. Available through the online database Ad*Access (http://scriptorium.lib.duke.edu/adaccess [accessed November 2001]).

7 "The Insult That Made a Man Out of Mac" (see Gaines 1982: 70–1) appeared in countless magazines and comic books, including almost every copy of *Superman* (Kimmel 1996: 211–12).

8 Information is from the Jack La Lanne website (http://www.jacklalanne.com [accessed January 2002]).

9 It bears noting that although the YMCA became more inclusive along gender and religious lines (considering, at one point, dropping "Christian" from its mission altogether), it was slow in opening its doors to Black Americans; the YMCA was not integrated until 1967 (Putney 1997).

10 Figures on the number of health food stores come from *Yellow Pages* listings for Manhattan, which were surveyed for 1960, 1965, 1970, 1973 (the year the New York Health Club opened) and 1975.

3 Health clubs

1 New York Health Club advertisements ran in *New York Magazine*'s Classifieds section, each week between October and mid-December of 1973, a run that would have cost approximately $1300. In *The Village Voice*, they ran as half-page ads; the "Shape up your shape!" ad ran on October 18, 1973, page 12. The "Health and Beauty Through Pleasure" slogan and ad copy are from the NYHC quarter page ad in the 1975 *Yellow Pages*. Numbers and names of health clubs in New York City were gathered from the Manhattan *Yellow Pages* listings for 1960, 1965, 1970, 1973 (the year New York Health Club opened), and 1975.

2 "Physical Fitness in Style" is quoted from a Dan Lurie Health Studios ad, which ran in the 1973 Yellow Pages. Lurie, himself a bodybuilder and a leader in the weightlifting world, was part of the mainstreaming of bodybuilding in the 1970s (Roach 1977).

3 Information from Manhattan *Yellow Pages* and the Jack La Lanne website (http://www.jacklalanne.com [accessed January 2002]).

4 One of the first elite athletic clubs survives today: the New York Athletic Club was founded in 1868. The NYAC was a bastion not only of male privilege, but also of racial and religious exclusion. The rise of the new commercial health clubs in the 1970s can be seen, in part, as a democratization of club culture, and part of the broader attacks on the institutionalization of privilege through exclusionary membership policies.

5 The Health Roof Club for Men opened in 1931 – the advertisement is from the 1960 *Yellow Pages*. The Barclay ad is from the 1970 *Yellow Pages*.

6 Information is from the "History" link on the YMCA website (http://www.ymca.net [accessed January 2002]).

7 From the YMCA website, as before.

8 Information is from the International Health, Racquet and Sportsclub Association (IHRSA) website (http://www.ihrsa.org [accessed January 2002 and 2007]), and from the database *Gale's Ready Reference Shelf* (accessed October 2001), which provides information on all registered organizations and groups. The IHRSA site provides free access to selected data on the commercial health club industry.

9 Statistics, including excerpts from the 2005 IHRSA / American Sports Data Health Club Trend Report, are available through the IHRSA website (as before; accessed January 2007).

10 Data on the global health club industry come primarily from the IHRSA website (as before; accessed October 2006), and reflect 2005 data (for the US, Asia-Pacific and Latin America), and 2002 data for Europe (these data are no longer available for free access on the IHRSA site). IHRSA industry data do not include data for Canada; the figure of 1,658 comes from the 2002 Canadian Business Directory database, and includes non-commercial health clubs, such as YMCAs and fitness facilities in hotels.

11 Information is from the IHRSA website (as before; accessed January 2007), including data on memberships per industry sector: 2005 data show 20 per cent of all health club members belong to YMCAs/YMHAs, and 52 per cent to commercial fitness or commercial multi-purpose clubs. The proportion of commercial clubs to YMCAs is based on a 2005 count of 29,069 commercial clubs (from the IHRSA website; accessed January 2007) and 2,617 YMCAs (from the YMCA website, as before, accessed January 2007). The proportion in 2000 was seven to one: 17,000 commercial clubs and 2,400 YMCAs (based on the IHRSA and YMCA websites; as before, accessed January 2002).

12 Indeed, an over-subscription to dominant bodily norms may precipitate users to drop out, thanks to the unattainability of their goals (see Sassatelli 1999a).

13 From the IHRSA website (as before, accessed January 2002 and 2007): non-dues revenue for IHRSA clubs was 24 per cent in 1998 and 1999, 27.2 per cent in 2003, and 28.1 per cent in 2004, suggesting both continued reliance on membership dues as well as continued attempts to diversify revenue sources. Personal training is the most common of such attempts: 94 per cent of IHRSA clubs in 2002 offered personal training and over half rated it as their most profitable program/service.

14 Data from IHRSA website (as before, accessed January 2007).

15 "No Judgments" is the slogan of Crunch; "Compromise is just a polite word for surrender" and "110%" come from Equinox ads; "Look Better Naked" was the slogan of David Barton gyms; "All Fitness. No Attitude" is the slogan of Manhattan Plaza Health Club and "More gym, less money" is a slogan for Lucille Roberts. All are taken from print advertisements between 1999 and 2002.

16 From the "What's the Skinny" pull-out chart in *Time Out New York Special Fitness Issue* (January 6, 2000: 19–21).

4 Fitness media

1 These are the 2006 activity recommendations from the US Department of Health and Human Services Centers for Disease Control and Prevention (CDC), endorsed by, among others, the American College of Sports Medicine and the 1996 Surgeon General's Report on Physical Activity (American College of Sports Medicine 1998: v). See also the CDC website (http://www.cdc.gov/nccdphp/dnpa/physical/recommendations/index.htm [accessed December 2006]).

2 The Center for Disease Control and Prevention provides a list of activities that qualify as moderate intensity, available online (http://www.cdc.gov/nccdphp/dnpa/physical/pdf/PA_Intensity_table_2_1.pdf [accessed December 2006]).

3 The findings of the *Perrier Study* were discussed in articles in *Time* (5 February, 1979, 113: 140) and *House and Garden* (June 1979, 151: 26).

4 *The New York Times* bestseller list began in 1935; *Publishers Weekly* began in 1919. Of books that were listed for 100 weeks or more on their combined bestseller lists (which include both hardcover and paperback editions), *Jane Fonda's Workout Book* is ranked 31st. Fonda's book was listed for 218 weeks, total, well ahead of any other fitness book. As a testament to the perennially strong markets for children and self-searching adults, the five top-selling books are *The Joy of Sex*, *The Road Less Traveled*, *Charlotte's Web*, *Winnie-the-Pooh*, and *Richard Scarry's Best Word Book Ever* (Justice 1998: 343).

5 Based on a subject search for "physical fitness" in ProQuest (accessed November 2001), the number of physical fitness features rose from 25 in 1980 to 63 (1985), 114 (1986), 331 (1990), 403 (1995), and 717 (2000); a sixfold increase between 1986 and 2000. The information on the increasing numbers of health magazines, and magazine titles in general, comes from the web site of the Magazine Publishers of America (http://www.magazine.org [accessed November 2001]).

6 As an indication of the growth of "do it yourself" media, the *New York Times* divided its nonfiction bestseller list into "general" and "advice, how-to and miscellaneous" in 1984 (Justice 1998: 10).

7 For example, according to the 2002 *Men's Health* media kit, a typical issue of *Men's Health* magazine was primarily composed of articles on culture and humanities (18 per cent), health (18 per cent), beauty, fitness and grooming (17 per cent), and fashion (13 per cent). The same point applies, to a lesser degree, to bodybuilding magazines. According to their 2000 media kit, half of the articles in *Muscle & Fitness*, one of the oldest and best-selling bodybuilding magazines, featured exercise, fitness and bodybuilding training techniques. The remaining content dealt with food and nutrition (27 per cent), psychological and sexual fitness (7 per cent), personal grooming and fashion (6 per cent), sports medicine and "women's" topics (5 per cent each). More "hard core" bodybuilding magazines, such as Weider Publication's *Flex*, have a much narrower editorial profile, and thus have less content that is not immediately relevant to training. That said, however, 25 per cent of *Flex*'s content is made up of profiles of bodybuilders, and news, gossip and commentary (according to the *Flex* 2000 media kit).

5 Personal trainers

1 A 2002 survey by the International Health, Racquet and Sportsclub Association (IHRSA) of 1,208 health clubs found that 94 per cent offered personal training services. Information is from the IHRSA website (http://www.ihrsa.org [accessed January 2007]).

2 A "2005 Salary Survey" (2,800 respondents) conducted by ACE is available online (http://www.acefitness.org/getcertified/certification_pt.aspx [accessed January

2007]), and found that 70 per cent of personal trainers are paid on an hourly basis.

3 The 1997 IDEA Personal Training Business Survey (which was based on a 48 per cent response rate to a survey of its 8,000 members in 1996; results appeared in *IDEA Personal Trainer* [8 (May): 25–40]) reported that 34 per cent of trainers are self-employed.

4 The IDEA website (http://www.ideafit.com/pft_recognition.asp [accessed January 2007]) provides the 2006 estimate of 100,000 trainers; in comparison, an IDEA survey in 1996 estimated that there were over 65,000 personal trainers in the US. Survey results cited here are taken from the "Personal Fitness Trainer Fact Sheet" on the IDEA website (http://www.ideafit.com [accessed June 2004 and now no longer available]), which reported findings from: the 1998 IDEA Personal Trainer Trendwatch; the 1997 IDEA Personal Training Business Survey (see note 3; see also Davis and Davis 2000: 5); and the 1997 IDEA Industry Report on Personal Fitness Training. In addition, findings on personal trainers' level of education and employment benefits come from the ACE "2005 Salary Survey" (see note 2).

5 BLS occupational employment and wage statistics are available online (http://www.bls.gov/oes; 2005 data [accessed January 2007]).

6 From "A Brief History of the YMCA Movement," available on the YMCA website (http://www.ymca.net [accessed January 2002]).

7 My thanks to Dahn Shaulis for bringing Artie McGovern to my attention. McGovern's biography is a fascinating one, weaving together several broad themes within physical culture of the 1900s: after a failed career in professional boxing, he followed the advice of a doctor and opened his first gymnasium, at which he trained both doctors and their patients. This led to working with Cornell University Medical College and during the First World War training soldiers and sailors who were deemed unfit for duty, as well as making a movie (with his wife, also a boxer) showing women how to defend themselves while men were away at war (Smith 1931: 71).

8 Information on the number of US health clubs is from the IHRSA website (see note 1).

9 Personal training studios had developed in tandem with the new lifestyle clubs, but at a much smaller, more exclusive scale, be it in terms of cost or the specialized target market. For example, Definitions, a Manhattan-based group of one-on-one studios, opened in 1983, and the Sports Training Institute – originally Nautilus Sports Medical – began in the mid-1970s with an emphasis on personal and professional instruction through individual appointments (Penney 1977; Hinds 1979; Levy and Shafran 1986: 62).

10 The phrase "fitness training for the masses" had been used three years earlier in an article in the *Los Angeles Times* (Calistro 1989: 30), reflecting the earlier development and expansion of personal training in the celebrity- and image-conscious Hollywood industry. As an indication of the lag between west coast innovation and eventual mainstream availability of personal training, press coverage of personal training for the middle class did not appear until the mid-1990s for places such as Pittsburgh (Devine 1995), Toronto, Vancouver and Ottawa ("Muscle Bound" 1995).

11 IDEA has changed its name several times to reflect its shift from a narrow focus on aerobics to serving a broad range of "fitness professionals." IDEA was "The Association for Fitness Professionals" at the start of the 1990s, "The Health & Fitness Source" by the late 1990s, and "The Health and Fitness Association" in 2001; the strategic addition of "health" in the 1990s was intended to reflect that "a number of members are in the allied health professions (for example, physical therapists, dietitians and athletic trainers) and fitness is, after all, a critical part of a healthy lifestyle" (Davis and Davis 2001: 3).

12 Although a Canadian personal trainer organization was formalized at a later date than the US counterpart, it bears mentioning that Canadian personal trainers were active as contributors and task force members in the IDEA personal trainer newsletter since its inception, suggesting that the rise of personal training as a middle-class service was probably simultaneous in the two countries, even if the high-profile celebrity trainers started on the west coast of the US.

13 Information on certifications is from the 1997 IDEA Personal Training Business Survey (see note 2), and on ACE certifications from an *IPT* article ("Evaluating Personal Trainer Certifications" 2000: 20). According to an ACE "certification specialist" (via an email exchange, February 2002), ACE was certifying over 5,000 trainers a year in 2002.

14 IDEA began to offer a referral service, connecting trainers and consumers, in 1995 (Davis and Davis 1995: 2); ACE also had its own professional registry by 1997 – offered both as an employment resource for personal trainers ("Earning our Personal Trainer Certification . . .", *IPT* 1997, 8 [May]: 53) and as a customer service for the public. IDEA began a Personal Trainer Recognition System in 2000, which was announced in a two-page advertisement in *IPT* promising to "help personal trainers receive the recognition they deserve and a way for the consumer to understand a trainer's credentials" ("Are All Personal Trainers Equal?", *IPT* 2000, 11 [September]: 6). Personal trainers were invited to apply for recognition; four tiers (professional, advanced, elite, and master) reflected various degrees of excellence in certifications, years of experience, education, industry contribution and quality of service. In addition, IDEA members can be listed in their online "Personal Trainer Locator," through which employers and clients can search through trainers' personal profiles. Information from the IDEA website (http://www.ideafit.com [accessed March 2002 and January 2007]).

15 Information on recommendations is from the 1997 IDEA Personal Training Business Survey (see note 2).

16 The IDEA code of ethics is available online (http://www.ideafit.com/pdf/Code_of_ethics_PFT.pdf [accessed January 2007]).

6 Lessons from the fitness field

1 Data on health club member incomes are taken from the IHRSA website (http://www.ihrsa.org [accessed January 2007]) and refers to 2005; the professional/managerial profile of personal trainers is based on the IDEA Personal Training

Business Survey (*IPT* 1997, 8 [May]: 25–40]); and the professional/managerial profile of fitness magazines is taken from online media kits (http://www.menshealth.com; http://www.shape.com; http://www.self.com; http://www.meredith.com [accessed January 2007]).

Bibliography

Abbott, A. (1988) *The System of Professions: An Essay on the Division of Expert Labor*, Chicago: University of Chicago Press.

Adelman, M.L. (1986) *A Sporting Time: New York City and the Rise of Modern Athletics, 1820–70*, Urbana, IL: University of Illinois Press.

American College of Sports Medicine (1992) *ACSM Fitness Book*, Champaign, IL: Human Kinetics.

—— (1998) *ACSM Fitness Book*, 2nd edn, Champaign, IL: Human Kinetics.

American Heart Association (1997) *Fitting in Fitness*, New York: Random House.

Anderson, W.T., Jr (1971) "Identifying the convenience-oriented consumer", *Journal of Marketing Research*, 8 (2): 179–83.

Athletic Business [no author] (1987) "More state regulation?", *Athletic Business*, 11 (4): 20–4.

Bailey, P. (1978) *Leisure and Class in Victorian England: Rational Recreation and the Contest for Control, 1830–1885*, London: Routledge & Kegan Paul.

Barbato, J. (1988) "Small waists, big $ales", *Publishers Weekly*, March 25: 16–24.

Baudrillard, J. (1981) *For a Critique of the Political Economy of the Sign*, St Louis, MO: Telos.

—— (1998) *The Consumer Society: Myths and Structures*, London: Sage.

Bauman, Z. (1996) "From pilgrim to tourist – or a short history of identity", in S. Hall and P. du Gay (eds), *Questions of Cultural Identity*, London: Sage.

—— (2000) *Liquid Modernity*, Cambridge: Polity.

Beck, U. (1992) *The Risk Society: Towards a New Modernity*, London: Sage.

Beck, U. and Beck-Gernsheim, E. (2002) *Individualization*, London: Sage.

Beck, U., Giddens, A., and Lash, S. (1994) *Reflexive Modernization: Politics, Tradition and Aesthetics in the Modern Social Order*, Cambridge: Polity Press.

Becker, H. (1982) *Art Worlds*, Berkeley: University of California Press.

Bee, P. (2006) "The BMI myth", *The Guardian*, November 28. Online. Available HTTP: < http://www.guardian.co.uk/health/story/0,,1958685,00.html> [accessed January 2007].

Bell, D. and Hollows, J. (2005) *Ordinary Lifestyles: Popular Media, Consumption and Taste*, Maidenhead, Berks: Open University Press.

Bender, M. (1967) *The Beautiful People*, New York: Coward-McCann.

—— (1968) "The 'health club' toasts its teacher with pouilly fuisse", *The New York Times*, October 30: 52.

Bernzweig, J. (1983) "The great American shape-up", *Madison Avenue*, 25 (11): 37, 39.

Billings, L. (1998) *Self's Better Body Book*, New York: Condé Nast Books.

Blau, F.D. (1978) "The data on women workers, past, present, and future", in A.H. Stromberg and S. Harkess (eds), *Women Working: Theories and Facts in Perspective*, Palo Alto, CA: Mayfield.

Blaxter, M. (2003) "Biology, social class and inequalities in health: their synthesis in 'health capital' ", in S.J. Williams *et al.* (eds), *Debating Biology: Sociological Reflections on Health, Medicine and Society*, London: Routledge.

Bordo, S. (1993) *Unbearable Weight: Feminism, Western Culture, and the Body*, Berkeley: University of California Press.

—— (1997) *Twilight Zones: The Hidden Life of Cultural Images from Plato to O.J.*, Berkeley: University of California Press.

—— (2001) *The Male Body: A New Look at Men in Public and in Private*, New York: Farrar Straus Giroux.

Bourdieu, P. (1984) *Distinction: A Social Critique of the Judgment of Taste*, trans. R. Nice, Cambridge, MA: Harvard University Press.

—— (1986) "The forms of capital", in J. Richardson (ed.), *Handbook of Theory and Research for the Sociology of Education*, New York: Greenwood Press.

—— (1990) *In Other Words: Essays Towards a Reflexive Sociology*, trans. M. Adamson, Cambridge: Polity Press.

—— (1993) *The Field of Cultural Production: Essays on Art and Literature*, ed. R. Johnson, New York: Columbia University Press.

Bourdieu, P. and Wacquant, L. (1992) *An Invitation to Reflexive Sociology*, Chicago: University of Chicago Press.

Brady, J. (2000) "Minding muscle: the technologies of bodybuilding from the turn-of-the-century machine-man to the new millennium's ULTRAGIRL™", unpublished thesis, New York University.

Braverman, H. (1974) *Labor and Monopoly Capital: The Degradation of Work in the Twentieth Century*, New York: Monthly Review Press.

Briedland, A. *et al.* (eds), (1996) *American Culture: An Anthology of Civilization Texts*, London: Routledge.

Brodeur, P. (1988) "Employee fitness: doctrines and issues", in J. Harvey and H. Cantelon (eds), *Not Just a Game: Essays in Canadian Sport Sociology*, Ottawa: University of Ottawa Press.

Brubaker, B. (1991) "Athletic shoe industry goes beyond big business", *The Los Angeles Times*, March 17: 3.

Bryman, A. (2004) *The Disneyization of Society*, London: Sage.

Buckley, C. (2001) "Beauty as a balm", *Miami Herald*, October 23: 1C.

Bunton, R. (1997) "Popular health, advanced liberalism and *Good Housekeeping* magazine", in A. Petersen and R. Bunton (eds), *Foucault, Health and Medicine*, London: Routledge.

Bunton, R. and Burrows, R. (1995) "Consumption and health in the 'epidemiological' clinic of late modern medicine", in R. Bunton, S. Nettleton, and R. Burrows (eds), *The Sociology of Health Promotion: Critical Analyses of Consumption, Lifestyle and Risk*, London: Routledge.

Burchell, G. (1996) "Liberal government and techniques of the self", in A. Barry, T. Osborne, and N. Rose (eds), *Foucault and Political Reason: Liberalism, Neo-liberalism and Rationalities of Government*, Chicago: University of Chicago Press.

Bureau of Labor Statistics (1999a) *1999 National Occupational Employment and Wage Estimates*. Online. Available HTTP: <http://www.bls.gov/oeshome.htm> [accessed March 2002].

—— (1999b) *Statistical Abstract of the U.S.: 1999. Occupational and Industry Employment*, Washington, DC: US Bureau of Census.

—— (2001) *Comparative Labor Force Statistics, Ten Countries, 1959–2000*, Washington, DC: US Department of Labor.

—— (2006) *Consumer Expenditures in 2004*. Online. Available HTTP: < http://www.bls.gov/cex/csxann04.pdf> [accessed January 2007].

Burggraf, H. (1986) "Personal trainers muscle into N.Y.", *Crain's New York Business*, February 3: 5.

Bush, G.W. (2003) "President Bush highlights health and fitness initiative", transcript of speech, Dallas, TX, July 18. Online. Available HTTP: <http:// www.gop.com> [accessed November 2004].

Cage, R. (1989) "Spending differences across occupational fields", *Monthly Labor Review*, December: 33–42.

Calistro, P. (1989) "Finding the right private trainer is the new challenge in physical fitness", *The Los Angeles Times*, July 9, Magazine: 30.

Campbell, C. (1987) *The Romantic Ethic and the Spirit of Modern Consumerism*, New York: Blackwell.

Campos, P.F. (2004) *The Obesity Myth: Why America's Obsession With Weight Is Hazardous to Your Health*, New York: Gotham Books.

Caplow, T. (1954) *The Sociology of Work*, Minneapolis: University of Minnesota Press.

Cavanaugh, J. (1979) "On the corporate treadmill", *The New York Times*, March 11, 23: 1.

Cerulo, E. (2006) "A case study in new yuppiedom", *Details*, December: 106.

Chin, E. (2001) *Purchasing Power: Black Kids and American Consumer Culture*, Minneapolis: University of Minnesota Press.

Clark, J. (1992) "Personal fitness trainers for the masses", *Kiplinger's Personal Finance Magazine*, 46 (June): 107.

Coakley, J. (2001) *Sport in Society: Issues & Controversies*, 7th edn, Boston, MA: McGraw-Hill.

Cohen, L. (1990) *Making a New Deal: Industrial Workers in Chicago, 1919–1939*, Cambridge: Cambridge University Press.

Cohen, L. *et al.* (2005) "Remember I'm the bloody architect!: architects, organizations and discourses of profession", *Work, Employment & Society*, 19 (4): 775–96.

Colman, D. (2000) "Your trainer's secret", *New York*, April 17: 44–7.

Committee on Ways and Means (1971) *Basic Facts on the Health Industry*, Washington, DC: US Government Printing House.

Cook, R. (2000) "The mediated manufacture of an 'avant-garde': a Bourdieusian analysis of the field of contemporary art in London, 1997–9", in B. Fowler (ed.), *Reading Bourdieu on Society and Culture*, Oxford: Blackwell.

Crabtree, B. and Miller, W. (1999) "A template approach to text analysis: developing and using codebooks", in B. Crabtree and W. Miller (eds), *Doing Qualitative Research*, Newbury Park, CA: Sage.

Crawford, R. (1979) "Individual responsibility and health politics in the 1970s", in S. Reverby and D. Rosner (eds), *Health Care in America: Essays in Social History*, Philadelphia, PA: Temple University Press.

—— (1980) "Healthism and the medicalization of everyday life", *International Journal of Health Services*, 10 (3): 365–88.

—— (1984) "A cultural account of 'health': control, release, and the social body", in J.B. McKinlay (ed.), *Issues in the Political Economy of Health Care*, New York: Tavistock.

—— (1994) "The boundaries of the self and the unhealthy other: reflections on health, culture and AIDS", *Social Science and Medicine*, 38 (10): 1347–65.

Critser, G. (2001) "Let them eat fat: the heavy truths about American obesity", *Harper's Magazine*, March: 41–7.

—— (2003) *Fat Land: How Americans Became the Fattest People in the World*, New York: Houghton Mifflin.

Cross, G. (2000) *An All-Consuming Century: Why Commercialism Won in Modern America*, New York: Columbia University Press.

Crossley, N. (2006) "In the gym: motives, meaning and moral careers", *Body & Society*, 12 (3): 23–50.

Csikszentmihalyi, M. (1990) *Flow: The Psychology of Optimal Experience*, New York: Harper & Row.

Dahlin, R. (2001) "Holistic rules the day", *Publishers Weekly*, November 26: 24–32.

Damjanov, M. *et al.* (1999) "The shape of things to come", *Time Out New York Fitness Special*, January 7: 10–13].

Davis, K. (2002) "A dubious equality: men, women and cosmetic surgery", *Body and Society*, 8 (1): 49–65.

Davis, K. and Davis, P. (1995) "Warm-up", *IDEA Personal Trainer*, 6 (January): 2.

—— (1996) "Stand out from the crowd", *IDEA Personal Trainer*, 7 (October): 2.

—— (1997) "Bring ethics to the workplace", *IDEA Personal Trainer*, 8 (January): 2.

—— (2000) "Scope of practice", *IDEA Personal Trainer*, 11 (October): 5.

—— (2001) "Ringing in the new year", *IDEA Personal Trainer*, 12 (January): 3.

Dean, M. (1999) *Governmentality: Power and Rule in Modern Society*, London: Sage.

Decker, J.L. (1997) *Made in America: Self-Styled Success from Horatio Alger to Oprah Winfrey*, Minneapolis: University of Minnesota Press.

Defrance, J. and Pociello, C. (1993) "Structure and evolution of the field of sports in France (1960–1990)", *International Review for the Sociology of Sport*, 28: 1–23.

Dent, M. and Whitehead, S. (eds), (2002) *Managing Professional Identities: Knowledge, Performativity and the "New" Professional*, London: Routledge.

Department of Health and Human Services (1996) *Physical Activity and Health: A Report of the US Surgeon General*. Online. Available HTTP: <http://www.cdc.gov/nccdphp/sgr/sgr.htm> [accessed January 2007].

Devine, L. (1995) "Personal trainer business is shaping up", *Pittsburgh Post-Gazette*, November 29: N9.

Dobbins, B. and Sprague, K. (1981) *The Gold's Gym Weight-Training Book*, New York: Berkley Books.

Douglas, M. (1966) *Purity and Danger: An Analysis of the Concepts of Pollution and Taboo*, London: Routledge & Kegan Paul.

—— (1982) *Natural Symbols: Explorations in Cosmology*, New York: Pantheon Books.

Douglas, M. and Isherwood, B. (1996) *The World of Goods: Towards an Anthropology of Consumption*, 2nd edn, London: Routledge.

Drucker, P.F. (1969) *The Age of Discontinuity: Guidelines to Our Changing Society*, New York: Harper & Row.

Drury, S.J. (1983) "Wellness can be the solution to rising health care costs", *Business Insurance*, 17: 25.

du Gay, P. (2004) "Devices and dispositions: promoting consumption", *Consumption, Markets and Culture*, 7 (2): 99–105.

du Gay, P. and Pryke, M. (2002) "Cultural economy: an introduction", in P. du Gay and M. Pryke (eds), *Cultural Economy: Cultural Analysis and Commercial Life*, London: Sage.

Duncan, M.C. (1994) "The politics of women's body images and practices: Foucault, the panopticon, and Shape magazine", *Journal of Sport and Social Issues*, 18 (1): 48–65.

Dunn, D.H. and Segal, T. (1988) "With a personal trainer, the gym comes to you", *Business Week*, January 11: 166.

Dunning, E. (1986) "Sport as a male preserve: notes on the social sources of masculine identity and its transformations", *Theory, Culture & Society*, 3 (1): 79–90.

Dutton, K.P. (1995) *The Perfectible Body: The Western Ideal of Male Physical Development*, New York: Continuum.

Dyer, R. (1996) *White*, London: Routledge.

Eide, M. and Knight, G. (1999) "Public/private service: service journalism and the problems of everyday life", *European Journal of Communication*, 14 (4): 525–47.

Elias, N. (1978) *The Civilizing Process*, trans. E. Jephcott, New York: Urizen Books.

—— (1987) *Involvement and Detachment*, trans. E. Jephcott, Oxford: Blackwell.

Elias, N. and Dunning, E. (1986) *The Quest for Excitement: Sport and Leisure in the Civilizing Process*, Oxford: Blackwell.

Ellis, B.E. (1991) *American Psycho*, New York: Vintage Books.

Entwistle, J. (1997) "Power dressing and the construction of the career woman", in M. Nava *et al.* (eds), *Buy this Book: Studies in Advertising and Consumption*, London: Routledge.

Epstein, H. (1998) "Life & death on the social ladder", *The New York Review of Books*, July 16: 26–30.

Euromonitor (2005) *Sports Equipment in the USA*. Euromonitor International Global Market Information Database. Online. Available HTTP: <http://www.gmid. euromonitor.com> [accessed January 2007].

Evans, R.G., Barer, M.L., and Marmor, T.R. (1994) *Why are Some People Healthy and Others Not?: The Determinants of Health of Populations*, New York: Aldine de Gruyter.

Ewen, S. (1976) *Captains of Consciousness: Advertising and the Social Roots of the Consumer Culture*, New York: McGraw-Hill.

—— (1999) *All Consuming Images: The Politics of Style in Contemporary Culture*, rev. edn, New York: Basic Books.

Falk, P. (1994) *The Consuming Body*, London: Sage.

Farley, T. and Cohen, D. (2001) "Fixing a fat nation", *The Washington Monthly*, (December): 23–9.

Featherstone, M. (1982) "The body in consumer culture", *Theory, Culture & Society*, 2: 18–33.

—— (1987) "Lifestyle and consumer culture", *Theory, Culture & Society*, 4: 55–70.

—— (1991) *Consumer Culture and Postmodernism*, London: Sage.

Fereday, J. and Muir-Cochrane, E. (2006) "Demonstrating rigor using thematic analysis: a hybrid approach of inductive and deductive coding and theme development", *International Journal of Qualitative Methods*, 5 (1): 1–11.

Ferguson, P.P. (1998) "A cultural field in the making: gastronomy in 19th-century France", *The American Journal of Sociology*, 104 (3): 597–641.

Fine, B. (1943) "Physical fitness work is spurred by colleges", *The New York Times*, March 21, E9.

Fisher, M.J. (1985) "Insurers pitch good health", *National Underwriter*, June 22: 4, 15.

Fishwick, L. (2001) "Be what you wanna be: a sense of identity down at the local gym", in N. Watson and S. Cunningham-Burley (eds), *Reframing the Body*, Basingstoke, Hants: Palgrave.

Flew, T. (2006) "The new middle class meets the creative class: the Masters of Business

Administration (MBA) and creative innovation in 21ˢᵗ-century China", *International Journal of Cultural Studies*, 9 (3): 419–29.

Florida, R. (2002) *The Rise of the Creative Class*, New York: Basic Books.

Fogarty, K.H. (1998) *Health Clubs: Architecture and Design*, Glen Cove, NY: PBC International.

Fonda, J. (1981) *Jane Fonda's Workout Book*, New York: Simon & Schuster.

Forman, J. (2001) "Attendance at fitness centers surges", *Boston Globe*, November 11: 4.

Foucault, M. (1977) *Discipline and Punish: The Birth of the Prison*, trans. A. Sheridan, New York: Vintage Books.

—— (1978) *The History of Sexuality*, Volume 1, *An Introduction*, trans. R. Hurley, New York: Vintage Books.

—— (1980a) "Body/power", in C. Gordon (ed.), *Power/Knowledge: Selected Interviews and Other Writings, 1972–1977*, New York: Pantheon Books.

—— (1980b) "The politics of health in the eighteenth century", in C. Gordon (ed.), *Power/Knowledge: Selected Interviews and Other Writings, 1972–1977*, New York: Pantheon Books.

—— (1985) *The History of Sexuality*, Volume 2, *The Use of Pleasure*, trans. R. Hurley, New York: Pantheon Books.

—— (1986) *The History of Sexuality*, Volume 3, *The Care of the Self*, trans. R. Hurley, New York: Vintage Books.

—— (1988) "Technologies of the self", in L.M. Martin, H. Gutman, and P.H. Hutton (eds) *Technologies of the Self: A Seminar with Michel Foucault*, Amherst, MA: University of Massachusetts Press.

—— (1991) "Governmentality", in G. Burchell, C. Gordon, and P. Miller, *The Foucault Effect: Studies in Governmentality*, Chicago: University of Chicago Press.

Fox, R.C. (1997) "The medicalization and demedicalization of American society", in P. Conrad (ed.), *The Sociology of Health and Illness: Critical Perspectives*, 5ᵗʰ edn, New York: St Martin's Press.

Frank, R.H. (1999) *Luxury Fever: Why Money Fails to Satisfy in an Era of Excess*, New York: Free Press.

Franklin, B. (1970) *Autobiography and Other Pieces*, ed. D. Welland, London: Oxford University Press.

Franks, B.D. and Howley, E.T. (1989) *Fitness Facts: The Healthy Living Handbook*, Champaign, IL: Human Kinetics.

Franks, B.D., Howley, E.T., and Iyriboz, Y. (1999) *The Health Fitness Handbook*, Champaign, IL: Human Kinetics.

Frew, M. and McGillivray, D. (2005) "Health clubs and body politics: aesthetics and the quest for physical capital", *Leisure Studies*, 24 (2): 161–75.

Frons, M. (1989) "Fit on the road", *Business Week*, December 4: 128.

Frum, D. (2000) *How We Got Here. The 70's: The Decade That Brought You Modern Life (For Better or Worse)*, New York: Basic Books.

Fukuyama, F. (1999) *The Great Disruption: Human Nature and the Reconstitution of Social Order*, New York: Simon & Schuster.

Gaines, C. (1982) *Yours in Perfect Manhood, Charles Atlas: The Most Effective Fitness Program Ever Devised*, New York: Simon & Schuster.

Gard, M. and Wright, J. (2005) *The Obesity Epidemic: Science, Morality and Ideology*, London: Routledge.

Garner, D.M. (1997) "The 1997 body image survey results", *Psychology Today*, 30 (1): 30–44.

Gault, Y. (1991) "Health clubs reshape strategy to boost profit", *Crain's New York Business*, August 26: 4.

Giddens, A. (1991) *Modernity and Self-Identity: Self and Society in the Late Modern Age*, Cambridge: Polity Press.

Gilbert, S. (1996) "Fitness helps, even for smokers", *The New York Times*, July 17: C7.

Gillick, M.R. (1984) "Health promotion, jogging, and the pursuit of the moral life", *Journal of Health Politics, Policy and Law*, 9 (3): 369–87.

Gimlin, D. (2002) "Aerobics: neutralizing the body and renegotiating the self", in D. Gimlin, *Body Work: Beauty and Self-Image in American Culture*, Berkeley: University of California Press.

Ginsberg, L. (2000) "The hard work of working out: defining leisure, health and beauty in a Japanese health club", *Journal of Sport and Social Issues*, 34 (3): 260–81.

Glassner, B. (1988) "Health club hawkers", in B. Glassner, *Bodies: Why We Look the Way We Do (And How We Feel About It)*, New York: G.P. Putnam.

Godbout, T.M. (1993) "Employment change and sectoral distribution in 10 countries, 1970–1990", *Monthly Labor Review*, October: 3–20.

Goffman, E. (1959) *The Presentation of Self in Everyday Life*, Garden City, NY: Anchor.

Goldberg, V. (1975) "Body building: is it an art, a sport or sheer exhibitionism?", *The New York Times*, November 30: 264.

Goldman, J. and Kennedy, L. (1983) *The New York Urban Athlete: Sports, Fitness, and Fun in the Big Apple*, New York: Simon & Schuster.

Goldstein, M. (1992) *The Health Movement: Promoting Fitness in America*, New York: Twayne Publishers.

Gottlieb, R. (1993) *Forcing the Spring: The Transformation of the American Environmental Movement*, Washington, DC: Island Press.

Grant, A.H.W. and Schlesinger, L.A. (1995) "Realize your customers" full profit potential', *Harvard Business Review*, 73 (5): 59–72.

Greco, M. (1993) "Psychosomatic subjects and the 'duty to be well': personal agency within medical rationality", *Economy and Society*, 22 (3): 357–72.

Green, H. (1986) *Fit for America: Health, Fitness, Sport and American Society*, New York: Pantheon Books.

—— (1989) "Introduction", in K. Grover (ed.), *Fitness in American Culture: Images of*

Health, Sport, and the Body, 1830–1940, Amherst, MA: University of Massachusetts Press.

Greene, R. (1986) "Does physically fit mean fiscally fit?", *Forbes*, 138 (6): 188.

Griffin, C.W. (1982) "Physical fitness", in M.T. Inge (ed.), *Concise Histories of American Popular Culture*, Westport, CT: Greenwood Press.

Gronow, J. (1997) *The Sociology of Taste*, London: Routledge.

Grover, K. (ed.) (1989) *Fitness in American Culture: Images of Health, Sport, and the Body, 1830–1940*, Amherst, MA: University of Massachusetts Press.

Guttmann, A. (1995) "Puritans at play? Accusations and replies", in D.K. Wiggins (ed.), *Sport in America: From Wicked Amusement to National Obsession*, Champaign, IL: Human Kinetics.

Haiken, E. (1997) *Venus Envy: A History of Cosmetic Surgery*, Baltimore, MD: Johns Hopkins University Press.

Haley, B. (1978) *The Healthy Body and Victorian Culture*, Cambridge, MA: Harvard University Press.

Hamermesh, D.S. and Biddle, J.E. (1994) "Beauty and the labor market", *American Economic Review*, 84: 1174–94.

Hardman, A. and Stensel, D. (2003) *Physical Activity and Health: The Evidence Explained*, London: Routledge.

Hardy, S. (1995) "Adopted by all the leading clubs: sporting goods and the shaping of leisure", in D.K. Wiggins (ed.), *Sport in America: From Wicked Amusement to National Obsession*, Champaign, IL: Human Kinetics.

Hargreaves, J. (1994) *Sporting Females: Critical Issues in the History and Sociology of Women's Sports*, London: Routledge.

Harris, L. *et al.* (1984[1979]) *Fitness in America – The Perrier Study: A National Research Report of Behavior, Knowledge and Opinions Concerning the Taking Up of Sports and Exercise*, New York: Garland Publishing.

Hellmich, N. (1993) "Body and book by Jake are designed to motivate", *USA Today*, 26 April: 4D.

Hepworth, M. and Featherstone, M. (1982) *Surviving Middle Age*, Oxford: Basil Blackwell.

Higginbottom, K. (2006) "Fat is the question", *The Guardian*, November 4, Work: 1.

Hinds, M.dC. (1979) "A gym exercising time-saving methods", *The New York Times*, July 3: C5.

—— (1980) "Where to shape up in Manhattan: a guide to health clubs", *The New York Times*, May 24: 48.

Hirsch, F. (1977) *The Social Limits to Growth*, London: Routledge & Kegan Paul.

Hobsbawm, E. (1990) *Nations and Nationalism Since 1780: Programme, Myth, Reality*, Cambridge: Cambridge University Press.

Hochschild, A.R. (1983) *The Managed Heart: Commercialization of Human Feeling*, Berkeley: University of California Press.

—— (1997) *The Time Bind: When Work Becomes Home and Home Becomes Work*, New York: Metropolitan Books.

Horsley, C.B. (1977) "A form of residential rehabilitation for New York: 'country clubs' ", *The New York Times*, May 25: D17.

Howell, J. (1990) "Meanings go mobile: fitness, health and the quality of life debate in contemporary America", unpublished thesis, University of Illinois at Urbana-Champaign.

—— (2005) "Generational marketing: fitness, health and lifestyle formations", in S. Jackson and D. Andrews (eds), *Sport, Culture and Advertising*, London: Routledge.

Howell, J. and Ingham, A. (2001) "From social problem to personal issue: the language of lifestyle", *Cultural Studies*, 15 (2): 326–51.

Howell, J. and Minor, S.L. (2000) "Health and fitness professions", in J. Harris and S. Hoffman (eds), *An Introduction to Kinesiology: Studying Physical Activity*, Champaign, IL: Human Kinetics.

Huizinga, J. (1955) *Homo Ludens: A Study of the Play Element in Culture*, Boston, MA: Beacon Press.

IDEA [no author] (1997) "IDEA personal training business survey", *IDEA Personal Trainer*, 8 (May): 25–40.

IDEA [no author] (2000) "Evaluating personal trainer certifications", *IDEA Personal Trainer*, 11 (November/December): 18–23.

Ilmonen, K. (2004) "The use of and commitment to goods", *Journal of Consumer Culture*, 4 (1): 27–50.

Ingham, A.G. (1985) "From public issue to personal trouble: well-being and the fiscal crisis of the state", *Sociology of Sport Journal*, 2 (1): 43–55.

Jackson, P. (1995) "The development of a scientific fact: the case of passive smoking", in R. Bunton, S. Nettleton, and R. Burrows (eds), *The Sociology of Health Promotion: Critical Analyses of Consumption, Lifestyle and Risk*, London: Routledge.

Jacobs, J.A. and Gerson, K. (1998) "Who are the overworked Americans?", *Review of Social Economy*, 56 (4): 442–59.

Jarvie, G. (1991) *Highland Games: The Making of a Myth*, Edinburgh: Edinburgh University Press.

Jarvie, G. and Maguire, J. (1994) *Sport and Leisure in Social Thought*, London: Routledge.

Jenkins, R. (1992) *Pierre Bourdieu*, London: Routledge.

Johnson, S. (1976) "A little weightlifting to get into feminine shape", *The New York Times*, December 13: 60.

Jordan, P. (1992) "Cher fitness", *American Fitness*, 10 (March): 30–3.

Justice, K.L. (1998) *Bestseller Index: All Books, Publishers Weekly and the New York Times Through 1990*, Jefferson, NC: McFarland & Company.

Kagan, E. and Morse, M. (1988) "The body electronic. Aerobic exercise on video:

women's search for empowerment and self-transformation", *The Drama Review*, 32 (4): 164–80.

Kaufman, B.P. and Kirchheimer, S. (1997) *Stronger Faster: Workday Workouts That Build Maximum Muscle in Minimum Time*, Emmaus, PA: Rodale Press.

Kaye, D. (1977) "Spring shape-up guide", *The New York Times*, March 27: F44.

Keat, R. and Abercrombie, N. (1991) *Enterprise Culture*, New York: Routledge.

Keller, K.L. (1998) *Strategic Brand Management: Building, Measuring, and Managing Brand Equity*, Upper Saddle River, NJ: Prentice Hall.

Kimmel, M. (1996) *Manhood in America: A Cultural History*, New York: Free Press.

King, N. (2004) "Using templates in the thematic analysis of text", in C. Cassell and G. Symon (eds), *Essential Guide to Qualitative Methods in Organizational Research*, London: Sage.

Klein, A.M. (1993) *Little Big Men: Bodybuilding Subculture and Gender Construction*, Albany, NY: State University of New York Press.

Kolata, G. (2003) *Ultimate Fitness: The Quest for Truth About Exercise and Health*, New York: Picador.

Kolbert, E. (2004) "Mother courage: kids, careers, and culture", *The New Yorker*, March 8: 85–7.

Kriegsman, M. (2001) "New York Health & Racquet Club (Whitehall Street location)", *Time Out New York Annual Fitness Special*, January 11: 18.

Krupa, D. (2001) "Sedentary death syndrome is second largest threat to public health", 29 May. Online. Available HTTP: <http://www.newswise.com/articles/2001> [accessed March 2002].

Kuczynski, A. (2001) "Oh, how far a magazine will go to stimulate newsstand sales", *The New York Times*, June 18: C1.

Kuzela, L. (1984) "Cashing in on the fitness boom", *Industry Week*, November 12.

Laberge, S. and Kay, J. (2002) "Pierre Bourdieu's sociocultural theory and sport practice", in J. Maguire and K. Young (eds), *Theory, Sport & Society*, Oxford: JAI, Elsevier Science.

Laberge, S. and Sankoff, D. (1988) "Physical activities, body *habitus*, and lifestyle", in J. Harvey and H. Cantelon (eds) *Not Just a Game: Essays in Canadian Sport Sociology*, Ottawa: University of Ottawa Press.

Lalonde, M. (1974) *A New Perspective on the Health of Canadians*, Ottawa: Department of National Health and Welfare.

Lamont, M. and Molnar, V. (2001) "How blacks use consumption to shape their collective identity", *Journal of Consumer Culture*, 1 (1): 31–45.

Lang, T. (2004) Interview, Radio 4, PM, February 11, London: BBC.

Larson, M. S. (1977) *The Rise of Professionalism: A Sociological Analysis*, Berkeley: University of California Press.

Lasch, C. (1979) *The Culture of Narcissism: American Life in an Age of Diminishing Expectations*, New York: W. W. Norton.

Lash, S. and Urry, J. (1987) *The End of Organized Capitalism*, Madison, WI: University of Wisconsin Press.

Laurence, L. (1996) "Fitness helps overcome other health risk factors", *Houston Chronicle*, July 31: 2.

Lears, T.J.J. (1983) "From salvation to self-realization: advertising and the therapeutic roots of consumer culture", in R.W. Fox and T.J.J. Lears (eds), *The Culture of Consumption: Critical Essays in American History, 1880–1980*, New York: Pantheon Books.

—— (1989) "American advertising and the reconstruction of the body, 1880–1930", in K. Grover (ed.), *Fitness in American Culture: Images of Health, Sport, and the Body, 1830–1940*, Amherst, MA: University of Massachusetts Press.

Lee, P. (1989) "Basic training", *Black Enterprise*, 19 (July): 52–3.

Leepson, M. (1978) "Physical fitness boom", *Editorial Research Reports*, 1 (14): 263–80.

Lehmann, P. (1979) "Health education", in Department of Health, Education, and Welfare, *Healthy People: The Surgeon General's Report on Health Promotion and Disease Prevention, Background Papers*, Washington, DC: US Government Printing Office.

Leicht, K.T. and Fennell, M.L. (1997) "The changing organizational context of professional work", *Annual Review of Sociology*, 23: 215–31.

—— (2001) *Professional Work: A Sociological Approach*. Oxford: Blackwell.

Leidner, R. (1999) "Emotional labor in service work", *The Annals of the American Academy of Political Social Science*, 561: 81–95.

Leiss, W., Kline, S., and Jhally, S. (1997) *Social Communication in Advertising: Persons, Products and Images of Well-Being*, 2nd edn, London: Routledge.

Levine, C. (2001) "America strikes back", *Patriot Ledger* (Quincy, MA), October 13: 15.

Levy, M.Z. and Shafran, J. (1986) *Gym Psych: The Insider's Guide to Health Clubs*, New York: Fawcett Columbine.

Lichtenstein, G. (1972) "Fraud complaints on health-spas rise", *The New York Times*, December 26: 1, 16.

Lipovetsky, G. (1994) *The Empire of Fashion: Dressing Modern Democracy*, trans. C. Porter, Princeton, NJ: Princeton University Press.

Long, R. (1997) "The fitness of the gym", *The Harvard Gay & Lesbian Review*, 4 (3): 20.

Luciano L. (2001) *Looking Good: Male Body Image in Modern America*, New York: Hill & Wang.

Lury, C. (1996) *Consumer Culture*, Oxford: Polity Press.

McCarthy, J. (1987) "An industry in transition", *Athletic Business*, 11 (4): 40–6.

McCarthy, J. et al. (1999) *50 Million Members by 2010: The American Fitness Industry's Plan for Growth*, Boston, MA: International Health, Racquet and Sportsclub Association.

McFall, L. (2004) *Advertising: A Cultural Economy*, London: Sage.

McGee, M. (2005) *Self-Help, Inc.: Makeover Culture in American Life*, New York: Oxford University Press.

McIntosh, P.C. (1968) *Physical Education in England Since 1800*, rev. edn, London: G. Bell & Sons.

Maclean's [no author] (1995) "Muscle bound: one trainer says clients 'want the energy to survive in the nineties' ", *Maclean's*, February 20: 48.

MacNeill, M. (1994) "Active women, media representations, and ideology", in S. Birrell and C.L. Cole (eds), *Women, Sport, and Culture*, Champaign, IL: Human Kinetics.

—— (1998) "Sex, lies, and videotape: the political and cultural economies of celebrity fitness videos", in G. Rail (ed.), *Sport and Postmodern Times*, New York: State University of New York Press.

—— (1999) "Social marketing, gender, and the science of fitness: a case-study of ParticipACTION campaigns", in P. White and K. Young (eds) *Sport and Gender in Canada*, Don Mills, ON: Oxford University Press.

Maguire, J. (1992) "Towards a sociological theory of sport and the emotions: a process-sociological perspective", in E. Dunning and C. Rojek (eds), *Sport and Leisure in the Civilizing Process: Critique and Counter-Critique*, London: Macmillan.

—— (2005) *Power and Global Sport: Zones of Prestige, Emulation and Resistance*, London: Routledge.

Maguire, J. and Mansfield, L. (1998) " 'No-body's perfect': women, aerobics, and the body beautiful," *Sociology of Sport Journal*, 15: 109–37.

Marchand, R. (1985) *Advertising the American Dream: Making Way for Modernity, 1920–1940*, Berkeley: University of California Press.

Marks, S. (1991) "Introduction", in M. Sudy (ed.), *Personal Trainer Manual: The Resource for Fitness Instructors*, San Diego, CA: American Council on Exercise.

Markula, P. (2001) "Beyond the perfect body: women's body image distortion in fitness magazine discourse", *Journal of Sport and Social Issues*, 25 (2): 158–79.

Mayo, J.M. (1998) *The American Country Club: Its Origins and Development*, New Brunswick, NJ: Rutgers University Press.

Miller, D. (1998) *A Theory of Shopping*, Oxford: Polity.

—— (2001) *The Dialectics of Shopping*, Chicago: University of Chicago Press.

Miller, L.K. and Fielding, L.W. (1995) "The battle between the for-profit health club and the 'commercial' YMCA", *Journal of Sport and Social Issues*, 19 (1): 76–107.

Miller, P. and Rose, N. (1997) "Mobilizing the consumer: assembling the subject of consumption", *Theory, Culture & Society*, 14 (1): 1–36.

Mills, C.W. (1959) *The Sociological Imagination*, New York: Oxford University Press.

Mitchell, A. (1983) *The Nine American Lifestyles*, New York: Macmillan.

Mobius, M.M. and Rosenblat, T.S. (2006) "Why beauty matters", *American Economic Review*, 96: 222–35.

Morris, V. (1997) "Interview with Doug Levine, president of Crunch gym chain mixes fitness with fun", CNNfn (Cable News Network Financial), *Business Unusual*, 18 July, transcript: Federal Document Clearing House.

Moss, L. (1986) "Meet Fred Manocherian: he's savvy but he's volatile, and those clubs are winners", *Crain's New York Business*, September 29: 1.

Mrozek, D.J. (1989) "Sport in American life: from national health to personal fulfillment, 1890–1940", in K. Grover (ed.), *Fitness in American Culture: Images of Health, Sport, and the Body, 1830–1940*, Amherst, MA: University of Massachusetts Press.

Muir, F.M. (1995) "Affording fitness: secretaries as well as stars now work out with personal trainers", *The Los Angeles Times*, September 8: B2.

Nasatir, J. (1996) "HLW La Palestra", *Interior Design*, January: 78–83.

National Center for Health Statistics (2005) *Health, United States, 2005*, Hyattsville, MA: Department of Health and Human Services.

Negus, K. (2002) "The work of cultural intermediaries and the enduring distance between production and consumption", *Cultural Studies*, 16 (4): 501–15.

Nestle, M. (2002) *Food Politics: How the Food Industry Influences Nutrition and Health*, Berkeley: University of California Press.

Nichter, M. and Nichter, M. (1991) "Hype and weight", *Medical Anthropology*, 13: 249–84.

Nixon, S. and Crewe, B. (2004) "Pleasure at work?: gender, consumption and work-based identities in the creative industries", *Consumption, Markets and Culture*, 7 (2): 129–47.

Nixon, S. and du Gay, P. (2002) "Who needs cultural intermediaries?", *Cultural Studies*, 16 (4): 495–500.

O'Brien, M. (1995) "Health and lifestyle: a critical mess? Notes on the dedifferentiation of health", in R. Bunton, S. Nettleton and R. Burrows (eds), *The Sociology of Health Promotion: Critical Analyses of Consumption, Lifestyle and Risk*, London: Routledge.

Oliver, J.E. (2006) *Fat Politics: The Real Story Behind America's Obesity Epidemic*, New York: Oxford University Press.

Oropesa, R.S. (1993) "Using the service economy to relieve the double burden: female labor force participation and service purchases", *Journal of Family Issues*, 14 (3): 438–73.

Pagano, P. (1985) "FTC drops attempt to regulate spa industry", *The Los Angeles Times*, December 19: 1.

Parker, S. (1976) *The Sociology of Leisure*, London: George Allen & Unwin.

Pavalko, R.M. (1971) *Sociology of Occupations and Professions*, Itasca, IL: F.E. Peacock Publishers.

Peiss, K. (1998) *Hope in a Jar: The Making of America's Beauty Culture*, New York: Henry Holt.

Penney, A. (1977) "Tough is good for you", *The New York Times*, 14 August, VI: 50–4.

—— (1990a) "Yes, it is possible", *Self*, January: 93.

—— (1990b) "You told me 'get real!' ", *Self*, March: 151.

Petersen, A. (1997) "Risk, governance and the new public health", in A. Petersen and R. Bunton (eds), *Foucault, Health and Medicine*, London: Routledge.

Pettinger, L. (2004) "Brand culture and branded workers: service work and aesthetic labour in fashion retail", *Consumption, Markets and Culture*, 7 (2): 165–84.

Pine, B.J., II, and Gilmore, J.H. (1998) "Welcome to the experience economy", *Harvard Business Review*, 76 (4): 97–105.

Pine, B.J., II, and Peppers, D. (1995) "Do you want to keep your customers forever?", *Harvard Business Review*, 73 (2): 103–13.

Plummer, J.T. (1984) "How personality makes a difference", *Journal of Advertising Research*, 24 (December/January): 27–30.

Prior, N. (2000) "A different field of vision: gentlemen and players in Edinburgh, 1826–1851", in B. Fowler (ed.), *Reading Bourdieu on Society and Culture*, Oxford: Blackwell.

Pronger, B. (1990) *The Arena of Masculinity*, New York: St Martin's Press.

—— (2002) *Body Fascism: Salvation in the Technology of Physical Fitness*, Toronto: University of Toronto Press.

Putnam, R.D. (2000) *Bowling Alone: The Collapse and Revival of American Community*, New York: Simon & Schuster.

Putney, C. (1997) "From character to body building: the YMCA and the suburban metropolis, 1950–1980", in N. Mjagki and M. Spratt (eds), *Men and Women Adrift: The YMCA and YWCA in the City*, New York: New York University Press.

Rader, B. (1997) "The quest for self-sufficiency and the new strenuosity", in S.W. Pope (ed.), *The New American Sport History: Recent Approaches and Perspectives*, Urbana: University of Illinois Press.

Real, M. (1999) "Aerobics and feminism: self-determination or patriarchal hegemony?", in R. Martin and T. Miller (eds), *SportCult*, Minneapolis: University of Minnesota Press.

Reichheld, F.F. (1996) "Learning from customer defections", *Harvard Business Review*, 74 (2): 56–67.

Riesman, D. (1950) *The Lonely Crowd: A Study of the Changing American Character*, New Haven, CT: Yale University Press.

Riess, S.A. (1989) *City Games: The Evolution of American Urban Society and the Rise of Sports*, Urbana, IL: University of Illinois Press.

Roach, M. (1977) "Bodybuilders labor to develop an image", *The New York Times*, March 20: 173.

—— (1978) "A few good places to get in shape", *The New York Times*, July 10: C10.

Roan, S. (1996) "Moderate exercise is too much for too many", *The Los Angeles Times*, July 12: E1.

Rocamora, A. (2002) "Fields of fashion: critical insights into Bourdieu's sociology of culture", *Journal of Consumer Culture*, 2 (3): 341–62.

Rose, N. (1990) *Governing the Soul: The Shaping of the Private Self*, London: Routledge.

—— (1996) *Inventing our Selves: Psychology, Power, and Personhood*, Cambridge: Cambridge University Press.

—— (1999) *Powers of Freedom: Reframing Political Thought*, Cambridge: Cambridge University Press.

Roseberry, W. (1996) "The rise of yuppie coffees and the reimagination of class in the United States", *American Anthropologist*, 98 (4): 762–75.

Russell, L.B. (1986) *Is Prevention Better than Cure?*, Washington, DC: Brookings Institution.

Ryan, P. (1995) "How can we judge quality?", *IDEA Personal Trainer*, 6 (July/August): 26–34.

Ryzik, M. (2006) "Don't hit on me, Mr Goodbody", *New York Times*, June 1: 8.

Sage, G.H. (1998) "The political economy of fitness in the United States", in K. Volkwein (ed.), *Fitness as Cultural Phenomenon*, New York: Waxmann Münster.

Sassatelli, R. (1999a) "Fitness gyms and the local organization of experience", *Sociological Research Online*, 4 (3).

—— (1999b) "Interaction order and beyond: a field analysis of body culture within fitness gyms", *Body & Society*, 5 (2/3): 227–48.

Sassen, S. (1990) "Economic restructuring and the American city", *Annual Review of Sociology*, 16: 465–90.

Schlosberg, S. and Neporent, L. (1996) *Fitness for Dummies*, Foster City, CA: IDG Books.

—— (2000) *Fitness for Dummies*, 2nd edn, Foster City, CA: IDG Books.

Schoen, E. and Cohen, A. (1973) "100 ways to stay warm", *New York Magazine*, 26 November: 42–8.

Schor, J. (1991) *The Overworked American*, New York: Basic Books.

Schulman, B.J. (2001) *The Seventies: The Great Shift in American Culture, Society, and Politics*, New York: Free Press.

Schwartz, J.E. (2001) "Social inequality, stress, and health", in J.R. Blau (ed.), *The Blackwell Companion to Sociology*, Malden, MA: Blackwell.

Shephard, R.J. (1986) *Economic Benefits of Enhanced Fitness*, Champaign, IL: Human Kinetics.

Sherry, J.F., Jr (ed.) (1998) *Servicescapes: The Concept of Place in Contemporary Markets*, Lincolnwood, IL: NTC Business Books.

Shilling, C. (1993) *The Body and Social Theory*, London: Sage.

Sidwell, M.J. and Kane, M.J. (1990) "Twentieth-century sport in the United States", in J.B. Parks and B.R.K. Zanger (eds) *Sport and Fitness Management: Career Strategies and Professional Content*, Champaign, IL: Human Kinetics.

Siegel, A. (1991) "Fitting in fitness", *Working Woman*, 16 (March): 67.

Simmel, G. (1950) "Secrecy", in K.H. Wolff (ed.), *The Sociology of Georg Simmel*, New York: Free Press.

Simonds, W. (1992) *Women and Self-Help Culture: Reading Between the Lines*, New Brunswick, NJ: Rutgers University Press.

Sivulka, J. (2001) *Stronger Than Dirt: A Cultural History of Advertising Personal Hygiene in America, 1875–1940*, Amherst, NY: Humanity Books.

Slater, D. (1997) *Consumer Culture and Modernity*, Cambridge: Polity Press.

Smith, B. (1931) "A broken knuckle gave him the winning punch", *American Magazine*, 112 (November): 68–71+.

Smith Maguire, J. (2001) "Fit and flexible: the fitness industry, personal trainers and emotional service labor", *Sociology of Sport Journal*, 18 (4): 379–402.

—— (2002a) "Body lessons: fitness publishing and the cultural production of the fitness consumer", *International Review for the Sociology of Sport*, 37 (3/4): 449–64.

—— (2002b) "Michel Foucault: sport, power, technologies and governmentality", in J. Maguire and K. Young (eds), *Theory, Sport & Society*, Oxford: JAI, Elsevier Science.

—— (2006) "Exercising control: empowerment and the fitness discourse", in L.K. Fuller (ed.) *Sport, Rhetoric, and Gender: Historical Perspectives and Media Representations*, New York: Palgrave.

Snowden, L. (1994) "I am not a trainer, this is not a gym", *Harper's Bazaar*, November: 84–6.

Solomon, M.R. (1998) "Dressing for the part: the role of costume in the staging of servicescape", in J.F. Sherry Jr (ed.), *Servicescape: The Concept of Place in Contemporary Markets*, Lincolnwood, IL: NTC Business Books.

Spielvogel, L. (2003) *Working Out in Japan: Shaping the Female Body in Tokyo Fitness Clubs*, Durham, NC: Duke University Press.

Sporting Goods Manufacturers Association (2000) *The SGMA Report: Tracking the Fitness Movement*, North Palm Beach, FL: Sporting Goods Manufacturers Association.

Stearns, P. (1997) *Fat History: Bodies and Beauty in the Modern West*, New York: New York University Press.

Steinberg, R.J. and Figart, D.M. (1999) "Emotional labor since *The Managed Heart*", *The Annals of the American Academy of Political Social Science*, 561: 8–26.

Stobbe, M. (2001) "Gym wars go toe-to-toe", *Charlotte Observer* (NC), 26 November: 1E.

Strobel, F.R. (1993) *Upward Dreams, Downward Mobility: The Economic Decline of the American Middle Class*, Lanham, MD: Rowman & Littlefield.

Sudy, M. (1991) *Personal Trainer Manual: The Resource for Fitness Instructors*, San Diego: American Council on Exercise.

Susman, W.I. (1979) " 'Personality' and the making of twentieth-century culture", in J. Higham and P.K. Conkin (eds), *New Directions in American Intellectual History*, Baltimore, MD: Johns Hopkins University Press.

Taylor, A. (1972) "From shimmying to standing on your head: ways of shaping up", *The New York Times*, March 24: 36.

—— (1974) "For those whose goals are firm muscles and a svelte body", *The New York Times*, September 16: 49.

Turner, B.S. (1994) "Preface", in P. Falk, *The Consuming Body*, London: Sage.

Turow, J. (2000) "Segmenting, signalling and tailoring: probing the dark side of target marketing", in R. Anderson and L. Strate (eds), *Critical Studies in Media Commercialism*, New York: Oxford University Press.

Unger, J.B. and Johnson, C.A. (1995) "Social relationships and physical activity in health club members", *American Journal of Health Promotion*, 9 (5): 340–3.

van de Mark, D. (1999) "Interview with Lucille Roberts, health clubs CEO", CNNfn (Cable News Network Financial), *Entrepreneurs Only*, June 25, transcript: Federal Document Clearing House.

Vanderbilt, T. (1998) *The Sneaker Book: Anatomy of an Industry and an Icon*, New York: New Press.

Veblen, T. (1959) *The Theory of the Leisure Class: An Economic Study of Institutions*, New York: Viking Press.

Vinikas, V. (1992) *Soft Soap, Hard Sell: American Hygiene in an Age of Advertisement*, Ames, IA: Iowa State University Press.

Volkwein, K. (ed.) (1998) *Fitness as Cultural Phenomenon*, New York: Waxmann Münster.

Wacquant, L.J.D. (1992) "The social logic of boxing in Black Chicago: toward a sociology of pugilism", *Sociology of Sport Journal*, 9 (3): 221–54.

—— (1995) "The pugilistic point of view: how boxers think and feel about their trade", *Theory and Society*, 24: 489–535.

Wallace, C. (1986) "Force-fit", *Madison Avenue*, 28 (3): 27–8.

Watkins, E. (1993) *Throwaways: Work Culture and Consumer Education*, Stanford, CA: Stanford University Press.

Weber, M. (1946) *From Max Weber: Essays in Sociology*, ed. H.H. Gerth and C.W. Mills, New York: Oxford University Press.

—— (1992) *The Protestant Ethic and the Spirit of Capitalism*, London: Routledge.

Wernick, A. (1991) *Promotional Culture: Advertising, Ideology and Symbolic Expression*, London: Sage.

Wharton, A.S. (1993) "The affective consequences of service work: managing emotions on the job", *Work and Occupations*, 20: 205–32.

—— (1999) "The psychosocial consequences of emotional labor", *The Annals of the American Academy of Political Social Science*, 561: 158–76.

White, P., Young, K. and Gillett, J. (1995) "Bodywork as a moral imperative: some critical notes on health and fitness", *Society and Leisure*, 18: 159–82.

Whorton, J.C. (1982) *Crusaders for Fitness: The History of American Health Reformers*, Princeton, NJ: Princeton University Press.

Wilensky, H.L. (1964) "The professionalization of everyone?", *American Journal of Sociology*, 70: 137–58.

Wilk, R. (2001) "Consuming morality", *Journal of Consumer Culture*, 1 (2): 245–60.

Williams, R. (1977) *Marxism and Literature*, London: Oxford University Press.

Wilson, P.S. (1979) "Editor's note", *Self*, January: 6.

Witz, A., Warhurst, C. and Nickson, D. (2003) "The labour of aesthetics and the aesthetics of organisation", *Organization*, 10 (1): 33–54.

Wolf, M.D. (1983) *Nautilus Fitness for Women*, Chicago: Contemporary Books.

Wolf, N. (1991) *The Beauty Myth: How Images Are Used Against Women*, London: Vintage.

Wolfe, T. (1982a) "The me decade and the third great awakening", in T. Wolfe (ed.), *The Purple Decades: A Reader*, New York: Farrar Straus Giroux.

—— (1982b) "The woman who has everything", in T. Wolfe (ed.), *The Purple Decades: A Reader*, New York: Farrar Straus Giroux.

Wood, L. (1988) "Fitness book purchasers", *Publishers Weekly*, March 25: 25.

World Health Organization (2000) *Obesity: Preventing and Managing the Global Epidemic*, Geneva: World Health Organization. Online. Available HTTP: <http://www.who.int/nutrition/publications/obesity/en/index.html> [accessed October 2006].

—— (2002) "Sedentary lifestyle: a global public health problem", *Move for Health Information Sheets*. Online. Available HTTP: <http://www.who.int/moveforhealth/advocacy/information_sheets> [accessed October 2006].

—— (2003a) "Annual Global Move for Health Initiative: A Concept Paper." Online. Available HTTP: <http://whqlibdoc.who.int/hq/2003/WHO_NMH_NPH_PAH_03.1.pdf> [accessed October 2006].

—— (2003b) "Risk factors: obesity, body mass index", *MONICA Monograph and Multimedia Sourcebook*. Online. Available HTTP: <http://whqlibdoc.who.int/publications/2003/9241562234_p198-238.pdf> [accessed June 2006].

—— (2004) *Global Strategy on Diet, Physical Activity and Health*. Geneva: World Health Organization. Online. Available HTTP: <http://www.who.int/nutrition/publications/obesity/en/index.html> [accessed October 2006].

Wynne, D. (1998) *Leisure, Lifestyle and the New Middle Class: A Case Study*, London: Routledge.

YWCA. (2001) *Briefings: Obesity*. Autumn (3). Online. Available HTTP: <http://www.ywca-gb.org.uk/docs/Obesitybriefing.pdf> [accessed October 2006].

Zald, M.N. (1970) *Organizational Change: The Political Economy of the YMCA*, Chicago: University of Chicago Press.

Zelizer, V. (2005) "Culture and consumption", in N. Smelsner and R. Swedberg (eds), *The Handbook of Economic Sociology*, 2nd edn, Princeton, NJ: Princeton University Press.

Zukin, S. (1995) *The Cultures of Cities*, Cambridge, MA: Blackwell.

—— (2004) *Point of Purchase: How Shopping Changed American Culture*, New York: Routledge.

Zukin, S. and Smith Maguire, J. (2004) "Consumers and consumption," *Annual Review of Sociology*, 30: 173–97.

Zuzanek, J., Beckers, T., and Peters, P. (1998) "The "harried leisure class" revisited: Dutch and Canadian trends in the use of time from the 1970s to the 1990s", *Leisure Studies*, 17: 1–19.

Index